Small Towns
and Big Business

Small Towns and Big Business

Challenging Wal-Mart Superstores

Stephen Halebsky

LEXINGTON BOOKS

A division of
ROWMAN & LITTLEFIELD PUBLISHERS, INC.
Lanham • Boulder • New York • Toronto • Plymouth, UK

ROWMAN & LITTLEFIELD PUBLISHERS, INC.

A division of Rowman & Littlefield Publishers, Inc.
A wholly owned subsidiary of The Rowman & Littlefield Publishing Group, Inc.
4501 Forbes Boulevard, Suite 200
Lanham, MD 20706

Estover Road
Plymouth PL6 7PY
United Kingdom

Copyright © 2009 by Lexington Books

All rights reserved. No part of this publication may be reproduced, stored in a retrieval system, or transmitted in any form or by any means, electronic, mechanical, photocopying, recording, or otherwise, without the prior permission of the publisher.

British Library Cataloguing in Publication Information Available

Library of Congress Cataloging-in-Publication Data

Halebsky, Stephen, 1954–
  Small towns and big business : challenging Wal-Mart superstores / Stephen Halebsky.
    p. cm.
  Includes bibliographical references and index.
  ISBN-13: 978-0-7391-2240-2 (cloth : alk. paper)
  ISBN-10: 0-7391-2240-1 (cloth : alk. paper)
  ISBN-13: 978-0-7391-3347-7 (electronic)
  ISBN-10: 0-7391-3347-0 (electronic)
  1. Wal-Mart (Firm) 2. Discount houses (Retail trade)—United States. 3. Small cities—Economic aspects—United States. 4. Big business—Social aspects—United States. 5. Quality of life—United States I. Title.
  HF5429.215.U6H35 2009
  381'.1490973—dc22   2008039297

Printed in the United States of America

∞^{TM} The paper used in this publication meets the minimum requirements of American National Standard for Information Sciences—Permanence of Paper for Printed Library Materials, ANSI/NISO Z39.48–1992.

To Barb

Contents

Tables and Figures		ix
Acknowledgments		xi
1	Introduction: Communities, Corporations, and Local Social Movements	1
2	Big Retailers, Aggressive Retail Development, and the Roots of Local Protest	27
3	How Superstores Affect Small Towns	51
4	Gig Harbor, Washington, and Petoskey, Michigan: Do the People Want It?	71
5	West Bend, Wisconsin, and Ottawa, Ohio: A Superstore in the Neighborhood?	99
6	Ashland, Wisconsin, and Eureka, California: Economic Benefit for Whom?	129
7	Explaining Success	165
8	The Local State, Corporate Retailing, McDonaldization, and Local Anticorporate Activism	187

Appendix	211
Bibliography	215
Index	229
About the Author	235

Tables and Figures

TABLES

Table 2.1. Number of Wal-Mart Stores in the U.S., by Region, 1975–2007

Table 7.1. Explanatory Variables

FIGURES

Figure 2.1. Retail Trade, 1963–1992: Number of firms and establishments

Figure 2.2. Retail Trade, 1963–1992: Percentage of total sales by firms with at least 100 units

Figure 2.3. General Merchandise Stores, 1963–1992: Number of firms and establishments

Figure 2.4. General Merchandise Stores, 1963–1992: Percentage of total Sales by firms with at least 100 units

Figure 2.5. Stationery Stores, 1963–1992: Number of firms and establishments

Acknowledgments

This book took a long time to write. Fortunately, many persons helped me along the way. Starting at the University of Wisconsin, I want to thank my dissertation committee, Gary Green, Bill Freudenburg, the late Fred Buttel, Paul Lichterman, and Maria Caton Campbell, for excellent advice and guidance. Gary Green, my advisor, merits special thanks for his invaluable support, intellectual and otherwise. I would like to thank Gary Long, Jeff Jackson, and Kirsten Dellinger at the University of Mississippi; Ieva Zake at Rowan University; and Anne Vittoria and Bill Skipper at SUNY-Cortland for providing comments on parts of the manuscript. Thanks also to Suzanne Penuel, who expertly copyedited an early draft of part of the manuscript, and Hank Johnston at *Mobilization*, who improved the presentation of certain parts. Michael Sisskin at Lexington Books deserves thanks for guiding me through the publication process. The anonymous reviewer gave the entire manuscript a very fair reading and provided many constructive comments.

Research funding came from several sources. I would like to thank the Midwest Sociological Society for a Dissertation Research Award, the Department of Rural Sociology at the University of Wisconsin for a Crowe Dissertation Research Scholarship, the Department of Sociology at the University of Wisconsin for a Research Travel Award and a Small Grants Award, and the University of Wisconsin for a Vilas Travel Fellowship.

I appreciate also the efforts of the small army of readers, including Mark Halebsky, Thelma Halebsky, Max Halebsky, Barb Kirby, and Nancy Johnson, who helped me stay abreast of events by cutting out articles and sending them to me. And I want to thank Alice and Bret Halebsky for their moral support. Tiantian Zheng also deserves thanks for her encouragement.

I am grateful to all the people in Gig Harbor, Petoskey, West Bend, Ottawa, Ashland, and Eureka who shared with me their experiences and insights.

I thank my parents, Thelma and Max Halebsky, who provided support in various forms.

Finally, Barb Kirby deserves special thanks for helping me with so many parts of this project.

1

Introduction

Communities, Corporations, and Local Social Movements

In 1999 the residents of Eureka, California, heard some news that many found unwelcome: Wal-Mart Stores, Inc. planned to build a 130,000-square-foot superstore in their city. Located on the Pacific coast and within easy distance of Redwood National Park, the city wanted to project an image of itself as a tourist destination. A Wal-Mart superstore, identical to thousands all over the country, certainly would not contribute to that image. There were other reasons to reject Wal-Mart's plans. The land that Wal-Mart wanted was near the old industrial section of the waterfront that had once been a center of economic activity and which the city hoped to revitalize as a source of well-paying industrial jobs. To put a mere discount department store—and one that was known for low-wage jobs—on such a crucial piece of land seemed shortsighted from the standpoint of economic development. Eureka had a struggling but viable downtown that would be hurt by the proposed new store, and independent merchants all over the city feared that Wal-Mart would harm them, perhaps fatally. Another objection, more abstract but of equal importance to many residents, was that a superstore threatened to replace the diversity and vitality of real community life with corporate homogeneity. While Wal-Mart's vaunted low prices were attractive to some, others felt that bargains on milk and underwear could not make up for numerous disadvantages. Furthermore, the city already had its share of discount department stores, including Kmart and a huge new Costco that had failed to generate the impressive tax revenue its promoters had promised. And there were already Wal-Marts in the counties north, south, and east of the city. Convinced that the last thing Eureka needed was a Wal-Mart superstore, a group of local citizens organized to oppose the project.

But what could they do? Wal-Mart had successfully placed its stores all across the country. Local opponents could not possibly hope to match the company's resources. Wal-Mart had extensive experience siting its stores and could afford to buy any additional expertise it might need, from public relations to legal advice to assistance from local realtors. It had a reputation for getting what it wanted and certainly would not be dissuaded simply because its plans were contrary to the interests and desires of many local citizens. The predicament faced by Wal-Mart's opponents in Eureka raises the question, what *can* a community do when its welfare is threatened by a large corporation? During the 1990s and continuing into the present, this question was raised in hundreds of small towns and small cities as superstore protests spread from coast to coast.[1] Also known as "big box" stores, superstores are retail establishments that are significantly larger and more rationalized than those built before the last twenty-five years. They may be as large as 200,000 square feet (the size of four football fields), are usually built on the outskirts of a town or city, and are typically surrounded by expansive parking lots. In superstore conflicts small grassroots organizations fight to prevent corporate retailers such as Wal-Mart, Home Depot, and Rite Aid from building superstores in their neighborhoods, towns, and cities. These stores, according to their critics, harm local communities by putting local independent merchants out of business, weakening the vitality of downtowns and Main Streets, siphoning profits from local economies, providing substandard jobs, disrupting residential neighborhoods, contributing to sprawl, undermining local uniqueness, and generally detracting from small town appearance, atmosphere, and quality of life. The critics argue that national and international retail chains contribute little to local well-being and come to town only to milk the community for their own financial benefit. The views of many opponents can be summed up in the words of an activist in Eureka: "[We don't want to be] just one of 10,000 other big box profit centers."[2]

Local groups opposing corporate action usually have few resources compared to the companies they oppose, which means that most conflicts between large corporations and local protestors are resolved to the advantage of the former. Such outcomes are so common that reading the literature in this area can be rather depressing.[3] Rather than tell another story of a community that was steamrolled by a powerful corporation, I sought to find instances where local groups have successfully opposed corporate threats to their communities.

Controversies over the siting of superstores provide a number of such instances and many of these controversies have arisen as a result of local protests against Wal-Mart's plans to site a store. These controversies, which have taken place primarily in the small towns and small cities where the company prefers to place its stores, offer particularly striking contrasts between a large corporation and grassroots community organizations. These are decidedly David-and-Goliath affairs, as small local groups take on one of the biggest companies in the United States. With the advantage of overwhelming resources and experience, Wal-Mart usually places its stores exactly where it wants. By the late 1980s, however, it began encountering resistance and during the 1990s had to contend with protests at approximately two hundred locations. A survey of town planners found that a surprising number of local groups have been able to successfully counter the company's expansion plans and prevent it from putting a superstore in their town or city.[4] These successes present an excellent opportunity to examine challenges to corporate behavior by local opponents.

In this book I investigate controversies over the siting of Wal-Mart superstores in six small cities during the 1990s. Each controversy is a complex piece of local history and politics, enlivened by conflicting claims about who and what is truly in the best interest of the community. In Eureka, California, and Gig Harbor, Washington, local superstore opponents thwarted Wal-Mart's attempts to put a superstore in their cities; in West Bend, Wisconsin, and Ottawa, Ohio, the opponents prevented Wal-Mart from placing its store on the particular site that it wanted, although the store was built later at a different, less objectionable site; and in Ashland, Wisconsin, and Petoskey, Michigan, their efforts were unsuccessful and a Wal-Mart superstore has now been built in the city exactly where the company wanted. I consider the first two cases complete successes, the second two partial successes, and the last two failures. I classify the outcomes in West Bend and Ottawa as partial *successes* because even getting Wal-Mart to abandon its preferred site for another, less objectionable site is a significant accomplishment for a grassroots group. While the successes represent the outcome of most interest, the failures provide crucial comparisons.

My primary goal is to understand how some small groups were able to prevail against the world's largest retailer. Using these controversies as empirical evidence, I construct an explanation of their successes. I also present a model of the conditions under which it may be possible for local groups to partially neutralize corporate power. A secondary goal is to place superstore controversies in a social, historical, and economic context, and to explain the problems and consequences of superstores and corporate retailing—in other words, to explain what is at stake in these and similar controversies.

COMMUNITIES

A "community," as I use the term, may be a small city, a small town, or a neighborhood. Action taken by a large corporation, because of its scale of operations, can affect an entire community. All groups in a community, however, may not be affected similarly and effects that are considered undesirable by some may be welcomed by others. A corporate action with community-wide impact can stimulate local discussion about the relationship between corporations and communities. The type of action considered here—the introduction of a superstore into a small town—often affects the entire community and frequently prompts discussion on such topics as the costs and benefits of having corporations as neighbors, the relationship between corporations and local independent merchants, the motives large corporations have for coming to town, and the effects corporations have on communities. Discussion of these topics can, in turn, raise fundamental questions about the nature of a community and its fate: Who should exercise control over what is built in a community? How important is community appearance? Is every form of development necessarily good for a community? Do members of a community have an obligation to support each other economically? Questions of these sorts invariably arise during superstore controversies.

Vidich and Bensman's well-known 1958 study of the rural small town they called Springdale highlighted the effects of large nonlocal organizations on small towns.[5] They found that the town was tightly connected to various nonlocal governmental and business organizations and had effectively ceded much of its independence to them. Today the typical small town or small city is even more dependent on nonlocal organizations than was Springdale in 1958. While the lack of local autonomy in Springdale was neither widely known by most of its citizens nor publicly acknowledged by its leaders, today many small-town residents are acutely aware of the extent to which their lives depend upon nonlocal entities, especially large corporations. Corporate influence is most evident in retailing, dining, and lodging, as evidenced by the extent to which corporate chains dominate these sectors. While some accept this state of affairs as simply the nature of modern society, others object to what they perceive as a process of corporate colonization that is occurring without their input or approval. Many people are concerned not only about local autonomy, the issue raised by Vidich and Bensman, but also about economic well-being, community character, and local quality of life. Succinctly put, the penetration of community life by large corporations has become problematic.

CORPORATIONS

As the most powerful type of nongovernmental organization in the United States today and as the most dynamic form of organization in the world, the large corporation has enormous potential to affect communities for better or for worse. The corporation is not synonymous with business. What distinguishes the corporation from sole proprietorships and partnerships, the other two principal forms of business organization, is that it exists as a legal entity separate from its owners, who have no personal liability for its actions. Today the corporation is the preferred organizational form for large business enterprises and its economic dominance is beyond dispute. While sole proprietorships and partnerships account for the overwhelming *number* of businesses, corporations dominate the economy by *level of business activity*. In 2004, 84 percent of the total revenue received by all forms of business went to corporations.[6] Moreover, the overwhelming majority of large firms, those with at least five hundred employees, are organized as corporations. These large firms accounted for 61 percent of all business revenue in 2002.[7]

My emphasis on the corporation should not be construed as an unqualified endorsement of small business. It is not unusual for local independent businesses to be perceived as failing to operate in the best interest of the community. In fact, the case studies in this book reveal that many small retailers are rather unpopular with some of their fellow townspeople, who accuse them of charging high prices, stocking out-of-style merchandise, providing shoddy service, hiring only their relatives and friends, and having limited hours. In some superstore disputes the business practices and alleged self-interest of the local merchants are nearly as much a part of the story as Wal-Mart itself. Nonetheless, large corporations can affect communities in ways that few small businesses can. As a result of their sheer size and scale of operations, a few corporations, or even just one, can have a significant impact on a community. A big company may be the largest local employer, the single biggest local taxpayer, the leading purchaser of locally produced products, or the dominant seller of everyday consumer goods (i.e., Wal-Mart). Big corporations differ also from small businesses in their ability to devote substantial resources to influencing public opinion through advertising and public relations. Their ability to influence politicians through campaign finance is well known.

But it is not only a matter of size, the corporation differs from small business qualitatively as well. The corporation, much more than the typical small business, embodies the relentless rationalization that characterizes so much of the modern world. Corporate rationalization results from a combination of bureaucracy, technological sophistication, and the drive to increase profits and market share. The behavior of the corporation is related to its peculiar organizational characteristics, which are both a cause and a consequence of its size. In some ways it is like an actual person: it can buy, sell, and own property, including other corporations; enter into contracts; sue and be sued; and take advantage of various constitutional rights (e.g., the right to free speech). Yet in other ways it is profoundly unlike a person: it can grow to any size; it can live forever, regardless of the deaths of its owners, directors, executives, and employees; it can easily change its name, its "home," its political allegiance, and its "occupation"; and its behavior cannot be influenced through moral suasion or threats of incarceration.[8] Critics maintain that these characteristics, combined with the limited liability of owners, have resulted in an organization that has many rights but few responsibilities. These sorts of criticisms are not new, but have become more salient in recent years.[9]

COMMUNITY-CORPORATE CONFLICTS

Community-corporate conflicts take various forms. What they have in common is that they involve local protest over corporate action (or inaction) that affects the local community, whether or not the corporation itself is headquartered locally. One type of community-corporate conflict common during the last several decades involves protests against decisions by corporations to shut down their local operations and relocate outside the community, often to another state or overseas. The reason given most often for such closings is that profitability can be increased by employing cheaper labor at the new location. The economic and social consequences of plant closings on communities can be enormous and have been well documented.[10] Success in preventing corporate relocation has been limited.

Another type of controversy involves the costs that cities feel they are forced to incur to attract or retain corporate employers. Given the lack of regional and national planning in the United States, cities and states often must compete against each other to attract corporate headquarters, production facilities (e.g., manufacturing plants), and branch establishments. As part of this competition, cities and states offer an array of costly subsidies to entice companies to locate locally, hoping their presence will increase employment and stimulate growth. This interlocal competition has been characterized as a "race to the bottom," as communities spend precious tax dollars on companies that are often already quite profitable. Corporations that have already established operations in a community have learned to play the game too and may threaten to leave if they are not granted various subsidies. Although some local officials maintain that these corporate subsidies are good investments, the overall effect of this competition is a net transfer of funds from public to corporate treasuries. Few communities have found a way to escape this costly competition.

Another type of dispute involves the actual or potential degradation of the local environment by corporations. In response, community activists try to prevent such degradation from occurring, compel corporations to clean up existing pollution, seek monetary damages, and press for adequate disclosure regarding the use of toxic substances. Two types of facilities that frequently provoke strong reactions are nuclear power plants and trash incinerators. These are not strictly community-corporate disputes because the decision to generate nuclear power or use trash incinerators often originates with government officials, and thus the opponents may be at odds with government officials as well as with the corporate manufacturers and operators of these facilities. During the last several decades local groups have been successful in preventing the construction of many new nuclear power plants and incinerators. But despite some success with these two particular threats, environmental problems of other sorts continue to be a point of contention between corporations and communities.

A final type of conflict arises in the course of urban development and growth. Cities are continually being shaped and reshaped by the actions of the individuals and organizations that profit from real estate development and growth. These individuals and organizations range from small local land speculators to multinational real estate development corporations. Large corporations, with their capacity to undertake large-scale development, sometimes pursue projects that have the potential to alter entire neighborhoods and even whole cities. Conflicts arise between corporations that benefit from development and growth and local actors who suffer from their adverse effects. While this is the general pattern, reaction to growth-oriented development varies between and within cities. A new factory, even a dirty one, might be welcomed in an impoverished city but scorned in a prosperous suburb. The destruction of low-cost housing and its replacement by expensive condominiums might be opposed in one neighborhood but embraced by another. The outcomes of conflict over urban development generally favor large corporations and the real estate interests that work on their behalf, although there are exceptions, as illustrated by some of the case studies presented here.

Superstore Controversies

Superstore controversies have some similarity with other forms of community-corporate conflict and have unique features as well. Like a plant closing, the siting of a superstore may result in the closing of local businesses as small merchants who cannot match its prices are eventually forced to close their doors. Like the competition between cities to attract manufacturing plants, a superstore siting may involve a competition in which municipalities offer various incentives to secure a superstore in the hope that it will generate jobs and tax revenue. In this competition, as with that over manufacturing plants, municipalities as a group are the losers. And, like other large-scale projects, a superstore can change the nature of a neighborhood, town, or city. Because of its size, a superstore in a small town represents a major development project. A unique aspect of superstore controversies is that some local residents simply do not want what the corporation is offering. Consider the contrast between disputes over waste incinerators and those involving superstores. Controversies over the siting of waste incinerators are often referred to as a type of "NIMBY" (Not In My Back Yard) dispute, where opponents concede that there is a need for such a facility, but do not want it built near *them* because of concerns about toxic chemicals, odors, traffic, and real estate values. Some of the participants in superstore controversies take a similar stance: they do not object to superstores, but feel that a particular site is inappropriate because of concerns about traffic, harm to downtown, damage to environmentally sensitive land, proximity to homes, and general incongruity with the surrounding landscape. Others, however, object to having a superstore built *anywhere* in their community. While current waste disposal arrangements make incinerators or other similar facilities inevitable, a superstore does not *have* to be built anywhere.[11]

Why reject a superstore? Adamant rejection may seem surprising, as the business being rejected is ostensibly nothing more than a large store that sells standard consumer goods. Behind this rejection, however, are a number of important concerns. First, in spite of the American preoccupation with shopping and consumption, some people feel saturated with commercial development. As one superstore opponent asked rather plaintively, "Why can't we have just a few places for the minority who do not need or want easy access to every commercial convenience?"[12] Others object to the effect superstores have on local small merchants. Still others are alienated by the business practices they consider characteristic of superstore retailers: low wages, lack of benefits, antiunionism, deceptive advertising, and predatory pricing. Finally, many reject superstores for their incongruity with the built environment (too big, too boxy, inappropriate architectural design, too much land paved over, too far from downtown, etc.) and their usurpation of public space. Taken together, these objections constitute a serious critique of contemporary corporate retailing.

The objections, however, go beyond retailing to encompass dissatisfaction with the contemporary corporate model in general, which is characterized by a fixation on short-term financial goals, extensive rationalization and bureaucratization, nonlocal ownership and control, a high degree of capital mobility, vigorous antiunionism, a drive toward low-wage and contingent employment, massive advertising and public relations, and aggressive political involvement (e.g., campaign contributions). Wal-Mart serves as a lightning rod for this dissatisfaction because it is not only the leading retailer, but also one of the largest corporations in the United States.[13] In the view of labor historian Nelson Lichtenstein, Wal-Mart has become the "template business setting the standards for a new stage in the history of world capitalism," replacing earlier template corporations such as General Motors and IBM.[14] Thus, to the extent that Wal-Mart represents the contemporary corporate model, superstore controversies are notable for their rejection of that model.

While superstore controversies raise these larger issues, I do not claim that the majority of participants in superstore controversies are motivated by an explicit critique of the corporate model. While some condemn the corporate model, others oppose only Wal-Mart and similar superstores, and still others claim agnosticism toward the company and object only to the particular site chosen by Wal-Mart. Regardless of their views, many superstore opponents direct considerable hostility toward Wal-Mart and this hostility tends to increase during the controversy as they become aware of the company's tactics, read its statements to the press, and interact with company officials. Whether participants object to the corporate model, to Wal-Mart, to superstores, or only to a particular site, the fact remains that they are opposing a very large corporation.

These controversies are also of interest because Wal-Mart exemplifies the phenomenon known as McDonaldization, "the process by which the principles of the fast-food restaurant are coming to dominate more and more sectors of American society as well as the rest of the world."[15] McDonaldization is the application of those principles (efficiency, calculability, predictability, and control), which have long dominated production, to consumption, with the result that today people are subjected to extensive rationalization as both consumers and workers. Wal-Mart is a nearly perfect example of McDonaldized retailing. Most people who oppose Wal-Mart, of course, have never heard of McDonaldization and many of their objections have little to do with it, but some of their objections are exactly those described by the McDonaldization thesis: homogeneity, impersonality, inauthenticity, stultifying work, and the degradation of personal interaction. These features strike many superstore opponents as particularly incompatible with the small-town quality of life they are trying to preserve, with the contrast between Wal-Mart and independent small merchants providing an especially stark illustration of the differences between McDonaldization and a non-McDonaldized alternative. Hence, opposition to the siting of a Wal-Mart superstore can be interpreted, at least in part, as a reaction against McDonaldization and raises the question, "What can be done about McDonaldization?" In the final chapter I discuss

McDonaldization at greater length and offer some propositions about the possibility of resistance.

LOCAL SOCIAL MOVEMENTS

Although superstore conflicts may be construed as taking place between communities and corporations, in reality communities do not act, individuals and organizations within communities act, and thus an investigation of successful opposition to corporate action requires an examination of the particular local efforts that constitute the opposition. The totality of such efforts in a given place may be characterized as a *local social movement*. Because few social movements succeed without some degree of organization, a *local social movement organization* is usually involved. Local social movements have not received as much attention from social scientists as national-level movements, but this should not be taken as a lack of importance. Some social movements exist solely as local endeavors—a "national" movement may, in fact, consists principally of local actions. Much of the early phase of the American civil rights movement, for example, consisted of a series of local movements. Some social movements may consist of a combination of national efforts and actions at the local level. In such instances, local actors may or may not have any significant connection with the larger social movement of which they are presumably a part. The activity of local social movement organizations may last anywhere from a few weeks to many years and the outcomes of such movements are often of vital importance to local participants, even if they are not significant at a higher level.

Local antisuperstore social movements have much in common with other social movements. Common features include collective action by a group that is neither a political party nor a governmental entity, extensive involvement by ordinary people, contending parties of vastly unequal power, and political activity that is based more on mobilizing people than on spending money. Opposition to superstores, may involve various challenges to the status quo, including challenges to consumerism, to landowner rights, to economic rationalization, to the presumption that commercial development promotes community welfare, and to corporate expansion and prerogative in general. And, like some other social movements, opposition to superstores involves the pursuit of goals that transcend the immediate interests of many participants. This is evidenced by the fact that in a typical dispute the opposition includes a wider array of local actors than the particular merchants who expect to be adversely affected or the particular homeowners who happen to live near the proposed site. While people from these two groups are actively involved in the opposition efforts, they are joined by many others whose interests are more diffuse. In the course of the controversy questions are raised about community welfare and corporate prerogative that go well beyond the interests of specific merchants or homeowners. Lastly, superstore conflicts have taken place all over the country, resulting in the emergence of a limited social movement infrastructure, which include books, videos, websites, copies of legal briefs, studies, and articles in the popular press, as well as the accumulated experience of other communities and activists. Because of these common features, findings about superstore controversies should be at least partially applicable to other social movements, especially those that are local.

To the extent that antisuperstore efforts are viewed as anticorporate, they have some affinity with a variety of other such movements, including movements that oppose corporate chains (e.g., protests against McDonald's and Starbucks[16]), accuse multinational corporations of taking advantage of the less developed nations, oppose corporate agriculture (e.g., protests against genetically modified food), protest environmental problems caused by corporations, and critique corporations in general for having undermined democracy. These movements, which have been labeled "anti-globalization" or "anti-corporate," encompass a range of views.[17] Some criticize specific actions or policies of particular corporations, while others offer a wholesale critique of the modern corporation and the corporate model.

While Wal-Mart and its practices are an issue for many opponents, from a legal standpoint the typical controversy does not turn directly on whether a town will decide to bar Wal-Mart, as it is illegal for a municipality to ban a specific company. Instead, it is usually fought out as a land use issue, most often involving zoning. The usual question to be decided by local officials or voters is whether Wal-Mart should be granted its request to have a particular parcel of land rezoned from its current designation (e.g., "residential" or "agricultural") to "commercial," thereby allowing a superstore to be built on the site. These controversies are intense local dramas involving a variety of players. As the case studies will show, there is sometimes considerable disagreement among local citizens about the desirability of a new superstore and the contention between local pro- and anti-Wal-Mart groups can be nearly as significant as the conflict involving Wal-Mart itself.

UNDERSTANDING THE OUTCOMES OF SUPERSTORE CONTROVERSIES

Social scientists (and everybody else) are perplexed when it comes to the question of how to limit corporate power, a question that globalization has made more pertinent and vexing than ever. Because corporations impinge on contemporary life in so many different ways, this question has been pursued in areas as diverse as labor law, environmental protection, consumer affairs, campaign finance, food and drug regulation, and antitrust. This book focuses on attempts to limit corporate power at the local level, with an emphasis on efforts to check unwanted, large-scale, retail development. Although various community-corporate conflicts have attracted the attention of social scientists, research on such conflicts remains disconnected and has not resulted in well-developed and well-established theories and findings (the growth machine perspective, discussed below, is a partial exception). While little is known definitively about how local groups might successfully constrain or modify corporate action, there are several areas of research that can be mined for leads and possible insights: research on social movement outcomes, research on siting controversies, and research on the growth machine. My purpose in examining this research is to identify factors (or "variables"—I use these terms synonymously) than can help explain how local groups might prevail against large corporations.

Social Movement Outcomes

Although scholars have generated an enormous amount of research on social movements during the last several decades, explanations for movement outcomes remain limited and tentative.[18] This is perhaps not surprising, given the variety and complexity of social movements. A starting point in the study of social movement outcomes is the realization that the relationship between what a social movement organization does and the outcome—i.e., whether or not it attains its goal—is not necessarily direct. The actions of a social movement organization may be minimally related to the outcome, while external forces, conditions, and actors may have a substantial impact. A distinction, then, can be made between those variables that are under the control of the social movement organization and those that are not. The first group includes organizational, framing, and action variables (i.e., mobilization, tactics, etc.). The second group, referred to as environmental variables, includes the stance of elites, actions by other organizations, the media, political opportunities and constraints, and a wide variety of other variables that vary from place to place and movement to movement.

The most thorough investigation of factors under the control of a social movement organization continues to be that of William Gamson, who found that challenging groups that are large, bureaucratic, and pursue reformist goals are most likely to succeed.[19] While his original study seemed to imply that violent tactics are associated with success, he later explained that "It is more accurate to interpret the results [of the original study] as 'feistiness works' rather than 'violence works,'" where feistiness "includes the willingness to break rules and use noninstitutionalized means—to use disruption as a strategy of influence."[20] While Gamson's findings remain influential and have generally been confirmed or accepted, it is unclear to what extent they apply to local movements contesting corporate action (all fifty-three social movement organizations in his sample operated at the national level).[21] If size and lack of bureaucratic structure are a disadvantage for local social movements, then they would seem to be especially disadvantageous in regard to community-corporate conflicts because such conflicts pit local protestors against organizations that are both large and bureaucratic, Wal-Mart serving as the prime example. To have a reformist goal, per Gamson, means to construe success in terms that do not include displacing the other party, referred to as the "target." His finding that movements with reformist goals are more likely to succeed applies well to community-corporate conflicts, as it is certainly easier to prevent or modify a particular corporate action than it is to eliminate a corporation entirely. Having said this, it is interesting to note that the goal of many local superstore opponents—to prevent a Wal-Mart store from being built in their town—is radical in the sense that it means flatly rejecting the company's presence, even if there is no attempt to eliminate the company as a going concern.

What about the effectiveness of disruption? This may depend, in part, on the extent to which a local social movement *can* disrupt a big company. It may be possible to disrupt the everyday business of a local independent company, and this tactic was used to advantage by protestors during the American civil rights movement, but it is more difficult to disrupt the operations of a large corporation that is headquartered elsewhere, has many establishments across the country or around the world, and has little need to cultivate the local population on a long-term basis. In any event, the anti-Wal-Mart activists in my case studies engaged mostly in "polite action" with little disruptive potential.[22]

Another factor under the control of a social movement organization is framing, the term used by social movement scholars to refer to the way an issue is packaged and presented. Every framing represents an attempt to define "the boundaries of the debate by placing the question [or issue] within a certain sphere of meaning."[23] In colloquial terms it is the spin given to an issue. Most social movement organizations carefully frame the issue to maximize the positive response from potential supporters, the public-at-large, the media, decision makers, and other parties. Framing is not limited to social movement organizations; other interested parties, including counter social movement organizations, construct and purvey their framings too, so that a dispute often involves competing framings. An examination of framing has become an important component of the analysis of a social movement, although the relationship between framing and outcomes remains understudied.[24] In the case studies that follow I pay close attention to the various framings used and assess how they affected the outcomes.

Many social movement organizations include legal challenges as part of their arsenal of tactics. While such challenges have worked well for some movements at the national level (e.g., the American civil rights movement and the women's movement), it is unclear to what extent they are effective at the local level, especially when the target is a large corporation. Legal challenges, usually in the form of lawsuits contesting the legality of zoning changes, have been used by opponents in a minority of superstore siting controversies. An important limitation of legal tactics—a limitation so general that it is rarely noted—is that a corporation can take any action it pleases unless that action is specifically prohibited by a law. The use of legal tactics presupposes the alleged violation of a law, but the particular corporate action that local opponents find so distressing may be perfectly legal. A major difficulty in deterring the expansion of corporate retailers is that for the most part it is well within the law. Another limitation is that legal tactics, even where feasible, may simply be ineffective. A small social movement organization taking on a large corporation is disadvantaged by the phenomenon identified by Marc Galanter: large corporations tend to prevail in legal contests because they are "repeat players" relative to their opponents.[25] This is clearly the case when local social movements confront superstores, although there has been some accumulation of legal experience by antisuperstore activists over the years. Another problem with legal tactics is that they may replace the engaged participation of movement supporters, leading to an eventual weakening of the movement.[26] Edward Walsh and Sherry Cable, who analyzed six years of protests by local activists in the wake of the Three Mile Island nuclear accident, maintain that "Litigation is seldom an effective SMO [social movement organization] tactic unless used in conjunction with community organizing and other political tactics."[27] While these observations indicate some potential drawbacks to the use of legal tactics in community-corporate conflicts, the topic deserves more study.

Turning to the environmental variables, there are, first of all, various actors that need to be considered. Prominent among these is the target itself, which meant paying close attention to Wal-Mart's actions during the controversies. I wanted to know what tactics it uses, how it employs its extensive resources to influence public opinion and decision makers, and how it frames the issue. Elites constitute another set of actors that may play an important role. Some scholars have argued that elites may be more important than the social movement organization itself in determining success or failure.[28] Government officials are one set of elites that can significantly affect outcomes; indeed, the decision by local officials to approve or deny a rezoning may itself constitute success or failure in superstore controversies. Another potentially important group, and one that includes elites as well as nonelites, is the growth machine, the coalition of locally based businesses with an abiding interest in local growth (see below). There may also be a counter social movement organization that is formed in response to the original social movement and deliberately seeks to frustrate its aims. While scholars have taken note of countermovements, research has concentrated on their origins and the interaction between movements and countermovements rather than on their effect on outcomes.[29] It is unclear how common and how influential countermovements are in community-corporate disputes. When I began my research I did not expect counter social movement organizations to be part of the story, as they are rarely mentioned in most accounts of superstore controversies. However, my field research revealed that such groups—local Wal-Mart supporters who organize to promote the store—are not an uncommon phenomenon and are worth paying attention to. The media are another important part of the environment and a potential resource for a social movement organization.[30] Every movement aspires to get favorable media coverage that will influence the target, elites, decision makers, and the public. Favorable coverage, of course, is not assured; the media may ignore, discredit, or distort the movement and its issue.[31] Today the national media are themselves large corporations or are owned by large corporations, thus predisposing them to support corporate initiatives and the corporate point of view. In small towns the dominant source of local news is the local newspaper, which usually covers superstore fights in detail. While American newspapers at all levels are notoriously probusiness, I was curious to see how the local papers would cover these controversies and what effect their coverage would have on the outcomes.

Siting Controversies

While an anti-Wal-Mart dispute may seem like an idiosyncratic form of local activism, such disputes have much in common with the larger category of siting controversies, which take place whenever citizens mobilize to protest the construction or placement of various facilities and projects in their communities. Siting controversies have erupted over waste incinerators, landfills, sewage treatment plants, waste transfer facilities, toxic waste storage facilities, and industrial hog farms. They also involve urban development projects such as roads, freeways, malls, condominiums, apartments, large parking garages, and sports stadiums.[32] Siting controversies have several common features. First, the proposed project is seen as a threat to health and safety, to the environment, to aesthetics, to the local economy, to the tranquility of residential districts, or to the overall quality of life by at least some of the persons who live in or near the host neighborhood, town, or city. Second, this threat spurs local citizens to organize and take defensive action, with opposition efforts acquiring many of the characteristics of a social movement. Third, the proposed project is typically initiated by an organization headquartered outside the neighborhood, town, or city, often a large corporation or governmental body. This leads to a fourth common feature: the unequal power and resources of the contending parties. It should be evident that superstore controversies possess all four of these features.

Although siting controversies have generated a considerable literature, it is not ideally suited to understanding the outcomes of community-corporate conflicts. One problem is that many authors do not distinguish clearly between corporate-initiated projects and state-initiated projects, making it difficult to comprehend the interplay of corporate action and local protest. Another limitation is that few studies systematically pursue an explanation of outcomes. There is also a methodological drawback: the typical study is a single-case study and thus the findings are of limited or uncertain generalizability. Given these defects, what can we extract from the siting literature? Many of these studies contain descriptive narratives that provide the interested reader an opportunity to attempt to identity potential explanatory factors.[33] My reading of these narratives points to three factors that may be associated with successful opposition. First, success tends to occur where there is a high level of mobilization by the opponents, relative to the size of the community. Success also seems to be associated with the actions of elites, in particular the public withdrawal of support for the project by one or more important public officials, or their conversion from active proponents to active opponents. And third, the opponents appear more likely to succeed when they employ a variety of political tactics rather than relying solely on lawsuits and other legal tactics, reinforcing the view of Walsh and Cable.

The Growth Machine

A third body of literature, taken from urban sociology, is the growth machine perspective.[34] Unlike much of the social movement literature, the growth machine perspective is concerned primarily with what happens locally; and unlike the siting literature, this perspective is focused on profit-driven business actors, although not necessarily on large corporations. There is some overlap between the growth machine perspective and the literature on siting disputes, as it is the growth machine that is often behind the siting of many controversial projects. According to this perspective the central issue in virtually every town and city, whether or not it is perceived as such by local residents, is growth, defined as an increase in economic activity or an increase in population, or both. Growth is pursued avidly by the growth machine, a loose coalition of landowners, landlords, developers, real estate brokers, financial institutions, utility companies, merchants, and other locally based businesses that benefit directly from growth. The growth machine and local government have a symbiotic relationship. Local government generally supports and facilitates the aims of the growth machine because it welcomes the job creation and tax revenue that are assumed to accompany growth. The growth machine, for its part, is actively involved in local politics to ensure that it will continue to secure the various approvals (e.g., zoning changes, building permits, etc.) it needs for its projects. While a new superstore in a small town represents a major commercial development, it may not be supported by the entire growth machine. The growth machine is generally expected to favor new retail development on the presumption that more stores means more people and more economic activity, but existing retailers who are threatened may not welcome a new store.[35]

While growth is profitable for the growth machine, it may be disadvantageous for other parties, in particular local residents who have to deal with the adverse consequences of growth such as more traffic congestion, more noise, loss of greenery, higher rents, loss of affordable housing, and the decline and disappearance of human-scaled places. Disputes ensue when local residents and others protest the initiatives of the growth machine. The growth machine is normally expected to prevail in these disputes because it benefits from a combination of financial resources, coalition building, political power, expertise, ideology ("growth is good"), and ongoing involvement that opponents can rarely match.

These findings provide an initial guide to some of the factors that might be associated with the success (and failure) of attempts by local groups to counter corporate action. The social movement literature suggests that large, bureaucratic, reformist groups that can disrupt "business as usual" are most likely to succeed. Framing may be important, but which framings are most effective is uncertain. The outcome may also depend on the actions taken by the target, the stance of elites, the treatment by the media, and the existence of a counter social movement organization. A reading of siting dispute narratives points to the importance of a high level of mobilization and the support of public officials, while suggesting that an over reliance on legal tactics may be counterproductive. The growth machine perspective does not tell us much about the success of local resistance groups because its emphasis is on how and why the growth machine prevails. However, it does furnish us with some insight into the dynamics of local politics and identifies a group of influential local actors. This review has indicated a number of factors that might explain the success of attempts by small local groups to fight off the world's biggest retailer. My task was to find out which of these factors actually do play a role in explaining outcomes, and which other factors, not identified above, play a role also. As I ventured into the field and delved into the archives I kept these factors in mind, but also remained open to other explanatory factors, some of which became apparent in the course of the research.

RESEARCH METHODS

Each of the six cities in my sample—Gig Harbor, Washington; Petoskey, Michigan; West Bend, Wisconsin; Ottawa, Ohio; Ashland, Wisconsin; and Eureka, California—experienced a controversy over the siting of a Wal-Mart superstore.[36] Each controversy is a case. I chose these cases because they have certain similarities and differences that make them suitable for study. The similarities, which may be thought of as the aspects being controlled, include the following: All six cities are small (population less than 30,000) and in rural areas, with the exception of Gig Harbor, which is part of the Seattle-Tacoma metropolitan area but is effectively isolated because it is located on a peninsula.[37] Thus, they all represent classic examples of a dispute pitting small-town opponents against a big company. Another similarity is that in all six cities the proposed siting provoked substantial controversy, operationalized as having occurred if (1) an organization was formed to oppose the proposed store or an existing organization took a public stand against the store, (2) at least fifty people attended an official meeting (e.g., city council) at which the proposed superstore was discussed, or (3) at least one hundred people signed a petition opposing the store. Also, all the controversies occurred in the mid-1990s, except Ashland, which occurred in the early 1990s, and Eureka, which took place at the end of the decade. Lastly, I deliberately did not choose cases where there had been significant involvement by college students. Although such involvement is perfectly legitimate, I wanted to focus on the residents, merchants, and others who have a greater long-term investment in local affairs.

The biggest difference among the cases is the outcomes: Gig Harbor and Eureka are complete successes (the store was not built), West Bend and Ottawa are partial successes (the store was eventually built, but not at Wal-Mart's preferred location), and Petoskey and Ashland are failures (the store was built at Wal-Mart's preferred location). I also chose cases that differed in various ways that I thought might have influenced the outcomes. Thus, in some cases the proposed superstore threatened a residential neighborhood; in others it was more of a threat to downtown. In some cases the opponents mobilized vigorously; in others their efforts were more limited. Local scenic beauty was considered an important asset in some cities and offered opponents additional grounds on which to object to a big box store; in other cities such concerns were not evident. Likewise, in some cities tourism and the resort business were a significant part of the local economy; in others they were much less important. In some cases the final decision was made by the city council or other official body; in others the matter was decided by a popular vote. Finally, while none of the cities could be considered exclusive, some had a significant affluent segment, while others were solidly middle and working class. I chose cities with different class demographics because I wanted to examine the popular notion that only the rich and upper middle class dislike Wal-Mart stores.

My method of data collection combined fieldwork and archival research. Most cases were located initially by examining back issues of *Sprawl-Busters Alert*, a publication that tracks superstore protests. Having identified a case that appeared promising, I sought additional information by telephoning local officials, the local librarian, and the local newspaper. Once it appeared that a case was suitable, I obtained and scrutinized microfilm copies of back issues of the local newspaper, which allowed me to reconstruct the events and identify individuals and organizations. I then contacted potential interviewees to request interviews. Finally, I traveled to each city and interviewed key participants representing various points of view, including mayors, city council members, planning commission members, planners, citizen-activists for and against Wal-Mart, local merchants, chamber of commerce officials, developers, real estate agents, and in one case a Wal-Mart official. I interviewed approximately a dozen persons at each location (see the appendix for a list of interviewees). I also examined relevant documents such as transcripts of official meetings, zoning maps, comprehensive plans, reports, and letters and petitions submitted to officials. As part of my fieldwork I visited the actual sites that had been proposed—some of which now contain a Wal-Mart superstore. Being in the cities where the disputes took place and observing the actual sites were crucial to understanding what happened.

My method of analysis is comparative historical.[38] This method, the essence of which is to systematically compare historical trajectories in search of "causal" factors, usually brings to mind studies of historical change at the national level, but it can be applied to events that are local and more recent as well. The cases presented here are recent history, but history all the same. To ensure that I had historical trajectories that could be compared, I chose only cases where the controversy had completely run its course and its history could be reconstructed. The fundamental comparison is between the complete successes and the failures, with the partial successes providing additional insight into both success and failure. I initially considered choosing only cases that were complete successes and then focusing on what they had in common. While such an approach has its advantages, I am glad that I decided to include both successes and failures in my sample because it was the comparison between these that proved most insightful.

PLAN OF THE BOOK

In chapter 2 I describe the economic, political, and social context of superstore controversies. Retailing has experienced extensive restructuring over the last several decades, resulting in an industry dominated by a small number of large, highly rationalized, technologically sophisticated corporations that bear little resemblance to their smaller noncorporate counterparts. The preferred format of the big retailers is the superstore/big box, which they aggressively site in small towns, suburbs, and cities in the United States and around the world. The big retailers have benefitted from controversial pricing tactics (predatory pricing, price discrimination, and resale price maintenance) that work to their advantage and against the interest of smaller retailers. They have benefitted also from changes in tax laws that have spurred the development of superstores at the local level. The transformation of retailing can be seen most clearly in the rise of Wal-Mart from Sam Walton's first few stores in Arkansas to its current status as the world's biggest retailer. While undeniably popular among a large segment of the population, the spread of superstores eventually led to a reaction as many people became concerned about retail saturation, sprawl, and the adverse effects of such stores on local quality of life. Wal-Mart, the biggest and most aggressive of the superstore retailers, became the target of antisuperstore opponents across the country.

Chapter 3 draws on the empirical literature in sociology, economics, and other areas to examine how superstores affect communities. I evaluate the major arguments in favor of a Wal-Mart superstore—that it offers low prices and a wide selection of merchandise, creates jobs, and generates tax revenue—and review the claims about its effects on small merchants and community welfare. I also explain how the placement, size, and design of superstores affects the built environment and note what planners and architects have said about what does, and does not, contribute to a satisfying urban milieu and sense of place. According to the critics, superstores adversely affect the built environment by contributing to sprawl and undermining the public realm.

Each of the next three chapters contains a pair of case studies: the two complete successes in chapter 4, the two partial successes in chapter 5, and the two failures in chapter 6. These cases convey the nature of these local dramas and provide the material for the analysis that follows. While there are similarities (and differences) among these cases, each reflects the uniqueness of a particular small town with a particular configuration of politics, geography, economic conditions, social class, local personalities, and history. Taken together, they provide a revealing view of local land use politics, especially in regards to zoning.

In chapter 7 I explain why each local social movement succeeded or failed. This explanation is based on a comparative analysis of approximately twenty variables, some suggested by the literature on social movement outcomes, siting controversies, and the growth machine; others I became aware of only in the course of conducting my research. The analysis reveals five key variables that explain why some superstore opponents succeeded and others failed. First, the successful opponents produced tangible evidence of widespread opposition. For example, in Eureka they took out a full-page newspaper advertisement listing dozens of local organizations that opposed the store, and in Gig Harbor they gathered more signatures on a petition than the population of the entire city. These sorts of tangible evidence constitute what might be called the *democratic argument*—the argument that the corporate action in question is opposed by a large segment of the community and not just by a few "extremists," "activists," or "greedy" small-business owners who might be easily discounted and dismissed. Second, success was more likely when the opponents framed the issue broadly. Emphasizing the adverse effects a Wal-Mart superstore would have on the whole town—whether in regard to land use, the economy, or quality of life—worked better than concentrating on the harm that it might cause for any particular subset of residents (i.e, small retailers, nearby homeowners, or downtown merchants). Third, most of the successful opponents received backing from the local media (i.e., the local newspaper). While the importance of the media is not surprising, what is perhaps unexpected is that local newspapers were willing to oppose a large-scale, corporate-sponsored development project. Fourth, the successful opponents did not have to contend with a counter social movement. A counter social movement organization, in the form of indigenous organized efforts to promote the proposed store, figured in three cases and in two of those it played serious havoc with the opponents' efforts by injecting competing framings into the debate and representing (or claiming to represent) large numbers of "silent" Wal-Mart shoppers. And fifth, the successful opponents benefitted from blunders made by Wal-Mart. While all of these variables contributed to success on the basis of their independent effects, three of them—evidence of widespread opposition, effective framing, and the media support—further contributed to success through a mutually reinforcing combination that enabled the movement to increase its reach and influence, and thereby increase its ability to prevail against a large corporation. I then offer a general model of the conditions under which communities may be able to deal with large corporations on more favorable terms. The four parts of this model are regulatory checkpoints, publicity, debate, and local decision making. I close the chapter by comparing my model with the recent project in political theory and practice known as deliberative democracy. Although I argue that deliberative democracy does not fully account for the impact of large organizations (i.e., the corporation) on deliberative processes, my overall assessment is that both my model and deliberative democracy are generally similar in their attempts to improve contemporary politics by implementing decision-making processes that are based on participation and reasoned debate.

I begin the final chapter with a discussion of what these controversies suggest about the importance of the local state. Here I argue that in spite of globalization the local state in the form of municipal governments continues to play an important role in conflicts between communities and corporations. I then return to the larger social issues raised by these disputes and explain why corporate retailing, above and beyond the issues involving Wal-Mart and superstores, is problematic, as manifested in the effects of organizational size, control, homogenization, fakery, and hypertrophy of consumption. This leads to a consideration of McDonaldization and the prospects for resistance. I find that some people will resist McDonaldization and their resistance can stimulate useful debate. However, resistance is hindered by the presence of supporters of McDonaldization, the difficulty of challenging business practices that are perfectly legal, and the simple fact that powerful corporations have found McDonaldization very profitable. I conclude by asking, and attempting to answer, two central questions about local anticorporate activism: Does it truly serve the community interest and can it effectively challenge the status quo? To the first, my answer is "yes"; to the second, "no, but it can contribute to that challenge."

NOTES

1. *Sprawl-Busters Alert*, a publication that tracks big box siting controversies, contained information on approximately two hundred such controversies between 1995, when it began publication, and 2000.

2. Patty Berg, quoted in *Humboldt Beacon* (CA), 1 July 1999.

3. See, for example, Crenson, *Un-Politics of Air Pollution*; Doukas, *Worked Over*; Gaventa, *Power and Powerlessness*; Jones and Bachelor, *Sustaining Hand*; and Wylie and Turnley, *Poletown*.

4. In 2000 I conducted a mail survey of local officials in municipalities where superstore controversies were reported to have occurred during the 1990s. The survey asked if there had been "at least one proposal to build a superstore in your area that was opposed by a local organization or group of persons" during the last ten years. Two hundred fourteen surveys were sent; 168 were returned (response rate of 79 percent). Of those returned, twenty-three were not usable, leaving 145 to analyze. Of these, 102 involved a Wal-Mart superstore. In eighty-five of these cases there was organized opposition, indicated by asking "Was a local organization formed specifically to oppose the superstore?" and "Did an existing local organization actively oppose the superstore?" In 33 percent of these eighty-five cases the store was built at the original site or at another site, in 48 percent it was not built anywhere, and in 16 percent it was "still under review." It is possible that the sample included a disproportionate number of well-organized and sophisticated opposition groups—that is, those with the best chances of prevailing—and thus the results may overstate the rate of success.

5. Vidich and Bensman, *Small Town*.

6. U.S. Census Bureau. *Statistical Abstract of the United States: 2008*. Table 721.

7. U.S. Census Bureau. *Statistics of U.S. Businesses: 2002*. http://www.census.gov.

8. British lord chancellor Edward Thurlow (1731–1806) remarked that "Corporations have neither bodies to be punished, nor souls to be condemned, they therefore do as they like." (quoted in Micklethwait and Woodridge, *The Company*, 33).

9. See Bakan, *The Corporation*; Clawson, Neustadtl, and Weller, *Dollars and Votes*; Court, *Corporateering*; Drutman and Cray, *People's Business*; Hartmann, *Unequal Protection*; Kelly, *Divine Right*; Mitchell, *Corporate Irresponsibility*; and Nace, *Gangs of America*.

10. See, for example, Bluestone and Harrison, *Deindustrialization of America*; Craypo and Nissen, *Grand Designs*; Nissen, *Fighting for Jobs*; Portz, *Politics of Plant Closings*; and Raines, Berson, and Gracie, *Community and Capital in Conflict*.

11. Some environmentalists argue that the extent to which proposed waste incinerators and other waste facilities *have* to be built somewhere is mitigated by the possibility of generating less waste in the first place, using alternative materials, and recycling more. See Freudenberg and Steinsapir, "Not in Our Backyards"; Gibbs, "Movement on the Move"; and Heiman, "From 'Not in My Backyard.'"

12. Letter to Pierce County Department of Planning and Land Services, dated 7 June 1996, file SPR 2–95, Pierce County Department of Planning and Land Services, Tacoma, Washington.

13. *Fortune*, "Fortune 500," 5 May 2008. In 2003 *Fortune* named Wal-Mart its "most admired" and "most respected" company. Useem, "One Nation Under Wal-Mart."

14. Lichtenstein, "Wal-Mart: A Template for Twenty-First Century Capitalism," 4.

15. Ritzer, *McDonaldization*, 1.

16. Starbucks may be viewed as a McDonaldized coffee shop.
17. See Starr, *Naming the Enemy*.
18. See Giugni, "Was It Worth the Effort?"; and Giugni, McAdam, and Tilly, *How Social Movements Matter*.
19. Gamson, *Strategy of Social Protest* (1975).
20. Gamson, *Strategy of Social Protest*, 2d ed. (1990), 156.
21. See Giugni, "Was It Worth the Effort?" An important dissenting view is Piven and Cloward, *Poor People's Movements*.
22. John Lofland identifies three degrees of contentiousness: polite action (i.e., lobbying, electioneering), protest action ("ostentatious, dramatic, and ambiguously legal or illegal nonviolent efforts"), and violent action. Lofland, *Social Movement Organizations*, 262.
23. Kruse, "The Movement and the Media," 68.
24. See Benford and Snow, "Framing Processes."
25. Galanter, "Why the 'Haves' Come Out Ahead."
26. See Gaffin, "Offending and Defending."
27. Walsh and Cable, "Litigation and Citizen Protest," 296.
28. See Burstein, Einwohner, and Hollander, "Success of Political Movements"; Jenkins and Perrow, "Insurgency of the Powerless"; and Schumaker, "Policy Responsiveness."
29. See Lo, "Countermovements and Conservative Movements"; Meyer and Staggenborg, "Movements, Countermovements"; Mottl, "Analysis of Countermovements"; Rucht, "Movement Allies"; and Zald and Useem, "Movement and Countermovement Interaction."
30. See Baylor, "Media Framing of Movement Protest"; Carroll and Ratner, "Media Strategies"; Gamson, *Strategy of Social Protest*, 2d ed. (1990); Gamson, "Bystanders"; Gamson and Wolfsfeld, "Movements and Media"; and Klandermans, "Introduction: Organizational Effectiveness."
31. See Molotch, "Media and Movements."
32. There are also large-scale projects such as mines, airports, dams, nuclear power plants, high-speed railroads, and pipelines that may affect a large territory and stretch over many jurisdictions. See Rucht, "Mobilization Against Large Techno-Industrial Projects."
33. Relevant studies include Bonanno and Constance, "Mega Hog Farms"; Cable and Degutis, "Movement Outcomes"; Clingermayer, "Electoral Representation"; Couch and Kroll-Smith, "Environmental Controversies"; DeLind, "Parma"; Furuseth and O'Callaghan, "Community Response"; Gaffin, "Offending and Defending"; Gordon and Jasper, "Overcoming the 'Nimby' Label"; Kaminstein, "Resource Mobilization Analysis"; Kearney and Smith, "Low-Level Radioactive Waste Siting"; Kurtz, "Politics of Environmental Justice"; Leong, "The Struggle over Parcel C"; Merritt, "Common Cause"; Mobert, "Co-Opting Justice"; Murphree, Wright, and Ebaugh, "Toxic Waste Siting"; North, "'Save our Solsbury!'"; Shemtov, "Taking Ownership"; Simmons and Stark, "Backyard Protest"; and Walsh, Warland, and Smith, *Don't Burn It Here*.
34. Molotch, "City as a Growth Machine"; and Logan and Molotch, *Urban Fortunes*.

35. See Halebsky, "Superstores."

36. Although I refer to all the municipalities as cities, Ottawa is officially designated a village.

37. The population figures for the cities in the year the controversy began are as follows: Gig Harbor: 5,470 (1995); Petoskey: 6,625 (1994); West Bend: 27,714 (1994); Ottawa: 4,352 (1994); Ashland: 8,744 (1990); Eureka: 25,429 (1998). U.S. Census Bureau, "Population Estimates for Places." http://www.census.gov.

38. See Ragin, *Comparative Method*, for an explication of the method.

2

Big Retailers, Aggressive Retail Development, and the Roots of Local Protest

How did superstores become so controversial? How did Wal-Mart become the world's biggest retailer and get involved in so many siting controversies? Why did superstore controversies start to occur in the late 1980s? This chapter will answer these questions and provide the context for the controversies examined in following chapters. The superstore story has several parts: changes in the retail industry, leading to the dominance of big retailers; legal and legislative wrangling between big retailers and other merchants; the rise of Wal-Mart; aggressive retail development; and eventual reaction as local citizens became increasingly concerned about retail saturation, sprawl, the fate of small merchants, and threats to local quality of life.

CHANGES IN THE RETAIL INDUSTRY

Increased Retail Sales

Although the American economy has not regained the rapid growth rate of the "golden age" of American capitalism that lasted from the end of WWII to the early 1970s, during the last several decades it has continued to grow at an impressive rate. Gross domestic product (GDP) per capita, adjusted for inflation, increased 75 percent between 1972 and 2000, tracked closely by retail sales per capita, which increased 77 percent during the same period.[1] A significant portion of total GDP, about one-third, goes to retail sales. This includes eating and drinking places, which, although they seem ubiquitous, account for only about 10 percent of all retail sales. The average American spent about four thousand dollars more in retail establishments in 2000 than in 1972 (in 1996 dollars). This increase in retailing is also related to the increased commodification of life: as more and more of what we need and want takes the form of commodities, shopping becomes correspondingly more important. While alternative forms of retailing such as TV shopping, catalog sales, and Internet shopping have increased in recent years, they have not significantly undermined the importance of store shopping.

Rationalization and Restructuring of the Retail Industry

Not only has retailing increased, but the types of stores and the companies that run them have changed as well. For a long time retailing was a traditional, labor-intensive industry that experienced few changes. However, the wave of economic restructuring that swept over much of American industry during the last several decades eventually reached retailing and has produced far-reaching changes. A variety of tasks such as ordering, accounting, and warehousing began to be rationalized in the 1960s as new technologies were introduced. The pace of innovation picked up during the last twenty years with the development and diffusion of techniques such as bar coding, scanning, electronic data interchange (which allows retailers to transmit sales data directly to suppliers), just-in-time delivery (a technique designed to minimize the holding of excessive inventory), and cross docking (a method to expedite warehousing). These sophisticated methods have enabled the big retailers to construct, monitor, and expand the far-flung global supply chains that undergird their operations.[2] The use of expensive and sophisticated technology to cut costs, along with mass advertising, has heavily favored the larger retail chains. The resulting uneven development has led to a restructuring of the industry as many independent retailers have vanished while mergers and acquisitions have resulted in a concentration of market share among a decreasing number of large retailers.[3] Retailers now rank among the very biggest American companies; nine of the fifty largest American corporations are now retailers.[4] Retailing has also gone global, with many of the big retailers now operating stores overseas. Wal-Mart, for example, now has stores in Argentina, Brazil, Canada, China, Costa Rica, El Salvador, Guatemala, Honduras, Japan, Mexico, Nicaragua, Puerto Rico, and the United Kingdom.[5]

We can track some of these changes by using data from the Census of Retail Trade, conducted by the U.S. Department of Commerce. Figure 2.1 shows the number of retail firms and establishments for selected years from 1963 to 1992. (A "firm," in the lexicon of the Department of Commerce, is a distinct legal entity engaged in business and may be organized as a corporation, a partnership, or a sole proprietorship. An "establishment" is a separate location where business is conducted. Thus, a small local retailer would be a firm with

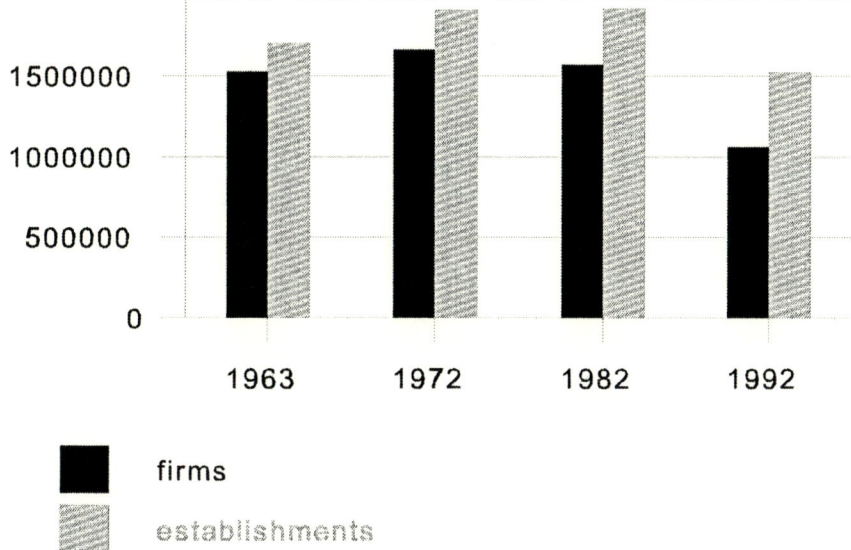

Figure 2.1. Retail Trade, 1963–1992: Number of firms and establishments
Source: *Census of Business,* 1963; *Census of Retail Trade* 1972, 1982, 1992.

probably just one establishment, while a chain would be a firm with many establishments. The multiple establishments that make up a chain are also referred to as "units.") Between 1963 and 1992 the number of firms and establishments declined, even though population increased by 36 percent and retail sales increased significantly. This decline in the number of firms is a result of many going out of business, merging with other firms, or being acquired. The surviving firms have tended to be the big chains, which have garnered an increasing share of the market. Big chains, defined here as firms with at least 100 units, accounted for 34 percent of all retailing by 1992 (see Figure 2.2). These data confirm what we see happening all across the county: big chains are taking over retailing.

The category within retail trade known as "general merchandise stores" encompasses department stores, variety stores, and miscellaneous general merchandise stores, and includes most nonspecialized retailers such as Wal-Mart. The trend here is similar to that for retail trade as a whole, but is even more pronounced (see Figures 2.3 and 2.4). The number of firms and establishments has declined significantly, while the large chains have expanded their share of the general merchandise market to 77 percent. Other Department of Commerce data reveal that by 1992 the fifty largest general merchandising firms, out of a total of 34,606 such firms, accounted for 92

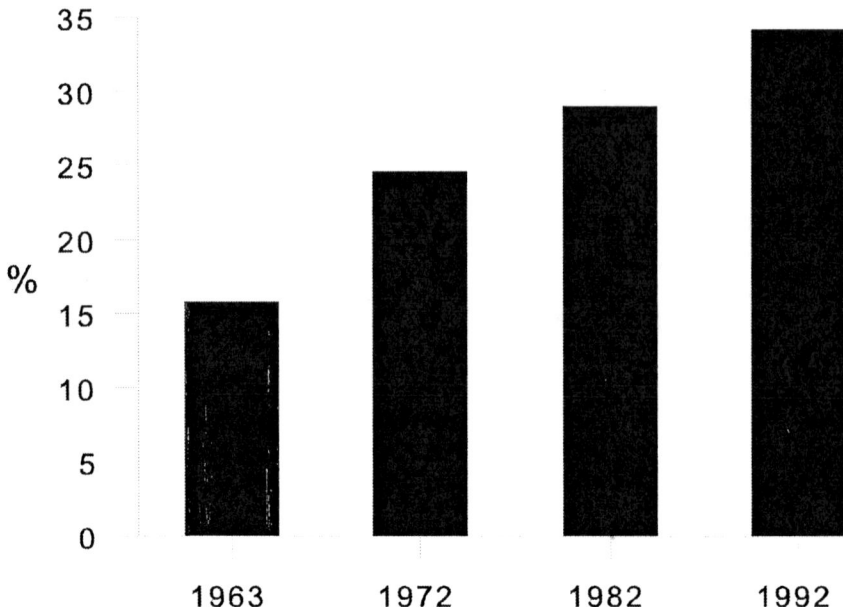

Figure 2.2. Retail Trade 1963–1992: Percentage of total sales by firms with at least 100 units
Source: *Census of Business,* 1963; *Census of Retail Trade* 1972, 1982, 1992.

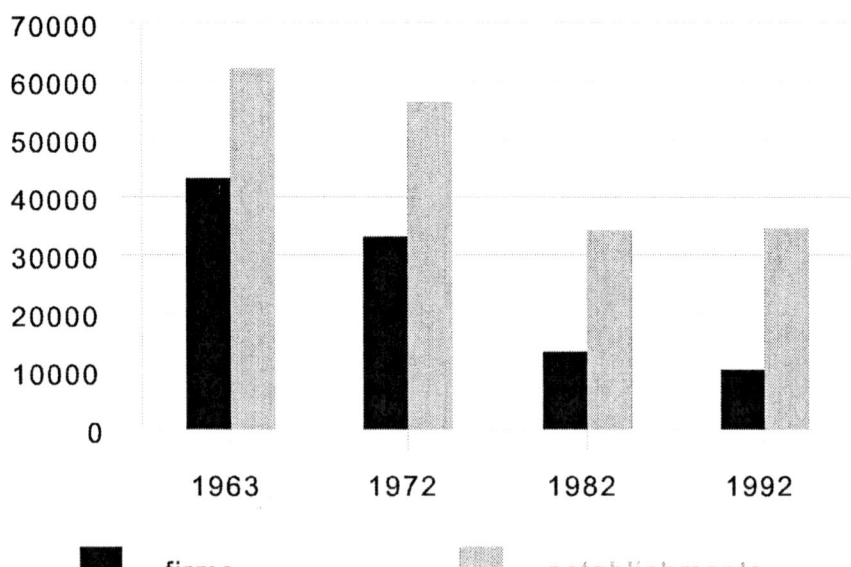

Figure 2.3. General Merchandise Stores, 1963–1992: Number of firms and establishments
Source: *Census of Business,* 1963; *Census of Retail Trade* 1972, 1982, 1992.

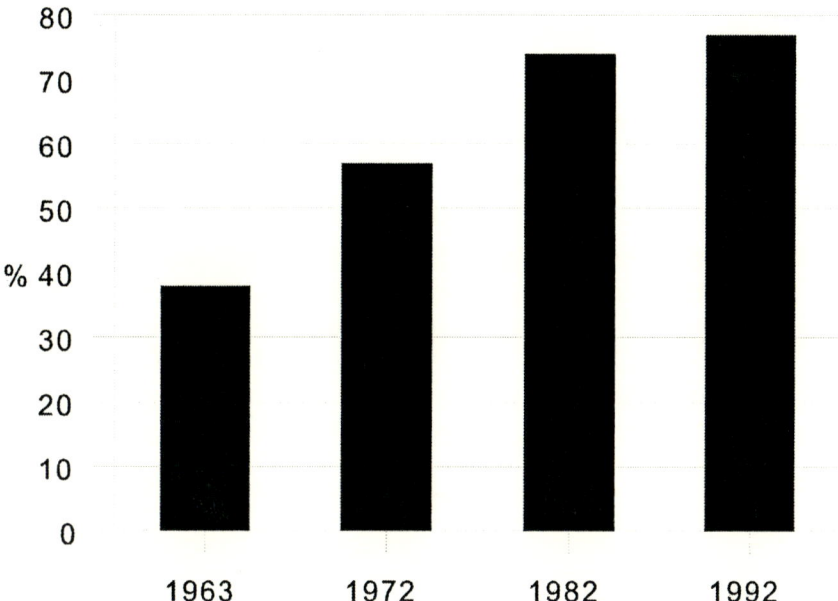

Figure 2.4. General Merchandise Stores, 1963–1992: Percentage of total sales by firms with at least 100 units
Source: *Census of Business*, 1963; *Census of Retail Trade* 1972, 1982, 1992.

percent of all sales in this category.[6] The trend toward concentration entered a new phase during the 1990s with the phenomenal growth of Wal-Mart, which by 1997 accounted for 32 percent of all general merchandise sales and by 2000 garnered nearly 4 percent of *all* retail sales in the United States.[7]

A simultaneous increase in retail sales and decrease in the number of stores can be reconciled in only two ways: more nonstore retailing or more sales per store. Both have occurred. Nonstore retailing (e.g., the Internet) has increased, but that increase has occurred only recently and was not a factor during the period under consideration here. The big change, and the one that has had the most significant implication for communities, is that stores have become bigger. Bigger stores normally generate more sales and this is reflected in the increased prevalence of superstores over the last several decades.

These general trends can be seen among specialty retailers also. Consider, for example, the fate of stationery stores. Between 1963 and 1992 the number of firms and establishments fell by 66 percent and 47 percent, respectively (see Figure 2.5), making the independent local stationery store an endangered species. This is an example of the consequence of many lines of retailing being taken over by specialty superstore chains known as "category killers" (e.g., Staples, Home Depot, Toys-R-Us, Best Buy). The declining number of

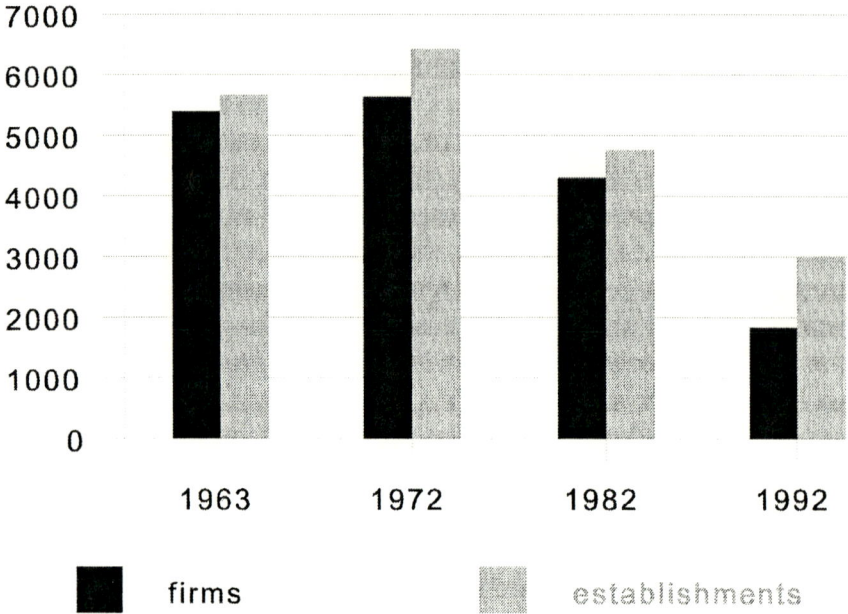

Figure 2.5. Stationery Stores, 1963–1992: Number of firms and establishments
Source: *Census of Business*, 1963; *Census of Retail Trade* 1972, 1982, 1992.

firms and establishments also reflects the fact that large general merchandise stores (i.e., Wal-Mart) have attracted many customers who formerly patronized specialty stores. Overall, the data indicate that retailing is increasingly dominated by large chains and large stores. Although superstore controversies did not begin until the late 1980s, some of the underlying changes occurred earlier, most markedly during the 1970s. Thus, there seems to have been some lag between changes in the retail industry and the growth of public opposition.

Growing Retail Clout

Another result of restructuring is a change in the relationship between the big retailers and the manufacturers and wholesalers that provide them with products to sell. The largest retailers have increased their size and power relative to manufacturers and increasingly dictate the terms of trade. Management guru Peter Drucker noted this in 1992 when he wrote that "Power in the economies of developed countries is rapidly shifting from manufacturers to distributors and retailers."[8] Wal-Mart's annual sales, for example, are six times those of Procter & Gamble, the leading manufacturer of personal care products, and nearly twenty-five times those of Nike, the largest apparel company. Toys-R-Us, the biggest retailer of toys and a leading category killer, has annual sales that are more than twice those of Mattel, the biggest toy manufacturer.[9] Concentration in retailing has led to a situation in which a single retailer can account for a large percentage of a manufacturer's total output. Seventeen percent of Proctor & Gamble's total sales, for example, are made to Wal-Mart, as are 23 percent of Clorox's, 20 percent of Revlon's, and 20 percent of RJR Tobacco's.[10] These disparities are even greater for the thousands of smaller companies that sell to the big retailers. Manufacturers face a strategic dilemma: if they play with the big retailers they have the opportunity to realize enormous sales by having their products reach a wide market, but the rules of the game are increasingly set by the retailers and make it difficult for the manufacturers, especially the smaller ones, to play the game profitably.

In traditional retailing the merchant's function was simply to sell goods directly to the public. Retailers generally had to take the products that manufacturers produced and had little room to maneuver in regard to quality, price, delivery, and payment. This has changed, at least for the big retailers.[11] Wal-Mart, for example, deals directly with many manufacturers instead of wholesalers and operates its own distribution centers, thus bypassing these two traditional links in the retail supply chain. Even more important, big retailers use their purchasing power to push manufacturers to lower their prices. Retailers also press them to provide special packaging and labeling, to pay fees to guarantee shelf space for their products, to provide long payment periods (while pushing for quick delivery), to invest in expensive technology, and to pay costly charge-backs for any mistakes in labeling, packaging, or delivery.[12] The manufacturers must comply with these demands or risk losing a large share of their market.[13] Moreover, major retailers now avoid some of the established manufacturers completely and contract directly with independent suppliers, often overseas, to have clothes and other products made to their specifications, which they sell under their own brand names.

The Spread of Superstores

One consequence of the rationalization of retailing, especially as pursued by discount merchandisers, has been the spread of superstores. Various aspects of their design and operation reflect the intense focus on minimizing costs that characterizes contemporary corporate retailing. First, large stores allow retailers to benefit from economies of scale and scope. Second, most superstores are built as inexpensively as possible, with architectural, construction, and landscaping costs kept to a minimum. Store designs are based on a limited number of master plans, which are replicated from site to site, with the result that most stores look alike and rarely conform to local architectural style. Third, retailers generally prefer to place their superstores near the outskirts of a city or even outside city limits. This allows for easy access to major roads and freeways, thereby facilitating the frequent truck deliveries that are necessary to keep the stores well stocked, which is integral to the rapid turnover of merchandise that has become crucial for success. Also, land on the outskirts is often cheaper than land located more centrally. Aside from considerations of costs, superstore retailers need a large chunk of land that is appropriately zoned (i.e., for large-scale commercial development) or that the retailer can convince local authorities to rezone, and the outskirts is often the best or only place to find such land. Land outside city limits in the surrounding county or rural township may be attractive because of lax or nonexistent zoning in such areas. Most of the controversies described in subsequent chapters revolved around attempts by Wal-Mart to have land rezoned to accommodate a superstore.

In the 1990s developers and retailers joined to create a new retail configuration, the "power center." A power center may be thought of as a shopping center made up exclusively of big box superstores. Located at the edge of a city or just outside city limits, it is composed of a number of freestanding big box stores surrounded by enormous parking lots. Shoppers must drive from store to store because of the distances separating them and the lack of sidewalks.

Changes in Tax Laws

Changes in state tax laws during the last twenty-five years also contributed to aggressive retail development and the spread of superstores.[14] During this period a number of states, especially in the West, enacted laws that limited the property tax liability of homeowners and owners of commercial property. The most well-known such law is California's Proposition 13, approved by the voters in 1978. During the next three years nineteen other states adopted property tax restrictions.[15] Devised as a grassroots response to citizen concerns about rising property taxes and the increasing size of government, Proposition 13 limited property taxes to 1 percent of the original purchase price and limited increases, where allowed, to no more than 2 percent each year.[16] Because property taxes have been a major source of revenue for local governments, Proposition 13 compelled many local politicians to search for other sources of revenue. One source that has become salient in some states is the sales tax. In California, for example, sales tax may be as high as 8 percent, with local governments entitled to keep 1 percent, based on the sales that take place within their boundaries. In the wake of Proposition 13 some cities and counties have become keen to promote retail development over other forms of development as a means of generating sales tax revenue.[17] According to Jeffrey Chapman, who studied this issue for the Public Policy Institute of California, "There are two popular ways (at least among elected officials) of generating a large amount of sales taxes from a small area: 'big-box' retail and car dealerships."[18] It is not uncommon for local officials to offer incentives to developers and retailers to ensure that high-volume superstore development takes place within their city boundaries. Thus, Proposition 13 and other similar measures have had the unintended consequence of contributing to the aggressive expansion of large-scale retail development.

AGGRESSIVE RETAIL DEVELOPMENT

All this brings us to the retail development that is the proximate cause of superstore siting controversies. The evidence presented above points to corporate retailers as the driving force behind the expansion of retail development in many communities. In spite of increasing concentration the retail industry remains fiercely competitive and a primary aspect of this competition is the search for new store sites. In conventional store retailing (as contrasted with nonstore forms of retailing), the principal way to expand market share is to open a new store or enlarge an existing store, regardless of whether or not a particular area is already served by existing merchants, and this is what has been occurring throughout the country. In some instances big retailers (i.e., Wal-Mart) have moved into small towns with a dearth of existing stores. In other instances, however, they have opened stores in towns and cities that already have a wide selection of stores. *American Demographics* declared in 1990 that "Most markets are now overbuilt with office, retail, and residential space" and "The furious pace of retail construction in the 1980s has led to . . . a glut of space in shopping malls."[19] Thus, the 1990s *began* with a surfeit of retail development. In spite of this surfeit stores continued to be built at a rapid pace throughout the 1990s. During this time industry analysts commented frequently that much of the country was "overbuilt" and "overstored."[20] An "overstored" market, as that term is used in the retail industry, means one in which there are so many stores that some will inevitably fail. Such a market, however, is not necessarily perceived as an obstacle by a large retailer intent on expansion. As these trends indicate, local residents correctly perceived that they were being subjected to a barrage of retail development.

As part of this surge in retail development, retailers have expanded into places such as museums, airports, parks, zoos, schools, and hospitals that previously contained few or no retail establishments. Newer forms of retailing (i.e., the Internet) and the reinvigoration of older forms (e.g., catalog sales) can be seen as other ways in which retailing has expanded and penetrated contemporary life. This enlargement of retailing has led to conflict as other parties object to the usurpation of space, real and virtual, by retail development. In a related trend, retailing has increasingly merged with other forms of consumption such as dining, entertainment, gambling, travel, and tourism. In the words of Paul Goldberger, we have entered the "entertainment-consumption age,"[21] characterized by the proliferation of retail and other consumption-oriented forms of urban development. Some scholars argue that the relative decline of manufacturing and the increased importance of consumption has resulted in cities that are now more accurately characterized as places of consumption than as centers of production.[22] Mullins et al. observe that:

> Over the past 30 or so years, consumption spaces have become an integral part of the emergent postindustrial-postmodern city ... [and constitute] a built environment that [has] replaced the earlier infrastructure of production ...
>
> Consumption spaces have emerged and continue to develop in response to the ever-increasing power of consumerism ... a cultural imperative demanding that all peoples in all countries buy and consume as many goods and services as possible.[23]

In the manufacturing-based economy that characterized most of the last century, companies that owned big local factories and other production facilities were often major players in local affairs, especially if their headquarters were local too. As the importance of consumption has increased, retailers have emerged as major players with whom other local parties must contend. Local economic development schemes now often involve retailing and other forms of consumption. Developers and big retailers often claim that a new shopping center, mall, or superstore will improve the local economy by transforming a town or city into a "destination" that attracts large numbers of consumers from far away. Local citizens and officials must now evaluate the costs and benefits of large-scale retail development and the often conflicting claims of the various parties involved.

THE POLITICS OF PRICING

As a result of these various trends many local communities have found themselves confronted with large and powerful retailers that are driven to maximize market share and are committed to ongoing rationalization in all aspects of their operations. The growth of the big retail chains, however, is not simply a story of increasing efficiency through better organization and more advanced technology. There is also a political dimension that involves contested legislation, court rulings, action (and inaction) by regulatory agencies, and interest group activism. Much of this involves various aspects of pricing by retailers and manufacturers. Pricing can be used as a weapon by one retailer against another; it is also part of the constant strife between manufacturers and retailers.

Various pricing tactics may provoke charges of unfair competition from those who are harmed directly as well as from others who consider such practices injurious to the public good. Anticompetitive pricing practices come under the purview of the Sherman Antitrust Act of 1890, which states that:

> Every person who shall monopolize, or attempt to monopolize, or combine or conspire with any other person or persons, to monopolize any part of the trade of commerce among the several States . . . shall be deemed guilty of a felony . . .

The Clayton Act of 1914 and the Robinson-Patman Act of 1936 also have provisions that apply to pricing. Questionable pricing practices are investigated by the Department of Justice and the Federal Trade Commission (FTC), which was established in 1914 and given the authority to investigate "unfair methods of competition." The extent to which questionable pricing practices have actually been curtailed has depended on the courts' interpretations of this legislation and on the propensity of the Department of Justice and FTC and to actively enforce legislation. Enforcement itself depends, in part, on presidential appointees and other political considerations. Attempts to prevent retailers and manufacturers from using pricing in an unfair manner have fluctuated widely over the last one hundred years and success at eradicating unfair tactics remains elusive. Part of the difficulty is that there is disagreement over what exactly constitutes "competition" or the lack thereof. If big retailers use low prices to drive small stores out of business, has competition and the public good been increased or decreased? Is efficiency, or mere size, being rewarded when big retailers are able to buy products from manufacturers at prices below those available to small retailers? In what follows we will look briefly at the three most common pricing issues: predatory pricing, price discrimination, and resale price maintenance.

Predatory pricing occurs when a dominant retailer sells goods below cost with the intent to force its competitors out of business and then recoup those losses by selling at higher prices (made possible as a result of eliminating competition). While predatory pricing can shade into the normal price-cutting practices of discounters, in its pure form it represents an attempt by a large retailer to dominate strictly on the basis of size. A large retailer, especially a chain, can afford to sell some products at a loss—even operate an entire store at a loss—for an extended period; its smaller competitors, even if equally efficient, do not have the resources to compete in this fashion and thus lose sales; some eventually go out of business.

Predatory pricing is illegal, but does it differ from normal "competitive" pricing? According to Terry Calvani, former commissioner of the FTC, "claims of predatory pricing were taken quite seriously" up until the 1970s.[24] Beginning in the mid-1970s, however, it became progressively more difficult for plaintiffs to prevail in predatory pricing cases. First, judges began to use a definition of "below cost" that was difficult for plaintiffs to establish. Later, in 1986, the Supreme Court cast doubt on the entire notion of predatory pricing by stating that "predatory pricing schemes are rarely tried, and even more rarely successful."[25] Then, in 1989, an important decision by the Court of Appeals removed the alleged predator's intent as a relevant consideration. Thus, it no longer mattered if the alleged predator had declared, "We will drive so-and-so out of business." Finally, in a landmark case in 1993, the Supreme Court affirmed these views and opined that the plaintiff must prove that the alleged predator will recoup its losses, where such proof required demonstrating that the alleged victim would be eliminated and that the market was susceptible to monopoly pricing. These standards of proof are so high that they have, in the words of one commentator, rendered the "death knell of predatory pricing" as a viable defense by its victims.[26] Although the courts have become increasingly unfavorable to claims of predatory pricing, such cases have continued. In fact, the number of cases brought before federal courts increased rapidly between the 1970s and the early 1990s, a trend that would appear to correlate with the expansion of discount retailers and indicates, at a minimum, a perception that predatory pricing is occurring.[27] Wal-Mart has had to defend itself against charges of predatory pricing more than once.[28]

Price discrimination occurs when a manufacturer sells the same goods to different retailers at different prices (i.e., selling to a big chain at a lower price than to a small retailer). The Robinson-Patman Act of 1936, enacted as a direct response to the rapid rise of chain stores during the 1920s and 1930s, especially A&P, was expressly intended to bar price discrimination when it harms individual businesses or the overall level of competition.[29] Although the original intent of Robinson-Patman was to prevent large chains from putting small retailers out of business, the courts and regulatory authorities have wavered in their adherence to that goal and consequently the overall effectiveness of the Act has been limited. Enforcement of the Act by the Department of Justice has been minimal during the last thirty years. One reason for the lack of enforcement is that the very intent of the Act has been questioned: should small independent retailers be protected when the ostensible alternative is lower prices for consumers? Under the influence of the Chicago School of law and economics, some regulators and judges have developed a conception of antitrust that construes consumer welfare as the *promotion of competition,* which is assumed to be evidenced by low prices, regardless of increasing industry concentration, and not as the *protection of competitors* (i.e., small merchants). Enforcement of the Act has always been hindered by its lack of clarity and the difficulty of identifying "discrimination," and since the 1990s the courts have made it even harder to successfully prosecute cases of discrimination by making them subject to some of the same stringent tests as predatory pricing.

A *resale price maintenance* (RPM) agreement exists when a manufacturer, acting independently or at the behest of one or more retailers, compels the retailers who sell its brand-name products to sign a contract obligating them to keep prices for those products *above* a certain minimum level; for example, if Mattel and Kmart signed an agreement which specified that Kmart will sell Barbie® dolls only at or above a certain price. The primary benefit of RPM for nondiscount retailers and small retailers is that it prevents discounters from underselling them.[30] Like price discrimination measures, RPM laws were passed initially during the 1930s to help small retailers combat the increasingly vigorous competition of the chain stores.[31] The supporters of RPM refer to pro-RPM legislation as "fair trade" laws, while the critics say such legislation encourages "price fixing."[32] RPM has always been denounced vigorously by the discounters—Rob Walton, a Wal-Mart executive, declared RPM a "great danger" to discounters.[33] In 1975 the discount industry persuaded Congress to pass the Consumer Goods Pricing Bill of 1975 which repealed RPM. In spite of the repeal, the status of RPM remains unclear. Harvard business historian Thomas McCraw observes that "[n]either Congress, the Justice Department, nor the Supreme Court has maintained a consistent position toward RPM over time" and "substantial disagreement persists on why it has been used in practice and what its actual effects have been."[34] Thomas Overstreet, in a 1983 review of the literature on RPM, concludes that it "does not appear ever to have been very pervasive in the U.S."[35] By contrast, Bluestone et al. argue that the repeal of RPM "precipitated a virtually total restructuring of the retail sector," including a rapid expansion of discounting, because it allowed discounters to sell name-brand merchandise and undersell regular department stores as well as small retailers.[36] David Boyd, in a complementary analysis, presents data showing that the total number of retail establishments declined dramatically and sales per establishment increased rapidly following the repeal of RPM.[37] These two changes are consistent with the shift to fewer but bigger stores that marks the rise of the superstore discount chains.

What can we conclude about the politics of pricing? The disputes over pricing have pitted discounters against regular merchants, big retailers against small retailers, and manufacturers against retailers. While local citizens have generally not been directly involved in these disputes and are unaware of this history, these disputes have had, and continue to have, important ramifications for communities because they affect the expansion or decline of various types of retailers, and thereby affect the size and power of the retailers that communities confront. While predatory pricing, discriminatory pricing, and RPM have been subject to legislative and judicial ups and downs, current arrangements, on the whole, clearly favor the discounters and large retailers. It is important to realize that these arrangements do not reflect the workings of the market but involve political action taken on the basis of group interests. The history of pricing disputes also shows that the notion of "competition" itself, as well as the connection between competition and the public interest, is open to interpretation.

WAL-MART

Wal-Mart, more than any other company, embodies the various changes in retailing discussed in this chapter. It has become the nation's leading retailer and has been a party to more siting controversies than any other company. In 2007 Wal-Mart's sales exceeded the combined sales of the next nine general merchandisers.[38] Hence, it is useful to review briefly the story of Wal-Mart and its well-known founder, Sam Walton.[39] Walton's retailing career began in 1945 when he became the franchisee of a Ben Franklin variety store in Newport, Arkansas. It was a small store located in the downtown of a small town and, as such, resembled most other small-town establishments of the time. Walton was astute and hardworking and soon made a success of the store. Because of complications with the lease, Walton was forced to sell the store (at a substantial profit) five years after opening it. He soon purchased another small store in another small town, this time a Harrison's variety store in Bentonville, Arkansas, that he renamed Walton's 5 & 10. Walton moved his family to Bentonville and remained there for the rest of his life. Today Wal-Mart is headquartered in Bentonville. Walton was immensely successful with his 5 & 10 and began to buy more variety stores. By 1962 he and his brother, Bud, owned and operated sixteen stores in Arkansas, Missouri, and Kansas.

Although successful at traditional retailing, Walton was ambitious and willing to try new methods. One new approach that piqued his interest was discount merchandising, which had begun to spread after WWII. Carried out successfully, discounting could be very profitable. The key was to combine low costs and high volume, two of the prime factors behind the eventual development of the superstore. Although most of the early discounters located in larger cities to ensure the requisite high volume, a significant number of Americans still lived in small towns and rural areas, leading some enterprising discounters, including Walton, to try placing stores there. As Vance and Scott note, putting a large store in a small town had "certain unique advantages. First, existing competition was limited.... Second, if a store were large enough to dominate business in a town and its surrounding area, other retailers would be discouraged from entering the market."[40] Sam Walton would prove beyond any doubt that money could be made by putting large discount stores in small towns. In 1962 Walton entered the discount business by opening a 16,000-square-foot store in Rogers, Arkansas, that he called Wal-Mart Discount City. The store was an instant success and Walton was off and running in the world of discount merchandising. He soon enlarged the Rogers store and began purchasing others. Walton prospered by leasing cheap buildings, spending next to nothing on store improvements, keeping costs as low as possible, attracting customers through low prices, and then selling at high volume and reinvesting the profit in more merchandise and more (and bigger) stores.

The success of the Wal-Mart discount stores convinced Walton that he could expand even faster if he had more capital. Walton needed a substantial amount of money and decided that the only feasible way to get it without incurring an oppressive amount of debt was to go public. With little fanfare the firm was incorporated in 1969 with Sam Walton as president and chairman of the board. Once incorporated, Wal-Mart raised money by selling stock to the public. Only about 23 percent of the common stock was sold to the public; the rest remained in the hands of Sam Walton, his family, and close associates. With an infusion of capital and the means to raise more in the future, Walton began to expand in earnest. Spreading outward from his base in Bentonville, Walton methodically built his empire, sometimes buying individual stores, sometimes entire chains. He continued to avoid the big cities and insisted on placing his stores in small towns, small cities, and, increasingly, the suburbs. By 1980 there were 276 Wal-Marts, most in the South (see Table 2.1). During the 1980s the company transformed itself from a regional to a national retailer. In 1988, after forty-three years of single-minded devotion to building his retail empire, Walton stepped down as chief executive; he died of cancer in 1992. His handpicked successor, David Glass, took over as president. By 1990 there were 1,525 stores in twenty-nine states, generating sales of over twenty-five billion. Under Glass's leadership the company continued to expand throughout the United States and began to venture overseas. At the end of 2007 Wal-Mart operated 4,022 stores in the United States and 2,757 in foreign countries.[41] It has been the nation's largest retailer since 1993, when it overtook Sears Roebuck.[42] In 2001 it passed Exxon Mobil to become the nation's largest corporation and the world's largest business and has been among the leaders ever since.[43] Walton's mastery of discount retailing made his family and him extremely wealthy. In 2006 Walton's widow, her three surviving children (John Walton is deceased), and John Walton's widow were among the richest eleven Americans, with a total net worth exceeding that of Bill Gates.[44] Forty percent of Wal-Mart stock continues to be owned by the Walton family, giving them control over the company.[45]

Sam Walton and Wal-Mart were, and to some extent continue to be, closely associated in the mind of the public. Walton's personal appeal, the essence of which was an earnest folksiness, was an unofficial corporate asset and contributed to the initial acceptance of his stores in many small towns. He visited his stores frequently, listened carefully to his employees, whom he referred to as "associates," and solicited their advice on ways to improve operations. The opening lines of the foreword to Walton's autobiography give a taste of his style:

> Hello, friends, I'm Sam Walton, founder and chairman of Wal-Mart Stores. By now I hope you've shopped in one of our stores, or maybe bought some stock in our company. If you have, you probably know how proud I am of what is simply the miracle that all these Wal-Mart associates of mine have accomplished in the thirty years since we opened our first Wal-Mart here in northwest Arkansas, which Wal-Mart and I still call home. As hard as it is to believe sometimes, we've grown from that one little store into what is now the largest retailing outfit in the world. And we've really had a heck of a time along the way.[46]

Walton's folksy act, however, concealed a sophistication and ruthlessness equal to that of any CEO in America. Whether under his control or that of his successors, Wal-Mart's operations have been marked by an extraordinary focus on profitability and growth, matched, according to the company's critics, by an equally extraordinary disregard for the well-being of

Table 2.1. Number of Wal-Mart Stores in the U.S., by Region, 1975–2007

YEAR REGION	1975	1980	1985	1990	1995	2000	2005	2007
South	62	186	584	1103	1363	1462	1784	1918
Midwest	42	90	159	357	711	798	942	1022
West	0	0	2	64	282	411	551	630
Northeast	0	0	0	1	198	314	425	452
Totals	104	276	745	1525	2554	2985	3702	4022

Note: Regions are U.S. Census Bureau regions.
Source: *Wal-Mart Annual Report*, various years

employees, vendors, host communities, and other retailers.[47] While Wal-Mart has from the beginning presented itself as the preeminent low-price retailer, the company's strategy has always been to keep its *costs* low, and it is its tactics for minimizing costs that have made it a target for many critics.[48] One secret of Wal-Mart's success at keeping its costs low has been its extensive use of advanced technology. While its competitors were still using traditional methods, Wal-Mart leaped into the world of high technology and invested heavily in data processing and communications equipment, including a satellite system that allows company headquarters to keep in touch with stores around the world. The use of state-of-the-art technology allows Wal-Mart to exercise exquisite control over all phases of its operations, including purchasing, pricing, shipping, warehousing, stocking, replenishing, and accounting.

Along with becoming a sophisticated and powerful retailer, Wal-Mart has developed expertise in site selection and real estate development, and augments that expertise by using an array of local, regional, national, and international firms to assist it with the siting and construction of its stores. These include public relations consultants, real estate agents, law firms, real estate developers, architects, site preparation specialists, environmental consultants, engineers, and various other experts. Thus, a local group that challenges Wal-Mart faces not only a huge, sophisticated retailer, but a daunting array of its business allies as well.

SUPERSTORE CONTROVERSIES

Having examined changes in retailing and the rise of Wal-Mart, I now consider how these factors, in combination with other social changes and concerns, led to the superstore controversies that emerged in the late 1980s and continue today. Some of these changes can be identified clearly; others are more general. While most superstore retailers have faced opposition at one time or another, I concentrate on Wal-Mart because it has expanded more aggressively than the others and has been involved in more siting disputes. There is no indication that Sam Walton shied away from the controversies that his stores sometimes provoked. Nevertheless, in his autobiography he stated that:

> Today . . . we have almost adopted the position that if some community, for whatever reason, doesn't want us in there, we aren't interested in going in and creating a fuss. I encourage us to walk away from this kind of trouble because there are just too many other good towns out there who do want us.[49]

These words, which have been picked up and repeated frequently by local Wal-Mart opponents, have haunted company executives and real estate developers since they were written in 1992. What the opponents intend to convey by citing Walton's words is clear: if Wal-Mart respects small towns, as Sam Walton claims he did, then it should take protests seriously and alter its plans. In this way local opponents have tried to use the Walton persona for their own ends, as against those of Wal-Mart officials.

The place to start is Wal-Mart's expansion. The company's growth during the 1980s and 1990s was truly phenomenal (see Table 2.1): 276 stores in 1980, 1,525 in 1990, and 2,554 only five years later! This meant that there were more Wal-Marts, in more towns, in more parts of the country, affecting more individuals and businesses, for better or for worse. As part of this expansion Wal-Mart moved farther and farther out of its base in the South and lower Midwest, eventually opening stores in every state. The increasing incidence of siting disputes coincides roughly with the move into other regions and most Wal-Mart siting controversies have taken place outside the South. Why should geography matter? It is difficult to identify the precise reasons, but there are several possibilities. First, many other parts of the country were more prosperous and therefore simply not as impressed with a big store whose main draw was that it had the lowest prices on underwear and other consumer goods. Also, people elsewhere probably knew less about Walton and identified less with his folksy country demeanor. Lastly, as Wal-Mart expanded outside the South, it probably encountered more towns and cities in which people felt a sense of political efficacy. Whether as a result of more education, higher income, or a stronger tradition of local political participation, people in these places were more likely to actively challenge proposed projects that they perceived as threats to their communities.

Superstores not only proliferated, they got bigger too. In 1980 the average Wal-Mart occupied about 45,000 square feet (excluding the parking lot).[50] In 1987 Wal-Mart introduced its first "Supercenter." Occupying up to 200,000 square feet, a Supercenter combines a regular Wal-Mart discount store and a full-size grocery store under one roof. The Supercenter marked Wal-Mart's entry into the grocery business and here, as in most of its other ventures, the company has been very successful. By 2003 it was the nation's leading grocer.[51]

Wal-Mart's increased use of Supercenters contributed to siting disputes in a number of ways. Because of their size, these retail behemoths seem even more out of place in small towns than standard superstores. Also, they carry more lines of merchandise and thus pose a threat to a wider range of local merchants. Because they sell groceries, Supercenters increase the likelihood of siting controversies for two reasons peculiar to the grocery business. First, whereas people are willing to drive to a big box department store at the edge of town or even outside town, they are much less willing to drive that far to buy groceries (assuming they have a choice). To compete with other grocers, Wal-Mart has been compelled to place its Supercenters closer to residential areas—sometimes in residential areas—and this has led to increased opposition from local homeowners and other residents. The controversies that took place in West Bend and Ottawa revolved around the objections of nearby homeowners. Second, grocery stores represent one of the few unionized sectors of retailing and Wal-Mart's increasing share of the grocery market has come partly at the expense of retail chains that employ unionized workers. United Food and Commercial Workers (UFCW), which represents grocery workers, has been alarmed by this loss of union jobs and has begun to take an active role in siting disputes, especially where unionized jobs are at stake.[52] Union opposition ties in with Wal-Mart's expansion out of the South, as many other parts of the country have higher rates of unionization.

There are other changes that are harder to pin down but whose common feature seems to be a concern that the quality of life at the local level is becoming degraded. An important part of this concern involves sprawl, the low-density development of housing, stores, office buildings, industrial facilities, and almost everything else that has become commonplace in the United States. Such development is typically found on the outskirts of town or in the surrounding rural area. The superstore format—large single-story buildings surrounded by acres of parking and located near the edge of town—represents the retail version of sprawl. While sprawl is not a completely new phenomenon, in the last several decades it has become more pronounced and has come to be perceived widely as a serious social and environmental problem. By the 1990s sprawl had become a key issue for organizations such as the Sierra Club, the Natural Resources Defense Council, and the National Trust for Historic Preservation.[53] In the 1970s local governments began to implement "growth management" measures, a term that refers to a range of proactive measures designed to regulate and control growth.[54] While considered radical at first, by the 1980s such measures were rapidly gaining acceptance. One type of measure aimed directly at curtailing sprawl is the growth boundary, which is "a line separating urban and rural areas. It represents a predesignated limit to urban sprawl and is usually designated to protect open space, agricultural land or other natural amenities. . . . The purpose is to promote compact urban development within and adjacent to existing urban areas . . . ."[55] A 1987 survey of growth management programs showed that growth boundaries were implemented at an increasing rate during the 1970s and 1980s, evidence that concern with the pattern of local development was becoming more widespread in the period preceding the outbreak of superstore controversies.[56]

By its very nature, sprawl acts as a centrifugal force, pushing people and businesses out of downtown and toward peripheral areas. This dynamic—with superstores an integral part of the process—almost invariably undermines the vitality of the downtowns and Main Streets that were once the heart of most towns and cities. Concerned about the widespread deterioration of downtowns, the National Trust for Historic Preservation created the National Main Street Center in 1980, which works to preserve, revitalize, and maintain downtowns. Over 1,200 communities across the country are now actively involved in Main Street Center programs.[57] This may be taken as further evidence of rising concern with the effects of superstores.

Perhaps as much as anything else, the spread of superstore controversies in the late 1980s and 1990s resulted from increasing awareness of those controversies that had already taken place, along with expanding knowledge of the issues. More and more people saw what had happened to small businesses and Main Streets in towns where Wal-Mart and other superstores had gained a foothold. They also read about superstore disputes, as more articles began to appear in the print media. In 1992 *Time* published an article titled "The Two Sides of the Sam Walton Legacy." Later that year NBC broadcast an exposé, "Wal-Mart: Made in the USA. Advertising Campaign Scam," on *Dateline* and in 1995 CBS News broadcast "Up Against the Wal-Mart" on *60 Minutes*. The latter proved, once again, the power of television as its dramatic portrayal of the negative consequences of Wal-Mart superstores on small towns immediately increased awareness of the issues nationwide. In fact, the video of this broadcast became a useful tool of anti-Wal-Mart activists. In Eureka, California, for example, the local opponents stoked anti-Wal-Mart sentiment at a town meeting by showing it on a big screen. Also, as mentioned earlier, a limited social movement infrastructure began to develop, comprised of books, videos, copies of legal briefs, and other items. An important part of this infrastructure is Al Norman, who started *Sprawl-Busters Alert*. Norman, who helped fight off a Wal-Mart store in his hometown of Greenfield, Massachusetts, in the early 1990s and was featured prominently in the *60 Minutes* broadcast, serves as a clearinghouse for the anti-big-box movement and offers his services as a consultant to local activists.

Lastly, the proposal to build a huge new Wal-Mart two miles outside of town, or perhaps within the city limits but right next to a pleasant residential district, may simply have been the final straw for many people. They were not hostile to all such stores, but their town already had all the shopping it needed, including more than enough chain stores and big boxes. They knew what had happened to other towns and could see the same thing beginning to happen to their town. And they had read or heard enough to know that citizens elsewhere had successfully repelled unwanted superstores. The prospect of a new Wal-Mart, the biggest of the big boxes and the most dominant of the chains, roused them to take a stand to save a part of their community that could still be saved.

CONCLUSION

This chapter has ranged widely in an attempt to situate superstore controversies among a number of economic, political, and social trends. One underlying trend is the continued increase in retail spending that parallels the increase in GDP and reflects the increasing commodification of contemporary life. The retail industry itself has changed as it has become highly rationalized, resulting in a restructured industry dominated by relatively few large chains. The stores themselves have grown bigger as most of the dominant chains have adopted the superstore format. These companies aggressively seek new sites in towns and cities across the country, even in places already saturated with retail development. Standing out from the others is Wal-Mart Stores, Inc., which has risen from Sam Walton's first 5 & 10 in Bentonville, Arkansas, to become the world's largest retailer. Wal-Mart and other powerful retailers have changed the American landscape, both literally and figuratively. These changes, however, have not always been welcomed and have led to numerous local protests. In the next chapter I examine the economic and social effects of superstores on communities.

NOTES

1. U.S. Census Bureau. *Statistical Abstract of the United States: 2003*. Tables HS-32, HS-36, and HS-40.
2. For changes in department stores before the 1980s see Bluestone et al., *Retail Revolution*. For later changes see Abernathy et al., *A Stitch in Time*.
3. Bonacich and Appelbaum, *Behind the Label*.
4. Those nine and their rank (by annual sales) among the top fifty corporations are Wal-Mart (1), Home Depot (22), CVS (24), Kroger (26), Costco (29), Target (31), Walgreen (40), Sears (45), and Lowe's (48). *Fortune*, "Fortune 500," 5 May 2008.
5. *Wal-Mart Annual Report 2007*. Wal-Mart pulled out of South Korea and Germany during 2006.
6. U.S. Census Bureau, *Census of Retail Trade*, 1992.
7. 3.95 percent = $133,522 million / $3,378,000 million. (Total 2000 Wal-Mart sales minus sales from international operations and sales from McLane's [a wholesaler owned by Wal-Mart] divided by total U.S. retail sales for 2000) Sources: *Wal-Mart Annual Report 2000*; U.S. Census Bureau, *Statistical Abstract of the United States: 2003*, Table HS-40.

8. Drucker, "Drucker on Management."
9. *Fortune*, "Fortune 500," 5 April 2004.
10. Useem, "One Nation Under Wal-Mart."
11. See Kumar, "Revolution in Retailing."
12. See Bonacich and Appelbaum, *Behind the Label* (Chapter Three: "Retailers").
13. Schifrin, "The Big Squeeze," 45–46.
14. I thank David Swanson for making me aware of this effect of Proposition 13.
15. Sokolow, "Changing Property Tax."
16. According to Lo, the bulk of tax savings went to businesses, not homeowners: "Landlords, farmers, and the owners of commercial and industrial property received 64 percent of the savings . . . ." Lo, *Small Property*, 21.
17. Lewis, "Retail Politics."
18. Chapman, *Proposition 13*, 12. Chapman's figures show that the percentage of aggregate city revenue coming from sales tax was about the same in 1977–1978 (11 percent) as in 1995–1996 (9 percent). Chapman, *Proposition 13*, 8, Table 5.
19. Hughes and Sternlieb, "Demographics vs. Development."
20. *Chain Store Age Executive*, "Retailers Keep Building," 168. See also Andreoli, "Store Counts Surge."
21. Goldberger, "Store Strikes Back."
22. The city as a site of consumption has been explored by Lowe and Wrigley, "Towards the New Retail Geography"; Miles and Paddison, "Urban Consumption"; Mullins et al., "Cities and Consumption"; Urry, *Consuming Places*; Wrigley and Lowe, "New Landscapes"; Wynne and O'Connor, "Consumption and the Postmodern City"; and Zukin, "Urban Lifestyles."
23. Mullins et al., "Cities and Consumption."
24. Calvani, "Predatory Pricing."
25. *Matsushita Electric Industrial Co. v. Zenith Radio Corp*, 1986, cited in Calvani, "Predatory Pricing."
26. Glazer, "Symposium."
27. By the early 1990s there were approximately three times more cases filed each year than in the early 1970s. Gundlach, "Price Predation," 281, Figure 1.
28. In the mid-1980s five small-town drugstore owners in Oklahoma sued Wal-Mart over predatory pricing. The company's response was distinctly political: it spent "$80,000 in a campaign to convince the Oklahoma legislature to repeal the law" (Vance and Scott, *Wal-Mart*, 147–48). The court ruled in favor of the drugstore owners, in spite of Wal-Mart's efforts. In 1993 a group of independent drugstores in Arkansas alleged that Wal-Mart had engaged in predatory pricing of various pharmaceutical products. Although a lower court ruled initially in favor of the druggists, Wal-Mart appealed the case to the Arkansas Supreme Court, which reversed the lower court and allowed the company to continue its pricing practices. The company's practice of pricing certain goods below cost was not in dispute (its stated policy was to "Meet or beat the competition without regard to cost") and the evidence showed that Wal-Mart had sold up to 30 percent of its pharmaceutical products at prices below cost (Hawker, "Wal-Mart and Divergence," 142). But under the legal conception that had come to prevail by 1995 (the year the case was decided), this evidence was not

sufficient to allow small retailers to successfully seek redress as victims of predatory pricing.

29. Known formally as the Great Atlantic and Pacific Tea Company, A&P was a nationwide dry-goods-and-grocery chain that had expanded to about 17,000 stores by 1929. In many ways the Wal-Mart of its day, A&P was considered a significant threat by small independent grocers, who felt disadvantaged by its ability to use its purchasing power to force manufacturers to sell to it at prices that were unavailable to smaller merchants. Opposition to the "chain store menace," as it was called, was widespread. See Hendrickson, *Grand Emporiums*.

30. A secondary benefit of retail price maintenance is that it may prevent discounters from free riding on the services provided by full-service retailers. Full-service retailers maintain a knowledgeable sales staff that is able to provide expert assistance to customers. Also, a full-service retailer may carry a full line of a manufacturer's products, instead of just the one or two best selling models. These two forms of service are costly and must be figured into prices—this, in part, is why full-service independent merchants charge more than discount chains. If consumers get information and assistance from a full-service merchant, but then buy from a discounter, the discounter is free riding on the efforts of the full-service merchant.

31. Vance and Scott, *Wal-Mart*.

32. Retail price maintenance is an instance of what economists call vertical price fixing: an agreement between a buyer and a seller to maintain prices at a certain level. Price fixing *among* a group of sellers (or buyers) is horizontal price fixing.

33. Quoted in Vance and Scott, *Wal-Mart*, 147.

34. For a recent review of the literature see McCraw, "Competition."

35. Overstreet, *Resale Price Maintenance*, 7.

36. Bluestone et al., *Retail Revolution*, 126.

37. Boyd, "From 'Mom and Pop" to Wal-Mart," 225.

38. *Fortune*, "Fortune 500," 5 May 2008.

39. This account of the early years of Wal-Mart draws on Vance and Scott, *Wal-Mart;* and Ortega, *In Sam We Trust*.

40. Vance and Scott, *Wal-Mart*, 41.

41. *Wal-Mart Annual Report 2007*.

42. Based on sales. *Fortune*, "Fortune 500," 18 April 1994.

43. Based on sales. *Fortune*, "Fortune 500," 15 April 2002.

44. *Forbes*, "400 Richest Americans," 21 September 2006.

45. *Wal-Mart Proxy Statement 2003*.

46. Walton, *Sam Walton*, xi.

47. Book-length critiques of Wal-Mart include Bianco, *Bully of Bentonville*; Dicker, *United States of Wal-Mart*; Norman, *Case Against Wal-Mart* and *Slam-Dunking Wal-Mart*; Ortega, *In Sam We Trust*; and Quinn, *Destroying America*. Two edited volumes that take a critical approach are Lichtenstein, *Wal-Mart*; and Brunn, *Wal-Mart World*.

48. For example, Wal-Mart minimizes labor costs by paying low wages, offering few benefits, and forcefully (and successfully) repelling all attempts at unionization (Ortega, *In Sam We Trust*; Zellner, "Wal-Mart Keeps Unions at Bay"; and Zimmerman

and Maher, "Wal-Mart Warns of Democratic Win"); siting costs by seeking inexpensive land on the periphery of town and then pressuring local officials to rezone it for commercial use; building costs by constructing its stores as simply and inexpensively as possible; warehousing and distribution costs by operating its own computerized state-of-the-art distribution centers throughout the country; advertising costs by printing its own flyers instead of advertising in local newspapers; and cost of goods sold by using its size and purchasing power to obtain the lowest possible prices from its vendors. Schiller et al., "Clout!" See also Fishman, "Wal-Mart You Don't Know."

49. Walton, *Sam Walton*, 182.
50. *Wal-Mart Annual Report 1980*.
51. Weir, "Wal-Mart's the 1."
52. Wal-Mart's entry into the grocery market was the indirect cause of the bitter 2003 strike that pitted the UFCW against Safeway and other unionized grocers in Southern California. The grocers claimed that they could not compete against Wal-Mart if they continued to pay wages and provide benefits at existing levels. The workers refused to grant the concessions demanded by their employers, precipitating the strike. Raine, "Southern California Supermarkets."
53. Gillham, *The Limitless City*. See also Bruegmann, *Sprawl*.
54. Porter, *Managing Growth*; see also Zovanyi, *Growth Management*.
55. Ruane and Gray, *Community Responses*, 18.
56. Ruane and Gray, *Community Responses*, 18, Figure 8.
57. National Main Street Center. http://www.mainstreet.org (9 July 2005).

3

How Superstores Affect Small Towns

"There's one thing you can't buy at Wal-Mart—small town quality of life."

—Al Norman

Wal-Mart superstores have been both lauded and criticized for their effects on small towns. While many issues are specific to particular towns, others come up in town after town and involve claims and counterclaims about shopping options, jobs, tax revenue, effect on small merchants, Wal-Mart's business practices, corporate retailing in general, and the impact of superstore placement, size, and design. Since small town controversies came to prominence in the early 1990s the number and complexity of the arguments and counterarguments has increased and the original question, "Is a Wal-Mart superstore good for our town?" has expanded, first, to "Are Wal-Mart superstores good for small towns in general?" and, eventually, to "Is Wal-Mart good for America?" Journalistic and academic writing on superstores and Wal-Mart has increased significantly over the last decade. There are now about a dozen books about Wal-Mart, some devoted entirely to a wide-ranging criticism of everything about the company. My goal here is to present an overview of the major points of contention, especially those that pertain to superstore conflicts in small towns, and review the relevant literature from the social sciences and other areas. When conducting the case studies I found that Wal-Mart supporters tended to emphasize a few key benefits while the opponents disputed some or all of those benefits and emphasized a wide array of costs. Also, the opponents were more likely to expand the issue from Wal-Mart's effect on a particular town to Wal-Mart's effect on small towns in general and the country as a whole.

Much of the literature has focused on Wal-Mart, sometimes rather obsessively. This is both helpful and not so helpful: helpful because Wal-Mart has been involved in the greatest number of small town "store wars" and was involved in all six of the controversies recounted here; not so helpful because Wal-Mart itself is really not the issue—the issue is the ability of local groups to successfully constrain undesired corporate behavior, an issue that extends beyond any particular corporation. Because of its size and aggressive tactics Wal-Mart has received the most attention, yet its modus operandi does not differ fundamentally from that of other big retailers or, viewed more broadly, other large corporations.

ARGUMENTS IN FAVOR OF A WAL-MART SUPERSTORE

There are three arguments in favor of a Wal-Mart superstore that appear in case after case: it will improve shopping options, it will create jobs, and it will increase tax revenue. Let's examine these in turn.

Shopping Options

Wal-Mart's strongest claim in regard to shopping is that it has low prices; a secondary claim is that it has a wide selection of merchandise. Low prices, more than anything else, have come to be associated with Wal-Mart and figure prominently in virtually every dispute. In a sense the entire controversy, whether at the local or national level, is about whether low prices—the major "benefit"—outweigh the "costs" incurred by independent retailers, workers, manufacturers, taxpayers, and others that make low prices possible.[1] While most observers agree that Wal-Mart undersells small retailers, conclusive evidence of the extent to which this occurs is surprisingly hard to find.[2] There are several reasons for this. First, there is a dearth of scholarly, peer-reviewed, price comparison studies; most price comparisons have been conducted by business consultants, trade journals and investment companies. These studies rarely specify the details of their research design, thus raising concerns about measurement validity and generalizability. Second, most studies compare Wal-Mart to other chain stores and omit consideration of independent retailers. Of course, some notion of how much Wal-Mart undersells the other major chains can be helpful because Wal-Mart presumably undersells the independents by at least as much. And third, many studies focus on particular types of consumer goods (e.g., food, drugs) instead of comparing prices across a broad array of items. These studies generally, but not always, find that Wal-Mart undersells its competitors, although not always by a wide margin.[3] Wal-Mart's ability to sell at low prices is based, in part, on its ability to negotiate advantageous deals with its vendors by dint of its large volume. Independent retailers, however, are able to do the same thing, if not to the same extent, by forming buyers' cooperatives.

Some critics argue that Wal-Mart's actual prices cannot be separated from the public's *perception* of its prices, which is heavily influenced by Wal-Mart's constant emphasis on "everyday low prices."[4] In addition to advertising constantly that it has low prices, Wal-Mart makes aggressive use of loss leaders, prominently displayed items deliberately priced below cost to attract customers and give the impression that the whole store is full of incredible buys. Wal-Mart's financial resources allow it to use loss leaders to an extent unavailable to other retailers, especially small retailers, who consider this tactic unfair because it is based on sheer size and not superior operating efficiency. The size and design of Wal-Mart stores also contribute to the appearance of low prices: huge, inexpensively constructed stores with merchandise piled high, some of it left on crates or still in boxes, give the impression of rock bottom prices.[5]

All parties agree that a Wal-Mart superstore offers a greater array of products under one roof than any single retailer. However, there are some considerations that mitigate this benefit. The selection within product lines may be more limited than elsewhere. Whereas an independent hardware store, for example, may offer a full line of power drills from each of several makers, Wal-Mart may "cherry pick" the best-selling models and not stock the others. Also, an independent hardware store is more likely to offer expert advice about choosing and using its products (which is one reason its prices are higher). To the extent that Wal-Mart puts other local merchants out of business, there will be decreased diversity *of retailers* and possibly a decline in the *overall* selection of products available in a town (unless it is a very small town).

Jobs

Does a new Wal-Mart store lead to a net increase in local employment? Several major studies have examined this question using large data sets. Neumark, Zhang, and Ciccarella analyzed all U.S. counties and found that the opening of a Wal-Mart store reduced local retail employment by about 3 percent.[6] In a similar study Basker examined 1,749 counties and found that retail employment increased by about 100 in the year after a Wal-Mart opened and then declined over the next several years to about fifty.[7] She also found that employment in wholesaling decreased by about twenty jobs. Basker is unable to conclude that this net increase is due to job loss in counties without Wal-Marts or whether it represents the replacement of full-time workers at other stores by part-time workers at Wal-Mart. Blanchard et al. examined 786 nonmetropolitan counties in which a retailer with 100 or more employees opened between 1977 and 1996. They found a decline in retail employment in counties in the southern and midwestern regions of the country, the two regions with the highest concentration of Wal-Marts and the longest presence.[8] There are several reasons why a new Wal-Mart store would result in a net decline in retail and wholesale employment: Wal-Mart's superior operating efficiency (fewer employees per sales dollar), a loss of jobs at other retailers, the centralization of nonstore employment (purchasing, accounting, finance, advertising, marketing, legal counsel, research and development, communications, information management, etc.) at Wal-Mart's headquarters, and Wal-Mart's use of its own warehouses instead of wholesalers.

There is also the issue of job quality. The company's high employee turnover rate and large number of employment-related lawsuits suggest significant employee dissatisfaction.[9] According to its critics, Wal-Mart's wages are so low and its benefits so inadequate or unaffordable that many employees must resort to public assistance in the form of food stamps, free school lunches, housing subsidies, emergency room medical treatment (instead of regular doctor's visits), state-funded children's health insurance programs, and federal tax credits for low-income workers.[10] Bernstein, Bivens, and Dube point out that the typical family spends more on housing, medical care, transportation, and education than on the consumer products sold by Wal-Mart, and thereby contend that low prices do not compensate for low wages.[11] The biggest difference between Wal-Mart and other retailers involves grocery jobs. While jobs at most other general merchandisers are nonunion, many jobs in the grocery sector are unionized, which means that Wal-Mart grocery workers earn substantially less than their counterparts at the major grocery chains. An evaluation of job quality should not be limited to a comparison with other retail jobs; it should also include nonretail jobs, because a small town's decision to allocate a large piece of land to a new Wal-Mart store may diminish its ability to attract other employers (i.e., a manufacturing facility) that offer jobs that pay more and are more likely to be unionized. Furthermore, a manufacturing facility would benefit the local economy more because it would bring in "new" dollars, compared to a retailer which typically only redistributes existing dollars.[12]

Tax Revenue

A third claim is that a new Wal-Mart superstore will improve a city's finances by generating sales tax revenue, property tax revenue, or both.[13] While a Wal-Mart superstore may generate more tax revenue than any other local retailer, the issue is the net effect: will the revenue generated by a Wal-Mart superstore exceed that lost from other stores? Most of the sales tax revenue from a Wal-Mart superstore represents revenue that would have been collected from other local retailers; a new superstore would spur an increase in sales tax revenue only if it attracted shoppers who ordinarily would have shopped elsewhere. The situation with property taxes is similar: while a superstore and the land on which its sits represent a large piece of real property, the value of that property must be set against the decreased value of other property.[14] Finally, there is the question of a superstore's overall fiscal impact: even if tax revenue goes up, will it offset the costs associated with a new superstore? One set of costs includes the construction and maintenance of infrastructure such as roads, lighting, signage, water lines, sewer lines, electric lines, and a stormwater system. Other costs include the resources that must be devoted to the crime and traffic accidents that occur at or near superstores. The financial responsibility for infrastructure varies from town to town and depends on the particular agreement worked out with the retailer; Wal-Mart may pay for it or it may be subsidized by the town. Some municipalities have provided Wal-Mart with other subsidies such as free or reduced-price land, property tax breaks, and sales tax rebates.[15] Thus, claims about tax revenue must be set against a number of possible costs to adequately gauge the effect of a superstore. It is impossible to make any sweeping conclusions about fiscal impact because tax structure, local costs, and use of subsidies vary from municipality to municipality, and because studies using large samples remain to be done.

WAL-MART'S EFFECT ON OTHER MERCHANTS AND ON COMMUNITY WELFARE

To the extent that Wal-Mart takes sales from other merchants, their fortunes will decline. Although Wal-Mart poses a threat to other corporate retailers, its effect on local independent retailers—and the ramifications throughout the community—is our concern here. The decline of small retailers described in chapter 2 strongly suggests that the spread of Wal-Mart superstores is causally connected to the decline of independent retailers. Of course, a single Wal-Mart store cannot always be blamed for everything, but it is an important contributing factor, especially in a small town. Although the situation in every town is different, the research generally supports the conclusion that there is an inverse relationship between the spread of Wal-Mart (and other corporate retailers) and the health of small merchants and overall community well-being. In some cases merchants selling a different type of merchandise may gain sales if a new superstore pulls people into the town who would not have shopped there earlier, although merchants in other towns will lose sales, an inevitable outcome given the zero-sum nature of retailing (see below).

In a series of studies beginning in the late 1980s, Stone used sales and tax data to examine Wal-Mart's impact on other merchants in Iowa, Mississippi, and other states, leading to the following "rules of thumb":

> *Rule of thumb number one* is that merchants selling items that differ from those sold by the discount mass merchandisers will not experience a loss of sales. . . .
>
> *Rule of thumb number two* is that merchants selling the same things that the discount stores are selling will probably experience a decrease in sales after the discounter opens. This applies not only to merchants in the local area, but to those in the outlying area. . . . [16]

Other researchers using a variety of research strategies have come to similar conclusions. Gruidl and Kline used aggregate sales tax receipts to analyze the effect of superstores in sixteen small towns in Illinois and found that "when a large discount store enters a small community, it quickly captures a large share of the retail market."[17] Peterson and McGee used survey data from 191 retailers in five small Midwestern cities with a Wal-Mart superstore and found that 52 percent of existing retailers reported a negative impact after the opening of Wal-Mart.[18] Their low response rate (45 percent) and the fact that retailers that had already gone out of business were not included in the sampling frame suggest that their results may underestimate Wal-Mart's impact. Davidson and Rummel used aggregate sales tax data to compare the effects of Wal-Mart on thirteen host towns, ten adjacent towns, and eighteen nonadjacent towns in Maine. They found that in host towns general merchandise stores grew much faster than other retail; in adjacent towns stores in both categories lost sales.[19] In the most global analysis yet, Basker examined 1,749 counties and found that the number of small and medium retail establishments declined after the arrival of Wal-Mart.[20] The decline of local merchants also means less business for all those local small businesses that provide them with services, such as accountants, financial advisors, lawyers, advertising agencies, printers, wholesalers, truckers, and information management specialists. Wal-Mart does not need the services of these small businesses because it centralizes all these functions at its headquarters in Bentonville, Arkansas.

The small merchants and the small businesses that provide services to them make up an important segment of the local community. What are the consequences of the decline of this segment? As research has accumulated it has become clear that the decline of small business has serious adverse consequences for the well-being of communities. Tolbert et al. analyzed 4,553 small towns and found that the presence of "local capitalists" in the form of small businesses, small manufacturing establishments, and family farms is associated with higher median income, lower poverty rate, lower unemployment rate, and greater population stability.[21] Narrowing the focus to retailers, Tolbert found the presence of small merchants to be negatively correlated with poverty, infant mortality, and crime.[22] Goetz and Swaminathan estimated the county-level decline in the poverty rate during the 1990s (a period of general economic growth and prosperity) associated with the presence of a Wal-Mart superstore and concluded that "the presence of Wal-Mart was unequivocally associated with smaller reductions in family-poverty rates . . . relative to places that had no stores."[23] In related research Shaffer examined 700 U.S. cities and found that "the average size of manufacturing and retail firms is negatively and robustly associated with subsequent growth rates of median household income."[24] In a subsequent study he found that "Income grew faster in those counties having a smaller average retail establishment size initially, or those having a larger proportion of small retail establishments."[25]

The decline of this segment can also be examined in terms of its effect on social capital and civic engagement. An analysis of 2,978 counties by Goetz and Rupasingha shows that social capital, as measured by indicators such as number of associations per 10,000 residents, turnout in elections, number of nonprofit organizations per 10,000 residents, and church adherence, declined during the 1990s in those with a Wal-Mart store.[26] Tolbert, in an analysis at the state level, found that "there is a quite strong relationship between share of employment in locally oriented [independent] retail and social capital as measured by [Robert] Putnam."[27] Lastly, the replacement of small retailers by chain superstores implies an increase in local economic concentration. Using county-level data on economic concentration and a nationwide survey of social capital, Blanchard and Matthews found that economic concentration is negatively associated with electoral participation and participation in protest politics, two important forms of civic engagement.[28]

What explains these rather striking findings? While a comprehensive explanation remains to be developed, some connections can be traced out. The association between Wal-Mart and poverty, income, and other measures of economic welfare appears to result from a combination of the following factors, many of which are a direct consequence of the decline of small merchants and other independent businesses: a decrease in local employment, the displacement of (relatively) high-wage jobs by low-wage jobs, downward pressure on local wages, the displacement of full-time by part-time work, reduced local charitable contributions, and profit flowing out of the local area. These economic effects are exacerbated by the erosion of civic engagement that occurs when independent businesses decline. The civic engagement of local businesses reflects their status as longtime residents with deep roots in their community and an abiding interest in the welfare of their community as well as the success of their businesses. They tend to be involved in civic affairs and support activities such as Little League baseball, Boy Scouts, Girl Scouts, nonprofit organizations, and charities to a greater extent than the average resident. They also take an interest in local government, admittedly sometimes with an eye for self-interest. The relationship local independent businesses have with each other and with the rest of the community represents a significant form of social capital, which contributes to community welfare. This segment of the local population has the motivation, the resources, and the experience to support the community as leaders and problem solvers. Blanchard and Matthews contrast the involvement of local business interests with that of corporations and note that when the latter predominate "local residents may become alienated because corporate goals are prioritized over the solution of local problems and general local well-being."[29]

RETAILING AS A ZERO-SUM GAME

Wal-Mart's effects on employment, tax revenue, and independent merchants can be better understood if we realize that retailing is what economists call a zero-sum game, a situation in which an increase in economic activity for one locale or population subgroup can occur only at the expense of another locale or subgroup; in other words, a situation in which there must be a "loser" for every "winner."[30] Applied to retailing this means that sales gained by one store must come inevitably at the expense of others. From this perspective the chief reason a Wal-Mart superstore does not necessarily result in a net increase in local employment is that it mainly *redistributes* sales, and therefore jobs, from existing retailers to the new superstore. The only way a new Wal-Mart could lead to a net increase in local employment is if total local retail sales were to increase. How might that occur? The most often proposed scenario is that a new superstore will be a "retail destination" and attract a substantial number of shoppers from other towns. While some people from other towns may come to shop at Wal-Mart, total local sales will increase only if the store attracts shoppers who would not have come to town otherwise. In most cases this is a relatively small number of people. Moreover, out-of-town shoppers will continue to make a special trip to shop at Wal-Mart only until there is a Wal-Mart (or other similar superstore) in their town or in another town closer than the town with the new Wal-Mart. Another scenario is that local shoppers who had been spending money out of town would now remain in town and spend their money at the new superstore. While certainly possible, this would be a significant factor only if a town had very few retail establishments. Moreover, in the absence of a local Wal-Mart (or other similar superstore) local residents may drive some distance to make special purchases, but few will make frequent out-of-town trips to buy everyday items.

For any specific town the smaller the effects of attracting outside shoppers and retaining local shoppers, the closer retailing approaches a zero-sum game. And while it is possible for one town to take sales from another, as the size of the territory under consideration increases the zero-sum nature of the situation becomes more evident. This analysis applies equally to tax revenue.

Suppose that a new superstore does attract shoppers from outlying areas who would not have come to town otherwise. This raises an important question: "Is that a good thing?" Should the citizens of one town rejoice because "our" new superstore has taken business away from independent merchants in a neighboring town? Is it desirable that out-of-town shoppers patronize a superstore in our town rather than the independent merchants in their town? While a certain amount of civic rivalry is healthy, this type of beggar-thy-neighbor attitude is detrimental to all communities in the long run.

SUPERSTORES AND THE BUILT ENVIRONMENT

In a small town a new superstore often represents a major development project and may significantly alter the local built environment. Wal-Mart and other chain retailers have developed a preferred format—very large single-story buildings with blank walls, surrounded by acres of parking and placed on the outskirts of town—that they have replicated thousands of times across the country. While the effect of the built environment on community well-being is difficult to quantify, research in sociology, architecture, and planning generally concludes that the typical superstore format adversely affects local quality of life by contributing to sprawl, degrading community appearance, undermining the vitality of downtown, and replacing public space with private space. What these critiques have in common is the view that there are deleterious, if not immediately obvious, connections between the quality of community life and the size, design, and placement of superstores.

Sprawl

Sprawl may be defined as "low-density, land-consumptive, automobile-oriented development located on the outskirts of cities and towns."[31] Superstores, in the view of many critics, epitomize sprawl.[32] Sprawl was a central concern of the opponents in Petoskey and Ashland, and an important but lesser concern in West Bend and Ottawa. A complex phenomenon, sprawl has been studied intensively, most often from a critical perspective. In *The Limitless City: A Primer on the Urban Sprawl Debate*, Oliver Gillham provides a comprehensive review of the literature.[33] Some of the problems reviewed by Gillham include the following: it consumes large amounts of land; it necessitates increased spending on infrastructure as centrally located roads, water lines, sewer lines, and other facilities are underused while new facilities must be built to accommodate peripheral development; it makes driving "mandatory" as new development can be reached only by car; and it creates a landscape that limits opportunities for social interaction. Driving is not only expensive and requires a nonrenewable energy source but results in increased air and water pollution, as well as the death and suffering caused by automobile accidents. Furthermore, heavy reliance on cars leads to overburdened roads, time spent in traffic congestion, and the stress of driving. To the extent superstores are a manifestation of sprawl and to the extent sprawl is a concern of local residents, superstores have been and will continue to be opposed by some portion of the population.

Superstore Size and Design

The general effect of superstore size and design is to accentuate the impersonality of corporate retailing. There are several additional problems specific to size. The first is that such large stores are out of character with the existing retail establishments in many small towns. Of course, if a town already has many superstores, then another one cannot be said, strictly speaking, to be out of character, but it would be out of character with those stores that embody traditional architecture. Another problem is the lack of human scale.[34] Huge buildings provide retailers with economies of scale and scope but do not satisfy basic human needs for intimacy and familiarity, needs that can be met only with structures that are scaled for real people, such as those found on traditional Main Streets. The problem of excessive size extends to the signs used by superstores. Because they are set so far back from the street and are oriented to drivers who are hurtling past on a boulevard or highway, their signs tend to be as large and eye-catching as possible. As the local landscape becomes cluttered with such signs it begins to lose its uniqueness and aesthetic appeal.[35]

The typical superstore is built with a minimum of ornamentation and architectural flair.[36] Wal-Mart superstores, in the words of John Rohe, are "architecturally uneventful."[37] Superstore design degrades the local built environment in several ways, beginning with the uncontested aesthetic judgement that they are unattractive. Sam Lubell, writing in *Architectural Record*, succinctly states the reason superstores take the form they do: "They are extremely cost-efficient and convenient to build."[38] One reason Wal-Mart superstores are so unsightly is that they are built cheaply, a result of the fixation on low cost and rationalization. Dunham-Jones, writing in *Harvard Design Review*, argues that "Wal-Mart's treatment of its stores and employees as disposable assets . . . exemplifies corporate strategies of flexible accumulation."[39] Cheapness indicates a lack of attachment to both buildings and communities; higher-quality buildings, by contrast, represent an investment in the community and indicate some sense of permanence and commitment. Another problem is that superstores are incongruous with local architectural styles, as corporate retailers generally make no effort to design buildings that will complement existing styles, thereby contributing to the problem of "places where nothing relates to anything else."[40] And to the extent that superstores replace local merchants, local architecture and style is replaced by corporate design. Another design issue is homogeneity—most superstores look about the same. As Sam Walton himself admitted, "we just started repeating what worked, stamping out stores cookie-cutter style."[41] Commenting on both size and design, Schwarzer argues that such buildings lead to a built landscape that is "extralarge, horizontal, orthogonal, and anonymous."[42] As corporate chains come to dominate retailing, communities across the country begin to look alike: "Never before could one travel such vast distances—from Houston to Salt Lake City, from the edge cities of Washington [DC] to the ever-spreading sprawl of Los Angeles—and experience built environments of such relentless efficiency and generic sameness."[43] Thus, superstore size and design detract from the uniqueness of particular communities and erode the sense of place that a town or city has for its residents.

There is nothing about large stores that necessitates the adoption of the superstore format; earlier department stores, in fact, were quite different. Until shopping malls began to spread after the Second World War, most department stores were built downtown. They drew people downtown, thereby enlivening the area and contributing to the critical mass needed for a vibrant downtown. These stores, especially those built during the classic period between the Civil War and the early years of the twentieth century, were architecturally quite different from today's big boxes.[44] Some were large, though not as large as today's superstores, but their size was more manageable because they were built upwards (multistory) instead of outwards. They were true "palaces of consumption," well-built and designed to complement other important downtown buildings.[45] "The new department-store grandeur," writes Boorstin, "gave dignity, importance, and publicity to the acts of shopping and buying."[46] Some of these beautiful buildings can still be found in downtowns around the country. The earlier department stores, furthermore, did not carry as many different types of merchandise as a Wal-Mart superstore and thus did not harm the sales of as many other merchants.[47] While small towns did not have palaces of consumption to rival those found in big cities, they had stores such as J.C. Penney's, Woolworth, and Montgomery Ward, which were located downtown and fit in architecturally with other buildings.

Effect on Downtown and Public Space

According to critics, the placement, size, and design of superstores interact to adversely affect urban ambience and the tenor of contemporary life in general. These effects are complex, sometimes subtle, and include the fate of downtown merchants, the vibrancy of downtown, the decline of public space, and the rationalization and commercialization of the built environment. The following critiques may be easier to comprehend if one thinks in terms of a contrast between, on one hand, a (somewhat idealized) downtown that is unique, open, lively, diverse, accessible, and comprised of public and private space devoted to commerce as well as to other pursuits; and on the other hand, a superstore, mall, shopping center, or power center that is privatized, homogeneous, highly rationalized, and devoted exclusively to selling. Put somewhat differently, the placement, size, and design of superstores combine to produce a built environment that is the antithesis of that which would most successfully promote a healthy civic and social life. While explicating all these issues fully is beyond the scope of the present work, I will sketch out their essence and note some of the relevant empirical research.

The place to begin is the observation that one consequence of placing a superstore on the outskirts of town is that customers are drawn away from stores located downtown or on Main Street (I use these terms synonymously here), leading to the demise of some portion of the downtown merchants, many of whom are independent merchants. The demise of these merchants may foretell the demise of downtown, an outcome with ramifications beyond the fate of particular merchants. A decline in the number of downtown shoppers is associated with a decline in downtown as a commercial center, which may contribute to its decline as a civic center, something that bodes poorly for a town or city. Whether or not it is situated in a town's geographic center, downtown represents the symbolic center of a town and serves as a "focus of civic identity."[48] As Peter Calthorpe observes, "The center of the traditional town integrated commercial, recreational, and civic life. It was what made a town a town."[49] Downtown serves as a civic center and is the venue for community events such as Fourth of July parades, Thanksgiving parades, homecoming parades, and other celebrations. While administrative functions traditionally located downtown such as city hall, police headquarters, and the court house may not be affected by the loss of commercial activity, other downtown facilities such as schools, museums, theaters, libraries, and art galleries may suffer from a loss of critical mass.[50] Also, downtown often contains some of the most significant local buildings and the best examples of local architecture. These represent the history and character of a town in a way that a big box store does not. Another reason downtowns are worth preserving is because they are compact, a result of the fact they were built before automobile use became widespread. Compactness enables walking, from home to store, from store to store, from store to post office, and so on, which has several advantages. For many persons, walking is simply more pleasant than having to drive everywhere. Another advantage is that those without access to cars or unable to drive are not excluded from participating in daily life. Superstores on the outskirts of town may be very inconvenient for those who lack cars, including preteens and many teenagers, older adults, and those unable to afford driving. Also, walking increases the possibility of running into friends and acquaintances and thus promotes contact between citizens, thereby strengthening social capital. Putting a superstore on the outskirts negates all these advantages. The overall result, then, of a decline in downtown commerce is a weakening of downtown's function as the center of local social life and the loss of an attractive, walkable district.

A crucial aspect of urban ambience and social life is the street life that characterizes intact thriving downtowns. Inspired by Jane Jacobs's seminal work on neighborhoods and street life, a number of planners, architects, and social scientists have empirically investigated street life and sought to identify the factors that contribute to, or detract from, it.[51] Probably the best-known investigation is that of William H. Whyte, carried out principally in New York City but applicable to other cities large and small. The basic elements of a good street (construed broadly to include sidewalks), according to Whyte, are:

Buildings flush to the sidewalk.
Stores along the frontage.
Doors and windows on the street.
Second-story activity–with windows so you can see it.
A good sidewalk.
Trees. Big trees.
Seating and ample amenities.[52]

Although Whyte conducted his research without regard to superstores (in fact, before superstores became prevalent), it is striking that a typical superstore represents the opposite of these elements. Another scholar of street life,

Allan B. Jacobs, systematically studied "great streets" in cities around the world. Jacobs notes that streets have many important functions: they "allow people to be outside . . . [they are] places of social and commercial encounter and exchange. They are places where you meet people . . . ."[53] In regard to social interaction, "Sociability is a large part of why cities exist and streets are a major if not the only *public* space for that sociability . . . ."[54] He identifies eight fundamental requirements for a "great street":[55]

- it must have places for people to walk with some leisure
- it must offer physical comfort to those on foot
- it mut be well defined
- it must engage the eye
- it must be transparent ("an invitation to view or know . . . what is behind the street wall"[56])
- its buildings and other structures must complement each other
- it must be well maintained
- it must avoid low quality in materials and design

Again, it is striking that the sort of built environment associated with a superstore is almost the exact opposite of what Jacobs describes. Complementary research has been carried out by Jan Gehl, who focuses on "life between buildings," which includes "not merely pedestrian traffic or recreational or social activities . . . [but] the entire spectrum of activities, which combine to make communal spaces in cities and residential areas meaningful and attractive."[57] Gehl emphasizes that what happens in public—the quality of public life—depends on the quality of public spaces. There is a continuum of urban design in regard to fostering life between buildings. At one end there are cities with "reasonably low, closely spaced buildings, accommodation for foot traffic, and good areas for outdoor stays . . . people coming and going, and people stopping in outdoor areas near the buildings because the outdoor spaces are easy and inviting to use. This city is a living city." At the other end are cities with "extensive automobile traffic, and long distances between buildings and functions." In such settings "Outdoor spaces are large and impersonal . . . [and] there is nothing much to experience outdoors."[58] A traditional downtown with its multitude of stores lining the sidewalk exemplifies the former design, while a typical superstore closely resembles the latter. Commenting specifically on buildings that are set back from the street and surrounded by large open spaces, Gehl observes that "Life has literally been built out of these new areas."[59]

Aside from being antithetical to a lively street life, big box design has specific adverse effects on shoppers and pedestrians. Long exterior walls make the area outside a superstore uninviting, an effect reinforced by the absence of windows (and window-shopping). Such a setting does not encourage one to stroll casually, stop to chat with others, or sit and observe the world go by, as one might do on Main Street. Superstores are usually separated from the street by a large parking lot and often lack sidewalks, creating a barrier to pedestrian traffic and a pleasant walking experience. As a result, such stores become alienating stand-alone structures that pose nearly insurmountable difficulties to achieving any sense of human scale and urban ambience.

Along with being a center, downtown serves a vital function as an important public space, understood as a space that is designed and intended for use by people in their role as members of the public. Streets, sidewalks, parks, civic buildings, and plazas, for example, are places that are not owned or controlled by a private interest such as a corporation. In such places persons are free to act as they please within the limits of the law. They may speechify on a soapbox, pass out political tracts, picket, sing, assemble, march, and generally engage in all the activities that are to be expected, if not universally appreciated, in a healthy democratic society. Public spaces are open to all members of the community and are not under the control of any particular individual or corporation. All of downtown, of course, is not public space, as many stores and other facilities are private (at least from a legal point of view), but public spaces are an essential part of the mix.

A superstore, by contrast, is a private space under the control of a large corporation and represents the rationalization of the built environment, in this case for the purpose of selling. The spread of such commercial spaces and their effect on communities have elicited concern from observers who are troubled by "what consumerism has done to American settlements."[60] One problem is the ubiquity and sameness of such forms of development. As Steven Miles comments, "Consumption has become so fundamental to the character of our urban environment that cities could in fact be construed to be 'unreal' in the sense that they could be anywhere; they have, in fact, lost a sense of place."[61] The critique of rationalized spaces of consumption has been developed most extensively in regard to malls, but applies as well to superstores such as Wal-Mart which are, in effect, one-store malls. Ada Louise Huxtable, former architecture critic for the *New York Times*, explains the logic of mall design:

> Established patterns are repeated rigidly and uniformly; no one tinkers with what works. The look, quality level, and general ambience are determined by meticulously researched consumer profiles . . . . This, in turn, sets the nature of the stores, their merchandise and mix, number and location. The deadly sameness that marks these places is absolutely intentional. . . . This standardization

of setting and goods is meant to guarantee a meticulously conceived and predictable profit formula and cash flow . . . .[62]

Sociologist Benjamin Barber concurs with this analysis and argues that the "mall stands as a powerful embodiment of the privatization and commercialization of space associated with the forces of what I have called McWorld, turning our complex, multiuse public space into a one-dimensional venue for consumption."[63]

Sociologist Lyn Lofland has written at length about the importance of what she refers to as the "public realm, a concept that includes public space,"[64] and argues that the built environment is a crucial component of the public realm as it can "encourage or discourage interaction."[65] The public realm has come under attack in contemporary America and one form of that attack has been architectural. Lofland points to five elements of post-WWII design that have contributed to the weakening of the public realm: "megamononeighborhoods," "autoresidences" (houses dominated by garages), "autostreets" (streets dominated by cars), "antiparks" (industrial parks, office parks, etc.), and "megastructures."[66] Superstores are clearly part of this panoply as they are collected in the megamononeighborhoods known as malls, shopping centers, and power centers; oriented exclusively to automobiles; and built at the scale of megastructures. They contribute to a landscape that lacks human scale, frustrates attempts at interaction, and undermines the public realm. Marketplaces have traditionally brought together in a central place a large number of buyers and sellers distributed among a plethora of shops and other selling venues, making shopping an activity with great potential as a source of lively social interaction. Shopping still attracts many people but opportunities to capitalize on its social potential are lost when retailing becomes dominated by superstores on the outskirts of town.

The idea of the "third place," developed by Ray Oldenburg, complements Lofland's notion of the public realm.[67] A third place is a place where people gather informally that is neither home nor work. Examples include pubs, cafés, taverns, bars, coffeehouses, barber shops, bookstores, and Main Streets. (Not every pub, café, etc., is a third place; there are several other requirements.) While a third place may be privately owned, one of its distinguishing features is that it is open to the public. One of the great virtues of third places is that they promote civic life by offering convivial and more or less neutral places for members of a community to meet and talk to each other. Third places, by their very nature, are non-McDonaldized and are rarely connected to large corporations. We might even say that a key function of a third place is to provide a venue for the sort of nonrationalized and non-McDonaldized interaction that is typically precluded in corporate settings such as superstores. Oldenburg argues that such places, which he also calls "great good places," are badly needed but in short supply in the United States. Downtowns tend to contain third places such as those described by Oldenburg, and downtown is itself a sort of all-purpose third place, as we would expect, given its role as a public space. Superstores negatively affect third places in a couple of ways. By contributing to the overall decline of downtown they contribute to its decline as an all-purpose third place. Also, the decline of downtown results in the elimination of many third places that are located downtown. Thus, to the extent that independent downtown businesses are replaced by corporate chains on the periphery of town, the net result is a loss of great good places.

As downtowns decline, then, the number of healthy public spaces declines and we find ourselves increasingly engulfed by privately controlled spaces, many of which are geared toward the promotion of consumption. It should be kept in mind that the effects of superstores on the local built environment are cumulative. While there is obviously always a first superstore built in any given town, the problem arises when such stores come to dominate local shopping. While one or two big box stores may be acceptable, a landscape dominated by such stores is much less attractive. As other venues are increasingly undermined, local uniqueness and charm begin to disappear.

NOTES

1. *Wal-Mart: The High Cost of Low Price* is the title of a documentary released in 2005.

2. Wal-Mart is not keen to have its prices subjected to a systematic comparison with other retailers. Vance and Scott, in their history of Wal-Mart, note that "the firm would evict anyone discovered in its stores with a notepad or a camera." Vance and Scott, *Wal-Mart*, 146. In one incident in Madison, Wisconsin, the owner of a competing grocery visited a local Wal-Mart and began recording a few prices. A Wal-Mart manager asked him to leave. He demurred, maintaining that he was bothering nobody, whereupon the manager called the police and had him removed. *Capital Times* (WI), "No Charges."

3. For example: The Prudential Equity Group found that a bundle of top-selling toys costs about 5 percent less at Wal-Mart than at Toy-R-Us (cited in Hays, "Toy Retailers"). *DSN Retailing Today*, a trade publication, found that Wal-Mart undersold Target, one of its major competitors, on nongrocery and grocery items by about 7 percent and 12 percent, respectively, and undersold Walgreens, a drugstore chain, by about 14 percent on drugstore items (nongrocery items: Desjardins, "Brand Basket"; grocery items: Heller, "Wal-Mart Outprices"; drugstore items: Troy, "Wal-Mart is Tops"; calculations by author). UBS Warburg, a consulting firm, found that several

dozen typical grocery items were 22–39 percent higher at major grocery chains than at Wal-Mart in several cities (Currie and Jain, "Supermarket Pricing"). By contrast, *Consumer Reports* found that Wal-Mart's prices on small appliances did not differ from those of independent merchants and its prices on computers did not differ from those of the major computer and office supply chains (appliances: *Consumer Reports*, "Where to Buy Appliances" September 2005; computers: *Consumer Reports*, "Computer Stores" December 2005).

Global Insight, an economic forecasting firm, estimates that Wal-Mart saved the average American household $2,329 in 2004 on food and other commodities. Global Insight, "Economic Impact." (The data for this study were supplied by Wal-Mart.) This figure is based on an analysis of Wal-Mart's presumed effect on the consumer price index, not on a direct comparison of actual prices. Bernstein, Bivens, and Dube of the Economic Policy Institute consider this figure "implausible" and offer a detailed critique of Global Insight's statistical analysis. Bernstein, Bivens, and Dube, "Wrestling with Wal-Mart," 1.

4. Other retailers have complained about Wal-Mart's claims about low prices. In 1994 an investigation by the Michigan Attorney General led to a settlement in which the company agreed to change the way it compared its prices to those of its competitors. Ortega, "Wal-Mart to Settle Dispute."

5. Cowgill argues that "Wal-Mart's business model is not really low-price, it is creating perceptions that prices are lower than they really are." Cowgill, "Case Study," 1.

6. Neumark, Zhang, and Ciccarella, "Effects of Wal-Mart."

7. Basker, "Job Creation."

8. Blanchard et al., "Suburban Sprawl."

9. The major lawsuits faced by Wal-Mart are described in the litigation section of its annual reports.

10. Estimates of these costs may be found in Miller, *Everyday Low Wages*.

11. Bernstein, Bivens, and Dube, *Wrestling With Wal-Mart*.

12. A manufacturing company typically sells the bulk of its products outside the city in which its plant is based. Depending on the particular product and scale of operations, it may have customers at the state, regional, national, or international level. Sales to these customers bring "new" money—and new jobs—into the city with the manufacturing plant.

13. The apportionment of sales tax receipts between local and state government varies from state to state.

14. Even if the opening of a new superstore does result in more sales and/or property tax revenue, it does not follow that local citizens will pay less property taxes, as municipalities do not typically respond to new sources of revenue by lowering taxes.

15. Karjanen and Baxamusa, *Subsidizing Wal-Mart*; Mattera and Purinton, *Shopping for Subsidies*.

16. Stone, *Competing*. Stone, Artz, and Miles, *Economic Impact*, offer the following comments to local officials:

> The findings of this study suggests that local officials should carefully weigh the costs and benefits of this type of development . . . . Quite often city councils and city staff are so

anxious to attract new businesses they will offer very attractive financial incentives and perhaps change zoning status in order to attract supercenter-type stores. Their primary motivation seems to be the belief that these new businesses will increase the property tax base, increase sales tax (where local sales taxes are in play), and increase employment. There are worthy goals, but many times the net increases are minimal as the new big box stores merely capture sales from existing businesses in the area. A reduction of sales for existing businesses usually translates into fewer employees, less sales tax, and lower property tax collections from the local stores.

17. Gruidl and Kline, "What Happens."
18. Peterson and McGee, "Survivors of 'W-day.'"
19. Davidson and Rummel, "Retail Changes."
20. Basker, "Job Creation or Destruction?"
21. Tolbert et al., "Civic Community."
22. Tolbert, "Minding Our Own Business."
23. Goetz and Swaminathan, "Wal-Mart and County-Wide Poverty."
24. Shaffer, "Firm Size."
25. Shaffer, "Establishment Size."
26. Goetz and Rupasingha, "Wal-Mart and Social Capital."
27. Tolbert, "Minding Our Own Business." Putnam's social capital index consists of fourteen indicators of "community organizational life," "engagement in public affairs," "community volunteerism," "informal sociability," and "social trust." Putnam, *Bowling Alone*, 291.
28. Blanchard and Matthews, "Configuration of Local Economic Power."
29. Blanchard and Matthews, "Configuration of Local Economic Power," 2245–46.
30. Shaffer, Deller, and Marcouiller, *Community Economics*.
31. Beaumont, *Superstore Sprawl*.
32. Al Norman, the nation's leading antisuperstore consultant, calls his organization Sprawl-Busters. http://www.sprawl-busters.com (22 April 2008). See also Beaumont, *Superstore Sprawl*; and Gratz, *Cities Back from the Edge*.
33. Gillham, *Limitless City*. Burchell et al., *Sprawl Costs*, calculate the costs of sprawl. Frumkin, Frank, and Jackson, *Urban Sprawl*, detail the health consequences of sprawl.
34. Sale, *Human Scale*.
35. Kunstler, "Zoning Procedures," refers to the result as a "cartoon of a human habitat."
36. More attractive superstores have been built in some cities, usually as a result of requirements by local officials. See Beaumont, *Better Models*; Hall and Porterfield, *Community By Design*; and Lubell, "Is There Hope?"
37. Rohe, "USA—What Went Wrong."
38. Lubell, "Is There Hope?"
39. Dunham-Jones, "Temporary Contracts," 9.
40. Kunstler, *Geography of Nowhere*, 185.
41. Walton, *Sam Walton*, 111.
42. Schwarzer, "Spectacle of Ordinary Building," 86.

43. Scwharzer, "Spectacle of Ordinary Building," 75. "Edge city" is Joel Garreau's name for the low density suburban cities that have sprung up around many central cities. Garreau, *Edge City*.
44. See Hendrickson, *Grand Emporiums*; and Leach, *Land of Desire*.
45. Boorstin, "Consumers' Palaces," 243–44.
46. Boorstin, "Consumers' Palaces," 243–44.
47. Gratz, *Cities Back from the Edge*.
48. Worpole, *Towns for People*, 4.
49. Calthorpe, *Next American Metropolis*, 22.
50. Worpole, *Towns for People*.
51. Jacobs, Jane, *Death and Life*.
52. Whyte, *City*, 101–2. See also Whyte, *Social Life*.
53. Jacobs, Allan B., *Great Streets*, 4.
54. Jacobs, Allan B., *Great Streets*, 4–5 (italics in original).
55. Jacobs, Allan B., *Great Streets*, Part Four, Chapter One.
56. Jacobs, Allan B., *Great Streets*, 285.
57. Gehl, *Life Between Buildings*, 16.
58. Gehl, *Life Between Buildings*, 33.
59. Gehl, *Life Between Buildings*, 49.
60. Lofland, Lyn, *Commodification of Public Space*, 17. See also Zukin, *Cultures of Cities*.
61. Quoted in Lyn Lofland, *Commodification of Public Space*, 18.
62. Huxtable, *Unreal America*, 104.
63. Barber, "Malled," 203. See also Crawford, "World in a Shopping Mall"; and Goss, "'Magic of the Mall.'"
64. Lofland, Lyn, *Public Realm*.
65. Lofland, Lyn, *Public Realm*, 182.
66. Lofland, Lyn, *Public Realm*, 200–205.
67. Oldenburg, *Great Good Place*.

4

Gig Harbor, Washington, and Petoskey, Michigan

Do the People Want It?

In this chapter and the next two I provide accounts of what actually happened in six small cities where Wal-Mart encountered significant opposition. The cases are presented in pairs, with each pair characterized by similarities or differences in respect to either the nature of the controversy or the outcome. Each controversy proved to be a complex local drama. While the big story is Wal-Mart versus local social movements, on the ground the situation is much more complicated. Wal-Mart itself is not always present, as it often hires a panoply of legal firms, realtors, developers, and public relations companies to deal with various aspects of siting a new store. In most of these cases there are local supporters as well as opponents, which means that there is conflict between community members as well as between Wal-Mart (or the companies working for it) and its opponents.

The cities in the first two cases, Gig Harbor, Washington, and Petoskey, Michigan, are both located in scenic settings: Gig Harbor on Puget Sound and Petoskey on the shore of upper Lake Michigan. A noticeable segment of the population in both cities could be described as upscale or upper middle class; in Petoskey this applies to those who vacation in the area as well. In the mid-1990s both cities were confronted with plans by Wal-Mart to place a superstore outside the city limits. There was organized opposition in both cities, but with different strategies and different outcomes.

Chapter 4

GIG HARBOR, WASHINGTON

"Did we need it?"

—Gretchen Wilbert, Mayor of Gig Harbor

The city of Gig Harbor is located on the southern part of Gig Harbor Peninsula. The peninsula itself, along with various harbors, bays, coves, narrows, and straits, is part of western Seattle-Tacoma. Gig Harbor (population 5,470) lies just across the Tacoma Narrows and is directly accessible from the mainland only via the Tacoma Narrows Bridge.[1] The city portrays itself as a quaint fishing village and a pleasant tourist destination. The local harbor is indeed filled with fishing boats and pleasure vessels, while the surrounding area is clean and picturesque, with restaurants and small stores. On the hills above the harbor are well-maintained houses that indicate an upscale citizenry.[2] The rest of the city is south of the harbor and slightly inland. Highway 16 runs north to south along the interior of the peninsula and cuts the city in two. Several miles south of the harbor and just off the highway is the city's busiest intersection, the corner of Point Fosdick Drive and Olympic Drive. Several shopping centers are located nearby, with well-known chains and independent stores. Less than half a mile south of the intersection, along Point Fosdick Drive and next to a shopping center, is a 19.5-acre parcel of wooded land that is vacant and undeveloped except for the Gig Harbor Motor Inn, a single-story rustic-style motel. It was on this piece of land that Wal-Mart proposed to build a 133,000-square-foot superstore with several acres of parking. At the time it would have been the largest retail building on the entire peninsula.

EARLY MOVES

In 1995, when the controversy began, the land was owned by Billie Webber of Oceanside, California, who had inherited it from her deceased sister, a former local resident. Webber, who was compelled to sell the land because of inheritance taxes, put it on the market in 1990. The land is just outside the Gig Harbor city boundary (and not within the boundary of any other city) and therefore all matters concerning development came under the jurisdiction of

Pierce County. In February 1995 the Pierce County Department of Planning and Land Services received an application to build a large retail establishment on the land. The size of the project and the proponent named on the application, Rick Barr, a broker with CB (Coldwell Banker) Commercial who had worked with Wal-Mart on other projects around the state, led the local newspaper to surmise that Wal-Mart was the likely retailer.[3]

Although Wal-Mart was indeed the principal party, company representatives made few appearances in the city. CB Commercial, a large real estate company with operations nationwide, negotiated an option on the land whereby Wal-Mart paid for the exclusive right to buy the land on or before a specified future date, in this case July 1996. Wal-Mart's strategy was to postpone buying the land until all the necessary approvals had been secured. CB Commercial hired Washington Land Design to oversee the engineering and design of the project, which hired the engineering firm of Huckell/Weinman to take the proposal through the county's lengthy environmental review process. Huckell/Weinman in turn used half a dozen independent specialists in areas such as traffic analysis, wetlands, water quality, air quality, sewage disposal, and geotechnical analysis. Wal-Mart also used Seattle-based Pacific Public Affairs to help with public relations and was represented by the Seattle law firm of Phillips, McCullogh, Wilson, Hill and Fikso.

THE LAND-USE APPROVAL PROCESS IN PIERCE COUNTY

The land in question was already zoned for commercial development, so Wal-Mart did not have to seek a rezoning (unlike most of the other cases). However, in Pierce County any proposal to build a commercial structure exceeding 8,000 square feet automatically triggers an environmental review. Thus, in this case the major regulatory hurdle for Wal-Mart would be getting through the county's environmental review. Local land use decision making, whether for rezoning or environmental review, typically entails a series of steps involving one or more official bodies, public hearings, and other opportunities for input by interested parties. The procedure for environmental review in Pierce County is as follows. First, the proponent submits a preliminary environmental impact statement (EIS) to the planning department, which circulates it internally for comment. Taking these comments into account, the proponent then revises the EIS and resubmits it. The planning department then issues a draft EIS (DEIS) for comments by other public agencies and the public, including a public hearing if requested by at least fifty persons. The DEIS, which is based to a large extent on material provided by the proponent, identifies possible adverse impacts of the project and proposes mitigating measures. The proponent then submits a final EIS that incorporates the comments made on the DEIS. The Pierce County Planning Advisory Council (PAC) reviews the final EIS and makes a nonbinding recommendation to the hearing examiner. Finally, the hearing examiner holds a public hearing, reviews all relevant material, and makes a decision.

Because the land in question was under the jurisdiction of the county, the citizens and elected officials of Gig Harbor were unable to directly affect the outcome of the environmental review process. The city, however, was allowed to have a representative on the PAC. The city's representative, Karen Biskey, was also an elected member of the county board of supervisors. From the opponents' point of view, she was probably the ideal PAC representative because she was a former president of the Peninsula Neighborhood Association (PNA), Gig Harbor's leading growth management advocacy group and the main organization in the fight against Wal-Mart.

Huckell/Weinman submitted the preliminary EIS in July 1995 and the revised EIS in January 1996. In April 1996 the planning department made the DEIS available for public comment. The opponents, however, did not wait for the DEIS, but began to critique the project as soon as they knew that Wal-Mart was behind it. The DEIS identified six broad areas of concern: "earth, water (including surface water and wetlands), aesthetics (including light and glare), air, noise, and transportation."[4] County land use regulations did not require any kind of economic impact statement, so the project was to be evaluated, ostensibly at least, solely on the basis of environmental considerations. The opponents, however, did not limit their criticisms to environmental matters, but criticized everything possible about the site and the store.

THE SUPPORTERS

Support from local businesses was scant.[5] Very few publicly announced their support or wrote to the planning department in favor of the store. Several of those who did support the store were classic growth machine actors: a local landowner who owned land near the site, local realtors, and the owner of a local building supply company.[6] The Gig Harbor-Peninsula Area Chamber of Commerce suffered internal dissension over the issue. A survey of the chamber's approximately 400 members found that 63 percent were opposed to the store. In spite of this, the chamber's board approved a resolution requesting Wal-Mart to "endorse and actively participate in an ongoing communication process . . . in an attempt to mitigate as many negative impacts . . . as possible."[7] For some members this resolution was tantamount to supporting the enemy. Brian Morford, owner of a small gift shop and a founding member of the chamber, resigned in protest, declaring, "This is a small-town community and they need to remember who made it what it is today, who made it successful. It wasn't the megagiants."[8] Fifteen other members, all retailers, quit in protest too.[9] According to its president, Lois Eyrse, the chamber did not want to discriminate against Wal-Mart and felt that since it was likely the store would eventually be sited, it was better to try to work with Wal-Mart than to be obstructionistic.[10] She hoped that by engaging in a dialog with Wal-Mart the giant retailer could be induced to build a "better store," meaning one that looked better and caused fewer environmental problems. In spite of these positive statements, Eyrse eventually submitted a letter to the county planning department stating that "The Chamber and its Board of Directors has never supported Wal-Mart in entering this community because of its tremendous impacts on traffic, environment and the economy."[11] If local business support was qualified, that of national and regional business actors was not. CB Commercial actively supported the project, as did Seattle-based Washington Land Design and its subcontractors, most of whom were based in the Seattle area too.

While local opponents appeared to greatly outnumber local supporters, some supporters tried to undermine the apparent strength of the opposition. First, they claimed that many local people and businesses really did want a new Wal-Mart superstore but had been silenced by the PNA, which applied "social pressure" to anybody who spoke out in support.[12] In this view, the PNA was just a "very vocal minority."[13] A second tactic, and one that we will encounter in other cases, is to claim that the opponents are snobs. This view was expressed by a few supporters who did not live in Gig Harbor but in small towns and rural areas elsewhere on the peninsula. According to one, the PNA consisted of "a few snobs who want to keep everybody out, especially 'those people', the people who want cheap underwear."[14] Another said that Gig Harborites were afraid that "every Billie Joe Bob and his live-in woman, Lillie June, will come on into the pristine city limits with their old pickup and shop at the eyesore Wal-Mart."[15] Eyrse also mentioned what she termed a "snob factor," which involved the invidious comparison of Gig Harbor with the blue-collar towns on the peninsula such as Port Orchard, where a Wal-Mart was being built unopposed.[16]

THE OPPONENTS

The Peninsula Neighborhood Association (PNA), which had been active since 1986 in trying to control unwanted or inappropriate growth in Gig Harbor, wasted no time in expressing its displeasure. The PNA was concerned about increased traffic, the possible demise of local independent merchants, environmental degradation of a scenic area, the unappealing scale and design of the proposed store, and the overall negative impact of a Wal-Mart superstore on Gig Harbor's small-town atmosphere. Tom Morfee, head of the PNA, began gathering signatures on a petition to be submitted to Pierce County officials. In June 1995 he called a public meeting to publicize the issue and organize protest. At the meeting, held at a local high school, more than 400 people showed up to hear an anti-Wal-Mart pep talk from Morfee, who had already managed to get 4,000 signatures on the petition. Ron Hayes, president of Local #367, United Food and Commercial Workers, spoke about Wal-Mart's poor record as an employer, passed out anti-Wal-Mart bumper stickers, and distributed thirty copies of a *60 Minutes* video called "Up Against the Wal-Mart," which critically examines Wal-Mart's effects on small towns.[17] This video was an important weapon in the arsenal of the anti-Wal-Mart forces in more than one case.

Another opponent was the mayor of Gig Harbor, Gretchen Wilbert, who had formerly been chair of the Gig Harbor Planning Commission and was supported by the local growth management forces. She was concerned with proper land use and urban design, which she considered crucial to preserving what was best about Gig Harbor.[18] Mayor Wilbert objected to the proposed store because it was out of scale for the city—"it did not fit"—and would negatively impact small retailers.[19] Also, it was simply not needed because a Wal-Mart was scheduled to open soon in Port Orchard, twenty minutes away. The fact that Wal-Mart was a large corporation attempting to locate in the community was not an issue for her; she said they "would have been happy to have [had] Microsoft."[20]

The *Peninsula Gateway*, the Gig Harbor newspaper, covered the controversy extensively. While at first cautious about the proposed store, it soon took a clear stance against it, as expressed in an editorial titled "It is time to join the fight to keep Wal-Mart out":

> Wal-Mart, the world's biggest retailer, wants to build a store in Gig Harbor.
> To this we say no.
> Gig Harbor is not a Wal-Mart community.
> The Peninsula Gateway joins the loud chorus of local residents telling Wal-Mart to stay out of our community. . . .
> . . .
> Do we really want to be just another Wal-Mart town?
> Do we want to be another Shelton, another Aberdeen, another Port Orchard?
> Or do we want to maintain our image of blending a natural setting with the splendor of our waterfront?
>
> November 15, 1995

During 1995 and 1996 the proposed store was a front-page story twenty-four times and the subject of at least ten editorials as well as numerous letters to the editor.

How did the people of Gig Harbor feel about Wal-Mart coming to town? The numbers, at least, would suggest that they were overwhelmingly against it. The PNA claims to have eventually collected 14,000 signatures on their petition, a significant number for a city of 5,470.[21] While the petition had no legal bearing on the eventual decision, it was often used by the PNA and others as a way of demonstrating the extent of public opposition. Very few people spoke up for Wal-Mart at the various official meetings and hearings, and of the roughly two hundred letters submitted to the county, only about half a dozen expressed support for the project.[22] The letters to the editor were overwhelmingly against the project.

FURTHER MANEUVERS

Wal-Mart, confident of eventual approval, officially came out in the open in October 1995 with a press release announcing its intentions:

WAL-MART PLANNED FOR GIG HARBOR AREA

Wal-Mart officials today announced the company is planning to build a store at the Gig Harbor area's Point Fosdick Center. The store is expected to be open in 1997. "We selected the Point Fosdick site because local residents are so under-served with retail options," Les Copeland, company spokesman said.

According to an economic study performed for the company, approximately $37 million a year is spent by local residents at stores outside the Gig Harbor area.

"This Wal-Mart will provide local residents with a convenient, low-cost, wide-selection choice that they don't currently have in the area. It means people will no longer have to cross the bridge to do their basic shopping," Copeland said.

Copeland said the fact that more shoppers will stay in Gig Harbor to do their buying should translate to more business for all area merchants. "What smaller communities usually find when Wal-Mart comes to town is that the people staying local to shop instead of leaving town spill over and buy at other retailers as well. . . . "

The 133,000 square-foot store is expected to employ 200 people. Wal-Mart typically hires local residents, pays competitive salaries and excellent benefits, and provides special opportunities for seniors, students and people with disabilities.

The Point Fosdick store will be designed with sensitivity to the local community, including leaving one-third of the property in open space, a landscaped parking lot, and an existing stand of trees buffering the view from State Route 16.

"Designing the site with this kind of sensitivity is just one of the many steps we will take to be a good neighbor in Gig Harbor," Copeland said.[23]

Wal-Mart also commenced a citywide direct mail campaign touting the store.

Later that month Pacific Public Affairs, the public relations firm hired by Wal-Mart, set up a meeting between Wal-Mart and the chamber. This was to be the first opportunity for anybody from the community to meet face-to-face with Wal-Mart representatives. Morfee found out about the meeting and requested that it be opened to the public: "If Wal-Mart is finally coming out of the closet, we want to give them a special clog-dancing, herring-tossing Gig Harbor welcome."[24] Although initially unreceptive to Morfee's request, the chamber acquiesced after he threatened to stage a demonstration. The *Peninsula Gateway*'s front-page story described the meeting as follows:

> They came, they signed petitions, they protested.
>
> Citizens showed up in force Tuesday night for a community forum at Peninsula High School to announce the planned opening of a Wal-Mart . . . .
>
> Originally called as a private meeting between Wal-Mart officials and member of the Gig Harbor-Peninsula Area Chamber of Commerce, the 90-minute session was open to the public.
>
> And the public was open about it.
>
> "We don't want you. We don't need you," one woman yelled while a Wal-Mart official addressed the crowd.
>
> "We don't want you here," a man cried out. "It's that simple."[25]

At the meeting, attended by 350 people, the PNA exhibited some of the tactics they would employ throughout the controversy. Some wore t-shirts and buttons that said "Against the Wal," while others brandished signs with anti-Wal-Mart messages. The PNA also used the meeting as an opportunity to continue collecting signatures on their petition. Several opponents unfurled a thirty-foot banner that read: "'If the community, for whatever reason, doesn't want us in there, we aren't interesting in going in and raising a fuss.' — Sam Walton." During the controversy the opponents also displayed bumper stickers, placed paid advertisements in the newspaper, set up a website, marched in the local Fourth of July parade, and packed the house at official meetings.

Les Copeland, public relations coordinator for Wal-Mart, made the case for a Wal-Mart in Gig Harbor. He said the city "in some ways but maybe not in character, is what Wal-Mart is all about."[26] According to Copeland, the new store would garner retail sales that were "leaking out" to other communities. He defended the store's size by explaining that it reflected anticipated future growth in the area and stressed that Wal-Mart expected to employ about 200 people.

Wal-Mart's arguments regarding convenience, low prices, and attracting more people to Gig Harbor were turned on their head by the opponents, who contended that these were actually *dis*advantages because they would negatively affect local quality of life. In response to the claim that a Wal-Mart superstore would lower the local cost of living, some opponents replied that they were interested in maintaining their quality of life, not reducing their cost of living. While the formal dispute involved land use, some residents raised larger questions about the kind of community they wanted to live in:

> The opposition to Wal-Mart is serious business. It represents an ongoing attempt of local residents to define their community.
> . . .
> For those of you who welcome Wal-Mart, I ask, "Why do you live here?"
> If you want to live in a community with convenient, discount shopping and do not mind the blight of expansive parking lots, cavernous commercial buildings, etc., those neighborhoods already exist. There is no need to create another one.[27]

From this perspective the additional shoppers who might be drawn to the city were seen mainly as the source of increased traffic in an already congested area.

Responding to criticism that its proposed store was aesthetically unpleasing and out of character with the surrounding neighborhood, Wal-Mart offered a new design. The original design had been a replica of a typical Wal-Mart superstore: a plain, single-story, rectangular, box-like building painted blue and grey with a huge red sign. The new design featured "earth tones" of beige and green, more natural-looking surface materials, faux dormer windows to give the illusion of a second story, a gabled entry, and a covered walkway in front. According to Wal-Mart:

> This is a symbol that Wal-Mart has the highest integrity and sticks to its word. . . . This one's unique. It's a stand-alone. When you consider the landscaping and open space, there's not another store like it.[28]

Critics of the project, however, were unimpressed. Morfee gleefully attacked:

> Now we have Wal-Mart's latest tactic to fool the gullible Gig Harborites: We'll put earth tones and a gabled roof on that big box, so it will blend in. Forget the 15 acres of asphalt . . . . 9,000 vehicle trips each day, six paved-over wetlands, an unknown number of small businesses down the tubes. . . .
> A big box of any other color is still a big box.[29]

Moreover, the *Peninsula Gateway* soon discovered that this "unique" design had also been proposed for a Wal-Mart in Fredericksburg, Virginia.[30]

THE ONGOING ENVIRONMENTAL REVIEW PROCESS

In April 1996 the county planning department issued the DEIS, the main vehicle used to solicit comments from interested parties. The concerns that it raised—traffic, wetlands, air quality, noise, water quality, and aesthetics—had all been brought up already by opponents. The issuance of the DEIS, however, was still important because it functioned as an official invitation to the opponents to make their point of view known. The PNA and others took advantage of this invitation to the fullest and criticized the assessment of problems and the proposed mitigations, as put forth in the DEIS and based on material supplied by the project's proponent. The PNA's critique was quite detailed because it was based on expertise and experience the organization had gained through various planning disputes during the previous ten years. The PNA made use of local volunteers with expertise in land planning and was prepared to hire outside experts if needed. Thus, Wal-Mart's expertise in site approval, and that of its professional allies (CB Commercial, Huckell/Weinman, etc.), was offset to some extent by the expertise that the PNA could muster.

Over fifty people requested in writing that a public hearing be held, thus ensuring that there would be at least one such hearing. The first public hearing was held on 14 May 1996, at a high school in Gig Harbor. More than 400 people attended, the overwhelming majority of whom opposed the proposed store. "In fact, no one took the podium to offer a kind word for the Arkansas-based retailer."[31] Because of the number of people who wanted to speak, six days later a second public hearing was held at which the project was heavily criticized again. Due to the continued high level of public interest, a rare third public hearing was held soon thereafter.

Although the city could do nothing about what was built on county land, it did have authority over what was built within city limits. In February 1996 the Gig Harbor City Council took preemptive action by approving an ordinance limiting the maximum size of buildings in commercial zones to 65,000 square feet—less than half the size of a typical Wal-Mart superstore. Because Wal-Mart insists on building stores larger than 65,000 square feet, this ordinance effectively prevents the company from putting a store in Gig Harbor in the future, should it want to do so. In the present, however, it was still possible that the city might annex the land (because it was adjacent to the city) and avoid the new ordinance because it had been passed after the application was originally submitted. However, the new ordinance gave the opponents a hook: if the land were annexed Wal-Mart would need to obtain sewage service from the city, and the city could then require the proposed store to meet its new size requirement. As it turned out, events never reached the point where such a situation could arise. The passing of the ordinance was significant, nevertheless, because it demonstrated that the city was willing to take an active role in preventing a superstore from being sited in or near Gig Harbor.

WAL-MART'S WITHDRAWAL

In July 1996 Wal-Mart's option on the land expired, with several important steps in the environmental review process not yet completed. Wal-Mart and the landowner discussed extending the option but were unable to come to an agreement. Wal-Mart was still free to purchase the land outright, but was hesitant to do so before it had in hand all the necessary approvals and permits. In August company representatives met with officials from Gig Harbor and Pierce County to discuss other possible locations. The site of most interest to Wal-Mart was in a relatively undeveloped area of the city known as Gig Harbor North. The city's recently enacted zoning ordinance, however, did not allow a store of Wal-Mart's usual size to locate in that area. In October the landowner acknowledged that she had granted an option on the property to another party, this time a local developer. In November Wal-Mart informed the *Peninsula Gateway* that it was withdrawing its application to build on Point Fosdick Drive. On 2 January 1997, the legal firm representing Wal-Mart sent a letter to the Pierce County Department of Planning formally withdrawing the application.[32]

PETOSKEY, MICHIGAN

> "There are two types of people in this area, the lunch buckets and the millionaires."
>
> —A Wal-Mart supporter

> "It's about more than just the price of toilet paper."
>
> —A Wal-Mart opponent

The city of Petoskey (population 6,625), long a favorite vacation destination, sits on Little Traverse Bay on the northeast side of Lake Michigan. Located 300 miles north of Detroit, the city thrives on tourism and the resort industry. In the summer people come to golf and sail; in the winter they ski and snowmobile.

Many of the houses in the area are second homes, used mainly in the summer. Rich Detroit industrialists and their families vacationed in Petoskey early in the twentieth century and that trend continues today, as evidenced by ads in the local paper for $400,000 pleasure boats and million dollar condominiums on the waterfront. One of the distinctive features of the city is the large number of restored Victorian homes, many situated on the hill which rises behind the city's downtown. According to a local saying, you part with "half your pay for a view of the bay."

Downtown Petoskey, known as the Gaslight District because of its period gaslights, is notable for its many restored commercial buildings and has been designated a National Historic District. The downtown is compact and picturesque, with a wide range of stores. Exclusive clothiers, art galleries, and jewelry stores are mixed in with standard retail establishments such as photo stores, drug stores, a J.C. Penney's department store, and a hardware store. The downtown is a fully functioning city center and includes city and county offices, a court house, a library, the the local newspaper, several churches, a number of schools, and the post office. While the downtown is compact, newer business development has spread north of the city along U.S. Highway 31 and south along U.S. Highway 131. Some of this development is in the rural township of Bear Creek (population 3,551), which surrounds most of the city. This newer development includes independent businesses as well as well-known national and regional chain stores. Petoskey is the county seat for Emmet County (population 26,944), which includes Bear Creek.

In August 1994 representatives of RG Enterprises, of Dayton, Ohio, presented to the Bear Creek Township Planning Committee their plan to build a strip mall on eighty-seven acres of undeveloped land off U.S. Highway 131, two miles south of downtown Petoskey, in Bear Creek Township. The mall would be anchored by a 130,000-square-foot Wal-Mart and a 65,000-square-foot Elder-Beerman, a full-line nondiscount department store. At the time it was proposed, it would have been the largest mall in the Petoskey-Bear Creek area and Wal-Mart would have been the largest single store in the area. The development, to be called Bear Creek Mall, would be approximately as large as the entire downtown Petoskey business district.

LAND USE ISSUES, THE APPROVAL PROCESS, AND EARLY MANEUVERS

RG Properties had worked with Wal-Mart on stores in several other locations in Michigan. The Gunlock brothers, Bo and Randy, who handled the project for RG Properties, had been looking for a site for a Wal-Mart store in the

Petoskey area for about six years. The parcel on U.S. Highway 131, on which they had an option to buy, had originally been farmland; by 1994 most of it was zoned residential. There were no homes on the property, although about twenty private residences abutted the site or were located nearby. Because the land was in Bear Creek Township, and because the township did not at the time have its own master plan, which would have included zoning ordinances, the land was subject to the zoning ordinances of Emmet County. Final approval for all development had to come from the Emmet County Board of Commissioners, an elected body made up of representatives from all parts of the county (including Petoskey). Townships in Michigan can devise their own master plans and thereby assume responsibility for zoning and other land use decisions, but are not obligated to do so. In instances such as this, where jurisdiction remained with the county, the county's philosophy was that it should "serve the townships' zoning needs."[33] In other words, the county had the final say, but it would be greatly influenced by the wishes of the township. When making its decisions, the Emmet County Board of Commissioners was required to consider the recommendations of three other official bodies: the Bear Creek Planning Committee, the Bear Creek Board of Supervisors, and the Emmet County Planning Commission. The proper sequence of events was for the township planning committee to recommend a proposed project to the township board, which then made a recommendation to the county planning commission, which then made its own recommendation to the county board of commissioners. In the two years following the Gunlocks' announcement, the Wal-Mart matter was discussed extensively by all four of these bodies at over two dozen official meetings and hearings.

A developer seeking to build a strip mall on land that is zoned residential normally must request to have the land rezoned to commercial. The Gunlocks, however, avoided having to seek a rezoning by using a planning device called a Planned Unit Development (PUD). With a PUD, a developer is allowed to place together on one site a mixture of building types that would normally be separated by different zoning districts. In particular, a PUD allows residential and commercial buildings to be placed on the same site, as long as they are part of the same comprehensive project. Whereas conventional zoning makes this sort of mixed-use development difficult, if not impossible, a PUD gives a developer the latitude to mix uses. In exchange for this latitude, the project is subject to extra scrutiny by local planning officials and legislative bodies, who can impose more stringent conditions on design and layout than they would be able to impose on development within a typical single-use zoning district. With a PUD, the existing zoning classification remains in effect; the PUD is considered an "overlay" placed on top of the existing zoning. Although the creation of a PUD in a residential zone, as occurred here, may result in a development that is predominantly commercial, it is technically not a rezoning. The significance of all this is that by requesting a PUD the developers were able to avoid the approval process that would have accompanied a conventional rezoning. Specifically, a rezoning request in Emmet County would have included the right of referendum; that is, it could have been submitted to a popular vote, if enough people requested such a vote. There was no such requirement for a PUD.

The approval process for a PUD in Emmet County consisted of three steps: preliminary approval, final approval, and site design review. A PUD takes effect when the "final approval" is granted, although construction cannot begin until the site review has been approved. One reason the Bear Creek Mall project was on the agenda at over a dozen meetings was because most of these three steps were discussed and debated by all four of the official bodies involved.

In August 1994 RG Properties informally presented their project to the Bear Creek Township Planning Committee. Even though there were some changes during the course of the controversy, the essential features of the proposed project remained the same throughout. The strip mall was to be constructed in several phases. The first phase would include the Wal-Mart superstore, the Elder-Beerman department store, 30,500 square feet of other retail space, and a senior living complex. Later phases would include a grocery store and more retail establishments, including some smaller retail along the highway. As part of their initial plan RG Properties proposed to donate twenty-one acres of the land to Northern Michigan Hospital, one of the area's largest employers, to build a senior living complex, which would include housing, offices, and medical services. Bo Gunlock told the Bear Creek Township Planning Committee that they approached the "city fathers" for suggestions on possible uses of land that was not needed for retail development and were told about the need for a senior living complex. According to Bo Gunlock, "This is not a public relations ploy . . . . We . . . are trying to give something to the whole community."[34] The hospital was initially pleased to receive the land, but soon declined the offer, apparently out of fear of being tainted by the controversy.[35]

In September 1994 the developers, their real estate broker, and a representative of Elder-Beerman made their first formal public presentation at a meeting of the Bear Creek Planning Committee. The developers emphasized the sales and property tax dollars the project would generate, the jobs it would create, and Wal-Mart's record of community giving. They claimed the stores would capture $100 million in buying power that was currently leaving the Petoskey area. Furthermore, they argued, the local population was increasing rapidly and could easily support the proposed mall. Finally, RG Properties was willing to pay for most of the infrastructure necessary to service the new mall.

THE OPPONENTS

Shortly after the project was announced some of the downtown merchants, along with others concerned about the direction that land use was taking in Petoskey, formed Urban Sprawl Alliance (USA), a nonprofit corporation whose stated purposes included the following:

1. To preserve the historic places and the traditional town commons threatened by urban sprawl.
2. To investigate threats to areas of existing economic and cultural vitality.
3. To discover and memorialize the history, artifacts and architecture of the downtown area.

. . .

5. To assure preservation of buildings, land, homes or other articles which may relate to the history and architecture of downtown areas.
6. To establish and maintain historic homes, building, artifacts and lands.
7. To hold meetings and other activities for the instruction and information of members and the general public.

. . .

10. [To] engage in and promote the study and education of history, natural history and natural resources.[36]

USA organized the opposition to the proposed mall and had a membership of over 1,000, which included people from the surrounding area as well as Petoskey. From its perspective the project represented the epitome of urban sprawl and everything negative associated with it. They argued that a new strip mall two miles south of the city would harm downtown. Unlike many small cities, Petoskey had a downtown that was viable, even thriving. But it was vulnerable. The downtown merchants were already competing with the strip development that was appearing along the highway and there was continual fear that Penney's, the only department store left downtown, would leave. To improve downtown's attractiveness, the city was launching a $4.5 million project to upgrade streets, sidewalks, lighting, and other downtown features.[37] As USA saw it, the central issue was sprawl, not Wal-Mart. A USA board member said, "I'm not against Wal-Mart. It would be great if they came downtown."[38] However, in Petoskey as elsewhere, concerns about the particular site and concerns about Wal-Mart inevitably became tightly intertwined.

There was also unease regarding the unresolved issue of the bypass that the Michigan Department of Transportation had proposed to build around Petoskey. Many people feared that the proposed bypass, if built, would lead to more strip development. Given these considerations, USA argued that it made little sense to build a big new mall with two major department stores on a highway two miles south of downtown.

USA's concerns about sprawl and the viability of downtown reflected a concern with local quality of life. As a downtown retailer remarked, "We're not gaining a store, we're losing a community."[39] Among USA's complaints: the project was out of scale with most other local development; it was ugly; it marred a scenic view leading into the Petoskey area; Wal-Mart would not maintain the same level of commitment to local affairs as locally owned businesses; and because it was a chain store, it would undermine local uniqueness and sense of place.[40] USA members felt that the proposed mall represented the type of mindless growth that had ruined so many other towns and cities in Michigan and across the country—it was precisely what both tourists and locals were trying to *escape* when they came to Petoskey. Another member of USA commented, "I'm an architect. I depend on growth. But people are starting to ask where you draw the line. When does growth turn into sprawl and threaten the things that make this community unique?"[41] Moreover, the project was not in keeping with the Petoskey-Emmet County Master Plan, which had been designed specifically to avoid sprawl. They also argued that it was a bad investment from a purely fiscal point of view because sprawl often leads to higher taxes to pay for expanded infrastructure, that it would take land that could be used for moderately priced residential housing, and that it was not needed because low-price shopping venues (e.g., Kmart) already existed in the area.

Members of USA used a number of tactics during the dispute. They offered comments at the many official meetings where the issue was discussed, wrote op-ed pieces and letters to the editor of the paper, held three "town hall" meetings featuring various planning experts, spoke on radio shows, appeared on a TV show, and, when all else failed, filed a lawsuit.

Throughout the controversy there were competing claims about the project's true popularity. At a special meeting of the county planning commission in October 1994, the Gunlocks presented what they felt was persuasive evidence that county residents favored their project. According to a telephone survey paid for by RG Properties, the project received a favorable rating from 56.6 percent of the residents of Bear Creek Township, 61.1 percent of Petoskey residents, and 57.5 percent of the whole county.[42] The opponents critiqued various aspects of the survey's procedures and questioned the validity of the findings, given that the developers had paid for the survey. At the same meeting William Germond, chair of the township planning committee, presented a survey of township residents undertaken before the Wal-Mart controversy, which showed they did *not* want a large commercial development in that part of the township.⁴³ The Gunlocks responded by attacking the township survey as unprofessional.

OTHER INTERESTED PARTIES

The members of the Petoskey Regional Chamber of Commerce had mixed feelings about the project, with many concluding that the overall effect on business in the Petoskey-Bear Creek area would be negative.⁴⁴ For many the problem had more to do with sprawl than with Wal-Mart. They argued that sprawl undermined the scenic qualities and small-town atmosphere that made Petoskey such an attractive destination for tourists and resorters, whose spending was crucial to the local economy. Too much sprawl development, although perhaps good for a few local businesses, could eventually destroy the very qualities that made the area a good place to do business. The chamber was definitely concerned that the proposed mall would contribute to the "erosion of . . . downtown."⁴⁵ Some merchants were afraid of being hurt by Wal-Mart; others, however, did not view Wal-Mart as a threat because their products and services were sufficiently specialized—and aimed at affluent customers—that they did not consider Wal-Mart to be a competitor. The chamber made a serious effort to get the Gunlocks interested in locating the Wal-Mart elsewhere in the area, preferably downtown. There was a downtown site that the chamber felt was a viable option, but the store would have had to be smaller than a typical Wal-Mart and would not have been able to have a parking lot of the usual size. The Gunlocks, however, were completely unmovable on all attempts to locate the Wal-Mart anywhere other than their chosen location. Under prodding from USA, the chamber's board of directors passed a resolution on 18 October 1994, stating that it

> . . . recognizes that the magnitude of the proposed RG Properties development will have a profound impact on the region. For this reason we encourage creative approaches to locating these businesses within the areas already identified for commercial development within the County Master Plans. As a land use issue, we affirm the existing process for zoning decisions. It is the Chamber's Mission to promote orderly economic growth and development while protecting the amenities of the area.⁴⁶

Chamber president Diane Litzenburger characterized the chamber's stance as neither for nor against the Wal-Mart, but the resolution clearly indicates that the chamber did not support the site chosen by the Gunlocks.

The Petoskey Gaslight-Downtown Association, a separate organization representing downtown interests, took a similar stance. It did not oppose Wal-Mart per se, but wanted new retail establishments to be located in "our downtown central business district or . . . [in] other areas the master plan has targeted as appropriate for such concerns."⁴⁷ The attempts by the chamber and the downtown association to coax Wal-Mart into locating downtown are understandable. Wal-Mart, however, has a long record of consistently and adamantly refusing to place its stores in the downtowns of small towns and small cities.⁴⁸

The local newspaper, the *Petoskey News-Review*, remained officially neutral during the controversy. This neutrality, however, was rendered somewhat questionable by its decision to print Wal-Mart's logo in colored ink on the front page as an accompaniment to six stories about the siting controversy.

THE SUPPORTERS

In November 1994 the Bear Creek Board of Supervisors unanimously adopted a resolution in favor of the proposed strip mall. This was an important vote because it showed strong support by the residents of the township, at least to the extent that their elected representatives reflected their views. Two main reasons were given for supporting the project. First, the bypass that the Michigan Department of Transportation had proposed to build around Petoskey and through Bear Creek would pass near the site in question and render it unsuitable for either housing or farming, thus making it suitable, by default, for commercial development.

The second reason involved shopping and a group I call the shoppers, those supporters who were narrowly focused on shopping issues and who wanted Wal-Mart—not just any big retailer, they wanted *Wal-Mart*. Although there was a Penney's in downtown Petoskey and a Kmart on the highway south of the city (not far, in fact, from the site of the proposed mall), some area residents said they needed more "shopping options." The Penney's was said to be too small and the Kmart, Wal-Mart's closest competitor and a very similar type of store, was said to be poorly managed and have an unsatisfactory selection of merchandise. The closest Wal-Mart was in Gaylord, about thirty-five miles away; some people said that the prices and selection there were so good that it was worth the drive. When the shoppers said that a Wal-Mart superstore would provide more "shopping options," they meant that it would provide them with more places to buy ordinary consumer items at discount prices, something they claimed was sorely needed by "working people"⁴⁹ with "moderate incomes" who lived in the area.⁵⁰ They felt that many downtown stores catered to the upscale resorters and affluent residents: "Petoskey looks out for resorters and people with money, but nothing for the year-round resident."⁵¹ According to several shoppers:

Petoskey is not made up of only wealthy persons. Their [sic] are many, many average working people that live here and love the area just as the wealthy do.... Both working men and women want and need to save a dollar wherever possible. Shopping downtown Petoskey is for the tourists and the wealthy and not for any average person.[52]

Some of the shoppers actively organized to ensure that the proposed Wal-Mart would become a reality. Several women got together, drew up a petition in support of the mall, and then went door-to-door, eventually collecting about one thousand signatures. They also attended the various official meetings and made their views known. When I asked a Bear Creek woman who had been one of the organizers about the various other issues raised by USA (i.e., sprawl), she dismissed them casually.[53] The shoppers are an interesting phenomenon and will reappear in some of the other case studies.

The Wal-Mart issue brought out the cleavage in the Petoskey area between what Al Foster, chair of the Bear Creek Board of Supervisors, referred to as the "two factions": the "rich" and the "working."[54] The working faction felt that downtown had priced them out. Now here was an opportunity to get something they wanted, a major discount department store, but the rich faction was trying to keep it from them, using various arguments about containing sprawl and saving downtown. The working faction, however, did not have a great deal of sympathy for downtown because they felt that downtown had never been very interested in them. As for the sprawl argument, they felt that USA and the other opponents had little credibility on this score because they had not objected to Bay Harbor, a large, sprawl like, upscale, planned community—including retail development—located approximately five miles west of Petoskey. They thought it was hypocritical for the opponents to cry "sprawl" over Wal-Mart when there had been no such uproar over Bay Harbor.

The supporters advanced several other arguments. They noted that strip development had already taken place outside of downtown.[55] They also maintained that the site, although mostly zoned residential, was not really suitable for housing because of the commercial development that had already occurred nearby, including a gravel pit and a truck refueling operation. They maintained, furthermore, that the site was advantageous for large-scale commercial development because all the necessary utilities were already in place, the developer was willing to pay for any necessary road construction, and the township would benefit financially from having Wal-Mart pay to tap into its sewer line. Foster emphasized that the "township paid for nothing."[56] Finally, some supporters felt that the downtown merchants only opposed the Wal-Mart because they feared it would cut into their business. In response to concerns about the store's appearance the Gunlocks promised, as had Wal-Mart in Gig Harbor, to build "a Wal-Mart store unlike any we've ever built. . . . [with an] all-brick front in the Michigan Victorian style."[57]

THE SECESSIONIST THREAT

Throughout all the official debates Bear Creek held a trump card: if the county did not approve the requested PUD the township could withdraw unilaterally from county zoning, implement its own zoning ordinances, and then approve the Gunlocks' project under its own authority. According to Foster, if the county had not ultimately granted approval the township would have taken this course of action "in a minute."[58] Bear Creek's ability to secede from county zoning undoubtedly weakened opposition to the project.

THE VIEWS OF TWO PROFESSIONAL PLANNERS

In January 1995 Mark Wyckoff, an outside planning expert, was invited by local officials to address a special public meeting on the issue. Wyckoff, an independent planner who had helped prepare the joint city/county master plan, was respected by officials in both Petoskey and Bear Creek Township. Wyckoff told the audience of 200 that the project was "huge in size. It is two or three times the size of what a community of your size could expect at this point of its development."[59] At the same meeting Max Putters, chief planner for the county, counseled against the project and offered an alternative whereby the Elder-Beerman could go downtown and the Wal-Mart could fit into an existing shopping center. The remarks of these two professionals did not appear to cause any significant change of opinion among the project's supporters.

Less than a week after Wyckoff and Putters spoke, the township planning committee voted 5–2 to recommend preliminary approval (step one) of the project. This vote was somewhat anticlimactic as the township board had already voted on, and approved, the same matter. About a week later the board voted 5–0 to recommend final approval (step two), thereby formally designating the site as a PUD. A month later, in early March, the county planning commission took up the matter. They tied, 4–4, on a vote for preliminary approval, the only occasion that a vote taken by any of the four deliberating bodies did not result in approval for the project.

THE NEIGHBORS

During March and April of 1995 the homeowners who lived near the site, and who were destined to become Wal-Mart's neighbors, finally spoke up. Dale

Meyer of USA presented to the county planning commission a petition against the project signed by several nearby homeowners. William Germond, a nearby homeowner (and also chair of the Bear Creek Planning Committee), expressed his views in a letter to county officials:

> To impose such a development on a fine residential neighborhood would be unthinkable according to current textbooks and most professional planners. Put yourself in the shoes of the families that have established homes and a lifestyle based on the belief they were secure in a residential neighborhood. . . . I doubt there is one among you that would want such a development frontyard [sic] or backyard, or are we so greedy for a few tax dollars that it's OK as long as it's not in "my backyard"? . . .
> Having built our home and spent the last thirty or so years landscaping and making the place a retreat from the daily grind, we are just getting ready to try retirement. . . . Instead, we will face the trauma of seeking a new home and starting over. . . . How do you compensate people for losses of quality of life? Who will pay? Certainly not the developer that is here today and gone tomorrow. . . .[60]

Another homeowner remarked, "I sure as hell didn't move out here to sit and look at Wal-Mart the rest of my life."[61] Unmoved by such sentiments, the township board voted in April to reaffirm its earlier decision in favor of the project. The shoppers were similarly unmoved, as shown by this report on a township meeting:

> . . . those Bear Creek Township residents [who lived nearby] were jeered by other folk of the township who want the project and the shopping choices it symbolizes. Some of them muttered the complainers ought to just move away.[62]

MORE VOTES IN FAVOR OF THE PROJECT

In April 1995 the county planning commission voted for preliminary approval of the project (on a vote of 6–2) and shortly thereafter the county board of commissioners voted for preliminary approval also (on a vote of 6–2). This last vote was important because it demonstrated that the county board, which had final authority over the project, was generally supportive of the project. During the next six months there was continued opposition by USA, continued support by the Bear Creek Board of Supervisors and the shoppers, and lengthy discussions over matters such as the exact layout of the project and the allocation of land for each type of use. Sensing that the project would eventually receive final approval from the county board, USA began sending out letters soliciting donations to help support a legal challenge. USA sent out over a thousand letters to local residents and owners of second homes in the Petoskey area. A member of USA described their fund raising efforts as generally successful and estimated that as many as one thousand persons made a donation.[63] In September 1995 the county planning commission voted 5–4 to grant final approval and on 12 October 1995, the county board of commissioners gave its final approval on a vote of 4–3. Although there was still one more step in the approval process (step three: site design), once a project had received final approval from the county board of commissioners there was little that could be done to stop it at the local level.

USA GOES TO COURT

The day after the county approved the project, USA and three nearby residents filed a suit in Emmet County Circuit Court against the Emmet County Board of Commissioners, the Bear Creek County Planning Commission, and RG Properties. The suit challenged the use of a PUD:

> . . . the county can't approve a planned unit development [PUD] that fundamentally changes the land use in existence; . . . no standards existed for the planners or commissioners to approve planned unit developments; . . . the zoning is [illegal] 'contract zoning,' changing zoning and land use in exchange for promises from the developer; . . . the rezoning is arbitrary and spot zoning, failing to follow the county's land use plan; . . . [and] there were no adequate findings as to why the property should be rezoned or that the project will not have a detrimental impact on the surrounding community.[64]

It took the court six months to rule on the suit, during which time the county planning commission approved the site design (step three), the last step in the approval process. Bear Creek Township, Emmet County, and RG Properties formally signed the PUD agreement in March 1996. The next month Judge Charles Johnson issued a ruling on the suit in which he agreed with USA, but only on a minor procedural point: that the county board had failed to provide written justification for its decision. The county board promptly met, put into writing its reasons for having approved the PUD, and then voted again to approve the project. USA then filed a second suit, similar to the first. Judge Johnson advised USA that it was not likely to prevail and Bo Gunlock threatened a countersuit, claiming that USA's second suit constituted "harassment."[65] Upon advice of its attorney, USA dropped its suit.

RG Properties began construction in May 1996 and Wal-Mart opened for business in January 1997. Elder-Beerman filed for bankruptcy before construction began; an Office Max was built in its place. Most of the rest of the mall never materialized.

Gig Harbor and Petoskey can be compared and contrasted in terms of the growth machine, the framing and tactics of the opponents, public reaction, and various case-specific and contingent factors. In both cities the businesses and government officials that would be expected to support growth, according to the growth machine perspective, offered very little support for the proposed Wal-Mart. In Gig Harbor, the chamber of commerce was an official supporter, but was wracked by dissension, with few businesses actually supporting Wal-Mart. Local businesses in Petoskey were similarly unsupportive and even the chamber failed to offer support. In both cities the store failed to get support from local government as well. In both cases the site was located on county land beyond the city limits, and thus, city officials had no authority over the disposition of the site. City officials in Gig Harbor, however, seem to have been more attuned to Wal-Mart's modus operandi. In the middle of the controversy they implemented new size restrictions on commercial development, a preemptive measure clearly designed to avoid superstores. In Petoskey, by contrast, city officials tried to get Wal-Mart to put its store downtown. Given Wal-Mart's record on the siting of its stores, which was wellestablished by 1995, this was a futile effort and indicated a lack of familiarity with how the company operates. The local newspaper, another typical growth machine actor, remained neutral in Petoskey but actively opposed the store in Gig Harbor.

A notable contrast between the two cases involves the framings used by the opponents. In Gig Harbor the PNA framed the situation as a fight between "between David and Goliath" for "our quality of life."[66] Many of the concerns that people had—traffic, environmental degradation, loss of small town atmosphere, sprawl—tied in well with the overall presentation of the issue as a matter of saving the unique Gig Harbor lifestyle. USA, in Petoskey, framed the issue in terms of proper land use and the containment of urban sprawl. While these two framings appear similar, they differed substantially in practice. The Gig Harbor framing was broader and had something for everybody, while the Petoskey framing resonated well only with the minority who were concerned with, and understood, sprawl.

These differences in framing are paralleled by differences in tactics. The PNA attacked everything it could about the store and the site, used colorful and dramatic actions, and tried to show that there was enormous grassroots opposition. These tactics generated a lot of negative publicity for Wal-Mart in Gig Harbor and throughout the Seattle-Tacoma area. USA was more constrained. It took an approach that was largely educational (i.e., town meetings featuring land use experts) and was careful not to attack Wal-Mart.

An additional contrast involves the local supporters. In Gig Harbor there was a conspicuous lack of publicly expressed support, with the exception of certain members of the chamber. In Petoskey, however, officials in the surrounding township and a self-organized group of shoppers made efforts to promote the store. They articulated a pro-Wal-Mart point of view and offered rebuttals to at least some of the arguments of the opponents. The actual degree of support among the area's residents was unclear as various surveys produced conflicting results.

There were also a few case-specific features that may have affected the outcomes. During the Gig Harbor dispute Wal-Mart opened a superstore in Port Orchard, a twenty minute drive from the city, which allowed the company to capture at least some of the sales dollars that would have been spent in Gig Harbor and perhaps lessened its resolve to put a store there. In Petoskey the developers' successful attempt to have the project approved as a PUD rather than a conventional rezoning meant that they were able to avoid a more rigorous approval process. Also, Bear Creek's ability to withdraw from county zoning at any time and assume authority for its own land use decisions undermined the efforts of the opponents.

Comparing the two cases, it is apparent that the framing and tactics used by the opponents in Gig Harbor were more effective. A real estate professional told me that Wal-Mart withdrew in Gig Harbor because it was becoming too costly.[67] While this may have been the proximate cause of Wal-Mart's withdrawal, it was related to the prolongation of the approval process, and *this* was a direct result of the actions by the opponents. Also, the size controls implemented by Gig Harbor officials raised another barrier and lessened the odds that Wal-Mart would prevail eventually. In addition to less effective framing and tactics, the opponents in Petoskey were confronted with an effective counter social movement (the shoppers), an approval process that was less rigorous, and probably more public support for the store.

NOTES

1. Population figures are from the U.S. Census Bureau, "Population Estimates for Places." http://www.census.gov. Population figures are for the year in which the controversy began, unless otherwise noted.

2. Per capita income in Gig Harbor in 2000 was $28,318, compared with $22,973 for the state of Washington. U.S. Census Bureau, "Fact Sheet, Census 2000." http://factfinder.census.gov.

3. Brian K. Miller, "Is Wal-Mart on the Way?" *Peninsula Gateway* (WA), 5 April 1995.

4. Pierce County Department of Planning and Land Services, *Draft Environmental Impact Statement for the Point Fosdick Center*, issued 19 April 1996.

5. Interview with Gretchen Wilbert, mayor, City of Gig Harbor.

6. Interview with Tom Morfee, president, PNA.

7. Resolution of the Gig Harbor-Peninsula Area Chamber of Commerce, n.d., file SBR 2-95, Pierce County Department of Planning and Land Services, Tacoma, Washington.

8. Quoted in Brian K. Miller, "Founding Chamber Member Resigns Over Wal-Mart Flap," *Peninsula Gateway*, 29 November 1995.

9. Interview with Lois Eyrse, president, Gig Harbor-Peninsula Chamber of Commerce.

10. Eyrse interview.

11. Letter from Lois Eyrse to Pierce County Department of Planning and Land Services, dated 20 May 1996, file SPR 2-95, Pierce County Department of Planning and Land Services, Tacoma, Washington.

12. Anonymous interview, Gig Harbor, Washington.

13. Eyrse interview.

14. Anonymous interview, Gig Harbor, Washington.

15. Letter to the editor, *Peninsula Gateway*, 13 December 1995.

16. Eyrse interview.

17. CBS News, "Up Against the Wal-Mart," *60 Minutes*, 3 September 1995.

18. Wilbert interview.

19. Wilbert interview.

20. Wilbert interview.

21. Morfee interview.

22. Based on examination of letters on file with the Pierce County Department of Planning and Land Services, Tacoma, Washington.

23. Wal-Mart press release dated 24 October 1995.

24. Brian K. Miller, "Wal-Mart to Go Public at Meeting?" *Peninsula Gateway*, 18 October 1995.

25. Tony Hazarian, "Wal-Mart Met with Round of Jeers," *Peninsula Gateway*, 25 October 1995.

26. Quoted in Tony Hazarian, "Gig Harbor 'is what Wal-Mart is all about' Spokesman Says," *Peninsula Gateway*, 25 October 1995.

27. Letter to the editor, *Peninsula Gateway*, 15 November 1995.

28. Quoted in Tony Hazarian, "Wal-Mart Alters Point Fosdick Store Look," *Peninsula Gateway*, 17 April 1996.

29. *Peninsula Gateway*, 1 May 1996.

30. Tony Hazarian, "Wal-Mart Alters Point Fosdick Store Look," *Peninsula Gateway*, 17 April 1996.

31. "Wal-Mart Not Wanted, Crowd Says," *Peninsula Gateway*, 15 May 1996.
32. Letter from John McCullogh to Pierce County Department of Planning and Land Services, dated 2 January 1997, file SPR 2-95, Pierce County Department of Planning and Land Services, Tacoma, Washington.
33. Interview with Max Putters, director, Emmet County Office of Planning and Zoning.
34. Quoted in Neil Stilwell, "Wal-Mart Gets Profane Reception," *Petoskey News-Review* (MI), 29 September 1994.
35. Brian McGillivary, "Hospital Backs Out on Wal-Mart," *Petoskey News-Review*, 7 October 1994.
36. Quoted in Neil Stilwell, "Alliance Plans Dec. 8 Town Meeting on Sprawl," *Petoskey News-Review*, 30 November 1994.
37. Neil Stilwell, "Petoskey Takes Close Look at Wal-Mart," *Petoskey News-Review*, 29 September 1994.
38. Quoted in Neil Stilwell, "Group Opposes Urban Sprawl, Says Wal-Mart OK Downtown," *Petoskey News-Review*, 30 November 1994.
39. Quoted in Brian McGillivary, "Developers Submit Plans for Petoskey Wal-Mart," *Petoskey News-Review*, 19 September 1994.
40. Anonymous interview, Petoskey, Michigan.
41. Quoted in George Cantor, "Wal-Mart: Consumer Savior or Downtown Destroyer?" *Detroit News*, 21 July 1996.
42. Results of survey by Marketing Research Services, Inc., file 124-94, Emmet County Office of Planning and Zoning, Petoskey, Michigan.
43. Brain McGillivary, "Wal-Mart: Emmet Residents Want Us." *Petoskey News-Review*, 19 October 1994.
44. Interview with Diane Litzenburger, president, Petoskey-Regional Chamber of Commerce.
45. Litzenburger interview.
46. Letter from Petoskey Regional Chamber of Commerce to Emmet County Planning Commission, dated 24 October 1994, file 124-94, Emmet County Office of Planning and Zoning, Petoskey, Michigan.
47. Letter from Petoskey Gaslight-Downtown Association Board of Directors to Bear Creek Township, Emmet County Planning Commission, Petoskey Regional Chamber of Commerce, and Petoskey News Review, n.d., file 124-94, Emmet County Office of Planning and Zoning, Petoskey, Michigan.
48. In recent years Wal-Mart has placed a few of its stores in big cities.
49. Interview with Al Foster, chair, Bear Creek Board of Supervisors.
50. Interview with Pat Mather, Emmet County Board of Supervisors.
51. Quoted in Neil Stillwell, "Bear Creek Board Wants Wal-Mart," *Petoskey News-Review*, 3 November 1994.
52. Letter to Max Putters, director, Emmet County Office of Planning and Zoning, 14 October 1994, file 124-94, Emmet County Office of Planning and Zoning, Petoskey, Michigan.
53. Anonymous interview, Bear Creek Township, Michigan.
54. Foster interview.

55. This could be an argument *against* more strip development also.
56. Foster interview.
57. Quoted in *Detroit News*, "Petoskey Area Residents Battle Wal-Mart Plan," 14 October 1995.
58. Foster interview.
59. Quoted in Brian McGillivary, "Planning Pros: Say No to Wal-Mart," *Petoskey News-Review*, 20 January 1995.
60. Letter from W.C. Germond to Emmet County Planning Commission and Emmet County Board of Commissioners, 22 March 1995, file 124-94, Emmet County Office of Planning and Zoning, Petoskey, Michigan.
61. Quoted in Brian McGillivary, "Neighbors of Proposed Wal-Mart Not Too Happy About Plan," *Petoskey News-Review,* 27 March 1995.
62. Neil Stilwell, "Bear Creek OKs Strip Mall Again," *Petoskey News-Review,* 6 April 1995.
63. Anonymous interview, Petoskey, Michigan.
64. Neil Stilwell, ". . . and So Is a Big Lawsuit," *Petoskey News-Review,* 13–14 October 1995.
65. Quoted in Brian McGillivary, "Wal-Mart Gets Ready to Build," *Petoskey News-Review,* 6 May 1996.
66. Morfee interview.
67. Anonymous interview, Gig Harbor, Washington.

5

West Bend, Wisconsin, and Ottawa, Ohio

A Superstore in the Neighborhood?

The city of West Bend, Wisconsin, and the village of Ottawa, Ohio, in contrast to the previous two cities, do not portray their environs as settings of great scenic beauty, at least not to the same extent. Another difference is that they are predominantly middle- and working-class towns. In West Bend and Ottawa, Wal-Mart wanted to put a store near a residential district and the ensuing controversies revolved around the threat posed to residential neighborhoods. The potential impact on the downtown merchants was not a major issue because of the salience of the residential threat, but also because the downtown in each city had already ceased to be the major commercial center. In West Bend the opponents faced a substantial growth machine in the form of local officials and business leaders who vigorously supported the store; in Ottawa they faced a counter social movement of local shoppers who ardently wanted a Wal-Mart, regardless of location. In both cases the opponents took essentially the same approach and obtained the same outcome.

WEST BEND, WISCONSIN

"Can you imagine giving people directions to my house and having to tell them, 'Turn at the Wal-Mart?'"

—Remark attributed to an opponent

> "We owe it to the people to follow the zoning laws ... or what is zoning for?"
>
> —West Bend Alderman Terry Vrana

The city of West Bend (population 27,714) is in southeastern Wisconsin, about thirty miles northwest of Milwaukee. During the early 1990s, in the runup to the controversy, the city's economy was healthy and its population was growing rapidly, as was that of surrounding Washington County.[1] On 7 November 1994, the mayor of West Bend, Michael Miller, announced that Wal-Mart intended to build a store in the city. The proposed store, to be open twenty-four hours a day, would include a McDonald's restaurant, a pharmacy, and an oil-change facility; the front of the site would contain restaurants of the type typically found on commercial strips. West Bend already had two discount department stores, Kmart and Shopko, as well as a large Fleet-Farm store that sold some of the same items as a discount department store. The proposed Wal-Mart, at 125,000 square feet, would be larger than any of these stores and would be the largest retail establishment in the city.

The site chosen by Wal-Mart was a 15.5-acre parcel of grassy and wooded land near the western edge of the city at the corner of West Washington Street and Valley Avenue (I will refer to it as the Valley Avenue site). The site is about two miles from downtown and was vacant except for an old farmhouse. The site consisted of three portions, each with a different zoning: multifamily residential, office park, and commercial. For Wal-Mart to build a store at the site all the land would have to be zoned commercial, which meant that about half of the site would have to be rezoned. Also, a small parcel had to be annexed from the town of West Bend. Wal-Mart intended to buy the land after all the various parts had been annexed and rezoned as necessary. There were a variety of structures and landscapes in the general vicinity of the site. Across West Washington was a large auto dealership and assorted commercial buildings, while across Valley Avenue was a branch of M & I Bank and the General Clinic, a medium-size medical facility. Valley Avenue, which begins at West Washington, curves gently past the site and winds slowly uphill into a recently built subdivision called Fox Ridge. The first part of the subdivision consists of duplex condominiums, which give way to single-family homes as one continues up the hill, with the size and value of the homes increasing the further up one goes. Wal-Mart's plans called for three entrances to be placed on Valley Avenue and for various changes to be made to the roads and traffic signals to accommodate the increased traffic that the store would generate. Valley Avenue is the main entrance to the Fox Ridge subdivision.

Wal-Mart's request to have the Valley Avenue site rezoned was considered at length by the Plan Commission and the Common Council, with the final decision to be made by the latter, an elected body whose members are known as alders. The city's planning department, known as the Department of Community Development (DCD), was actively involved and worked extensively with Wal-Mart to develop plans for the site. During the controversy numerous changes were made to the plans for the site. Whether or not *significant* changes were made was an ongoing point of contention between the supporters and opponents.

The Plan Commission held its first public hearing on 6 December 1994. Seventeen Fox Ridge residents expressed their views on the proposed rezoning; all were opposed except one, David Bohn, a developer who owned the land and had developed the entire Fox Ridge subdivision. The opponents voiced concerns about the traffic, noise, and litter that the new store would generate; the negative effects on the natural environment; and the incongruity of a large, busy, commercial development located next to a residential neighborhood. The DCD was in favor of the rezoning and maintained that commercial development at the corner of West Washington and Valley Avenue was consistent with the city's 2010 Land Use Plan. The Plan Commission denied recommending the rezoning on a 4–2 vote. Undeterred by this initial rebuff, Wal-Mart submitted a preliminary site plan a few days later. Company representatives also met with a group of residents, who again expressed their concerns about the adverse effects of a superstore in their neighborhood, and met individually with members of the Common Council.[2] The Common Council took up the rezoning about two weeks later. At a meeting attended by 150 persons, Wal-Mart representatives and interested members of the public presented their views to the council. Todd Murphy, of Todd Robert Murphy Communications, Inc., a Milwaukee public relations firm hired by Wal-Mart, stressed the extent to which Wal-Mart had made changes in the site plan in response to residents' concerns (e.g., repositioned the store) and said the company would continue to take their concerns into consideration. He presented the results of a canvassing of city residents, paid for and organized by his firm, that produced 1,408 affirmative responses for Wal-Mart, which were offered as proof that the project enjoyed support throughout most of the city, even if the residents in the immediate area were opposed.[3] Executives from two local companies that sold to Wal-Mart also expressed support for the store. Most of the members of the public who spoke were opposed to the Valley Avenue site, and many of those were Fox Ridge residents. After three hours of hearings and discussion, the council voted 7–1 to table the matter to give Wal-Mart and the project engineer a chance to revise their site plan (also known as a concept plan) to satisfy the various criticisms of the residents and alders. Wal-Mart submitted a revised plan in January 1995 and another in February.

SUPPORTERS OF THE VALLEY AVENUE SITE

The project had many supporters, including the following:

The Mayor and the Department of Community Development

The mayor and the DCD were major supporters of the project. They were pro-growth and for them a new Wal-Mart represented growth. Even before Mayor Miller formally announced the proposed store, the DCD had begun working with Wal-Mart on preparing plans for the site. For Miller, a major attraction of the store was the jobs that it would create. He also expected it to increase local tax revenue by expanding the tax base, while requiring only minimal city expenditure because Wal-Mart had agreed to pay for all necessary infrastructure.[4] The only expense to the city would be the expanded police coverage that the store would require. Mayor Miller, however, was mindful of his constituents and stated, "I would like to see a Wal-Mart in West Bend, but I also have to represent the people."[5]

The Local Newspaper

The major local newspaper, the *West Bend Daily News*, went on record early as a supporter.[6] The paper gave four reasons for supporting the store: it would keep shoppers in the city, draw shoppers from outside the city, create jobs, and add to the city's tax base.[7] Later, however, the newspaper became a critic of the Valley Avenue site.

The Chamber of Commerce

The West Bend Area Chamber of Commerce was another enthusiastic supporter. Betty Pearson, executive vice president of the chamber, said there was little negative reaction to Wal-Mart from other merchants in the city, whether located downtown or elsewhere. Moreover, the chamber did its own research and concluded that a Wal-Mart store "invigorated the retail environment," something West Bend needed at the time, according to Pearson.[8] At the height of the controversy the newspaper published a piece by Pearson in which she touted the store in explicit growth machine terms:

> Healthy communities—just like healthy individuals—grow. To not grow means to stagnate or go backwards. . . . .
> The West Bend Area Chamber of Commerce believes that growth is good, and that with careful planning communities and businesses can thrive. . . .
> To sustain growth, The [sic] West Bend Area Chamber of Commerce pledges to work with new and existing businesses on thriving and surviving here. . . . The entire world of work needs to focus on getting and keeping businesses healthy.
> Growth in our community should be planned for and heartily welcomed.[9]

The Landowner

As mentioned above, the landowner was David Bohn, a developer who had developed the Fox Ridge subdivision in 1992. Bohn also lived in Fox Ridge, but unlike his fellow subdivision homeowners he was an enthusiastic supporter of the Valley Avenue site.

Wal-Mart

As usual, Wal-Mart representatives emphasized the jobs that would be created, the addition to the tax base, and the improved retail environment that would result from keeping more shoppers in the city and attracting more shoppers from outside the city. Les Copeland, public relations coordinator for Wal-Mart, whom we met before in Gig Harbor, asserted that Wal-Mart was known for "raising money for local charitable causes, [promoting] environmental programs and spurring industrial development."[10] He did not explain how the presence of a Wal-Mart would spur industrial development in West Bend. As part of its promotion campaign, Wal-Mart sent a flyer to all residents advocating the Valley Avenue site.

The Public Relations Firm

Todd Murphy, the public relations specialist, promoted the store and the site at various official meetings and in the press. He illustrated the popularity of a Wal-Mart store by showing a video that portrayed the positive reaction that employees and shoppers had to a Wal-Mart in another Wisconsin community. Throughout the controversy he maintained that the Valley Avenue site was the only site in the city that Wal-Mart considered suitable, with the implication that if Wal-Mart did not get the Valley Avenue site it would drop the city completely and the people in West Bend would not get a Wal-Mart. This petulant attitude appears to be a standard Wal-Mart tactic and was evident in more than one controversy.

Local Employers

Wal-Mart itself was a customer of several local employers and used this fact as a lever to increase support for the Valley Avenue site. At least four West Bend companies sold to Wal-Mart: the West Bend Company, a manufacturer of small kitchen appliances and pots and pans; Enger Kress, a leather goods manufacturer; WESBAR, a metal products fabricator; and Amity, another leather goods manufacturer. Not only did these companies sell to Wal-Mart, but some of them subcontracted with other local businesses, thus extending down into the community the number of firms and individuals that had a stake in seeing Wal-Mart attain its goals in West Bend. Representatives of two of these companies intimated that their relationship with Wal-Mart might suffer—and by extension their role as local employers—if Wal-Mart did not get the rezoning it wanted.[11]

OPPONENTS OF THE VALLEY AVENUE SITE

The most vocal and most organized opposition came from the people who lived near the site, especially the residents of the Fox Ridge subdivision. Aware that Wal-Mart was proceeding as if it expected eventual approval, a group of Fox Ridge residents formed a nonprofit organization in April 1995. The new organization, called Citizens Advocating Appropriate Planning (CAAP), served as an organizing device for the opponents, whose primary concern was the disruption that a superstore would bring to their neighborhood. They argued that they had bought homes in the subdivision based on the zoning that was in effect at the time of purchase. That zoning provided for a careful and deliberate gradation of uses extending from West Washington up into the subdivision: the land along West Washington was zoned for commercial use; the land behind that was zoned for multifamily residential (i.e., apartments); behind that was a small environmentally sensitive area containing a creek; the area further back was zoned for duplexes; and finally, still further back and going up the hill, came single-family zoning. Under Wal-Mart's proposal most of the land from West Washington up to the duplexes would become commercial. What this meant for the Fox Ridge residents is that the undeveloped area separating them from West Washington would disappear and they would be nearly adjacent to large-scale commercial development.

One of the biggest problems, according to CAAP, was a substantial increase in traffic, both on Valley Avenue and in the subdivision itself. A study performed for the DCD estimated that traffic on Valley Avenue would increase to about 9,000 vehicles a day.[12] One Fox Ridge resident commented:

We just don't believe this is the right location for the store. The issue is not that we are trying to keep Wal-Mart out of West Bend, we want them to come to West Bend. But the store just doesn't have a place in a residential neighborhood area. It's just not appropriate for a neighborhood this size to deal with the 8,000 to 9,000 cars a day that Wal-Mart will attract.[13]

Throughout the controversy there was extensive discussion about how much effect this increased traffic would have on the residential area. Not only were the number of vehicles and the routes taken an issue, but residents were concerned also about the large trucks that would be making frequent deliveries to the store.

Some residents were worried that a Wal-Mart would lead to increased crime in their area. Aside from crime at the store, they feared that increased traffic in the subdivision would lead to an influx of "unknown" people, which was taken by some as a harbinger of crime. At one council meeting a girl expressed concern for the safety of the kids in the area and raised the possibility of "children disappear[ing] from neighborhoods, never to be seen again."[14] CAAP also expressed concerns about litter, noise, lighting, and the sheer size of the building. Regarding the importance of having a local Wal-Mart in West Bend, they pointed out that there were already four Wal-Marts within thirty-five miles of the city, with the closest only fifteen miles away.

In sum, the residents maintained that a Wal-Mart store would disrupt the transition from commercial to residential development in the area, was out of scale with surrounding development, would greatly increase traffic and noise, might lead to an increase in crime, and could cause their property values to decline. In other words, the Valley Avenue site was simply the wrong site for a Wal-Mart in West Bend. CAAP emphasized that it was not against having a Wal-Mart in West Bend or against Wal-Mart per se. An advertisement announcing the formation of CAAP stated that its purpose was to "promote appropriate zoning and re-zoning decisions in the City of West Bend so as to protect desirable existing development . . . [and that it was] not opposed to Wal-Mart building in West Bend at a site currently zoned for commercial development."[15]

CAAP framed the issue as a matter of maintaining the integrity of the 2010 Land Use Plan, which was designed to promote well-ordered development in the city. The 2010 Plan, formally adopted in 1992 after several years of discussion, represented a major effort by the city to plan for its future development. It was intended to be "the official guide to the decision-making of the City's officials concerning the development and redevelopment of the City and [its] environs" and "to be used as a tool to help guide the physical development of the community into a more efficient and attractive pattern, and to promote the public health, safety, morals, and general welfare of the community."[16] The particular instance of land use planning of most interest to CAAP, of course, was the proposed rezoning near Fox Ridge. Two leaders of CAAP, in a full-page opinion piece published in the *West Bend Daily News*, wrote:

> The project Wal-Mart would have the city adopt means the end of a citizen's ability to rely upon the 2010 Plan when deciding where to buy or build. If special interests are going to be given exceptions to the 2010 Plan's vision merely to enhance their bottom line, the 2010 Plan becomes meaningless . . . .
> . . . We are opposed to the city throwing out the comprehensive plan for the city's future because a large corporation wants to come to town. . . .
> We and our children will be here a long time after Wal-Mart comes and goes. . . .
> *If Wal-Mart gets the city to make an exception at the Valley Avenue site, it may not be long before other large corporations get exceptions to plan in your neighborhood*. . . (emphasis added).[17]

CAAP took pains to emphasize that the pertinent issue did not involve economics (whether a Wal-Mart would be good for the local economy) or shopping preferences, but was strictly a matter of zoning and appropriate land use. Some residents of other sections of the city agreed with CAAP on this issue:

> I sympathize deeply with those residents. I don't think this should be done to them. They bought and built their homes knowing that it was residential.[18]

The members of CAAP pointed to other available sites in the city and disputed Wal-Mart's claim that if it did not get the Valley Site it would drop all plans to build a store in West Bend. They pointed out that West Bend's demographics and growth rate made it an ideal city for Wal-Mart, so it was unlikely the company would abandon all plans of locating in the city if it did not secure the Valley Avenue site.

The opponents used various means to make their views known. They placed large signs on their lawns that said, "Our Backs Are to the Wal* No Rezoning" and wore buttons with the same slogan. They presented a petition to the city council signed by 90 percent of the subdivision's eighty residents.[19] They also brought up Sam Walton's now-famous promise not to build a store where it was not wanted and asked Wal-Mart to keep that promise in West Bend. They argued their case at the various meetings of the Plan Commission and Common Council, met privately with the members of the council, sent letters to the editor of the local newspaper, and spoke on a radio talk show. When the newspaper printed a full-page article by Todd Murphy in favor of the project, CAAP promptly prepared a rebuttal, which was given equal space.

DOWNTOWN WEST BEND AND THE DOWNTOWN MERCHANTS

West Bend has a well-defined downtown district centered on the northern end of Main Street. The downtown, however, is no longer the commercial center of the city; in fact, the city has no clearly recognizable commercial center, just strip development in several parts of the city. The downtown has an assortment of retail and service establishments, including a family-run hardware store, but has had no major department stores since J.C. Penney's left in the late 1980s. Downtown is also not the city's governmental center, as illustrated by the placement of the new municipal building in one of the areas dominated by strip development.

The downtown merchants remained almost silent throughout the controversy and their organization, the Downtown Marketplace Association, did not take a position on either Wal-Mart or the Valley Avenue site. Alderman Tom O'Meara III, who represented the district containing downtown, reported that he had heard very few objections from downtown business owners.[20] The hardware store, however, considered Wal-Mart a very serious threat and several downtown merchants displayed "Our Backs Are to the Wal" signs in their windows.[21] In the view of a longtime local observer, the downtown merchants were indeed concerned about Wal-Mart, but their organization was "weak" at that time and they simply were not prepared to engage in much political struggle.[22]

MORE ARGUMENTS OF THE PROPONENTS

The store's supporters offered two types of arguments: those related to the desirability of having a Wal-Mart in West Bend and those related to the land use concerns raised by CAAP. They argued that the proposed store would eliminate trips that some residents were making to Wal-Marts elsewhere, would keep more shopping dollars in the city, and would attract shoppers from the surrounding area. In response to fears that Wal-Mart might hurt local small businesses, the proponents argued that Wal-Mart might hurt sales at Shopko and Kmart, but would not have much effect on smaller businesses that occupied different niches. Les Copeland insinuated that those businesses that objected to Wal-Mart were poorly run: "Businesses that have a history of selling quality merchandise at a good price and providing service to their customers prosper."[23] This dig at the small merchants is a another standard Wal-Mart tactic.

On the zoning issue, Mayor Miller and others argued that having the site rezoned to commercial to accommodate Wal-Mart was not the "worst" thing that could happen.[24] What could be worse? Developing the site in accordance with the existing zoning, which included a designation of "multifamily residential" for about half the site. What was wrong with "multifamily residential?" It was the zoning designation for apartments. And what was wrong with apartments? The problem with apartments, according to the DCD, was that they changed the city's "traditional development pattern, which is a city of mainly single-family homes."[25] In other words, apartments attract *poor people* and thus, according to this logic, the Fox Ridge residents should not have been so upset with a proposed Wal-Mart superstore.

In response to assertions that the rezoning violated the 2010 Plan, the proponents argued that the rezoning was consistent with the plan because there was already extensive commercial development on the other side of West Washington. Alternatively, and somewhat inconsistently, they also argued that the 2010 Plan should be viewed as "flexible" because land use plans, by their very nature, have to be adaptable to change.

Those in favor of the store seemed convinced that a majority of the city's residents were on their side and portrayed the opposition as a relatively small number of people in Fox Ridge who were interested only in maintaining the tranquility of their upscale subdivision. The opponents, in other words, were cast as NIMBYists, and not just ordinary NIMBYists, but privileged NIMBYists. At one council meeting it was implied that they were essentially the "country club" set.[26] The members of CAAP who spoke at meetings were all clearly professionals, which may have contributed to the image that they were an elite group, and some of the homes in the subdivision were definitely larger and nicer than the average West Bend home, although none were grandiose. Although the members of CAAP strove to appear neutral on the question of Wal-Mart itself, Murphy portrayed them as "clearly anti-Wal-Mart people. They claim they are not opposed to Wal-Mart in West Bend, but they are."[27] This comment seemed designed to arouse resentment among others who wanted a Wal-Mart.

In West Bend there was no organized popular support for the store, as there had been in some other communities, so it was difficult to gauge popular sentiment. The project file at the DCD contained only a few letters from residents, all against the site.[28] Letters to the editor of the local newspaper were split fairly evenly for and against. Most declarations of popular support emphasized wanting a Wal-Mart in West Bend, not the suitability of the Valley Avenue site. The following comment is typical:

> I think Wal-Mart should be brought in. I think it's great. To drive 25 miles to get to a good store is ridiculous. West Bend needs more stores like Wal-Mart, and bigger shopping malls.[29]

THE CONCEPT PLAN AND THE FINAL VOTE

Let's review the events up to this point: The Plan Commission considered the rezoning in late 1994 but voted against it. Shortly thereafter the Common Council took up the matter but then tabled it to allow Wal-Mart more time to revise its plan. During the early part of 1995 Wal-Mart continued to submit revised plans. In the spring Fox Ridge residents formed CAAP. By this time the controversy had heated up and was receiving extensive coverage in the local paper, which later named it the top local story of 1995.[30]

To continue, in April the *West Bend Daily News* changed its stance and editorialized against the Valley Avenue site for the first time. The paper now stressed the importance of upholding the integrity of zoning and asked why Wal-Mart was so stuck on a site that seemed inappropriate.[31]

On 20 April the DCD recommended to the Plan Commission that Wal-Mart's latest concept plan for the Valley Avenue site be approved. The purpose of the concept plan, which addressed mainly questions of site layout and traffic mitigation, was to establish that a Wal-Mart store could fit on the site and could meet all necessary design requirements. The fact that the DCD recommended to the Plan Commission that it approve the concept plan, when the commission had voted down the rezoning, indicates that the DCD was pushing hard for the Valley Avenue site. John Capelle, director of the DCD, acknowledged that there were other possible sites in the city, but claimed that they all had major deficiencies.[32] On 24 April Wal-Mart placed a full-page advertisement in the newspaper noting that it had made "over 30 changes to . . . [the] proposed development,"[33] including eliminating the auto repair center, recirculating truck traffic, agreeing to pay for road improvements, and agreeing to screen the store from the subdivision. On 26 April the Plan Commission considered the concept plan. Before a crowd of 150, most of whom opposed the Valley Avenue site, the Plan Commission voted 6–1 to approve the plan.[34]

Two weeks later the Common Council met to finally vote on the rezoning. After hearing once again from all sides, the Council voted 5–3 to reject the rezoning. It was a very tough decision for the council, which had been caught between appearing to succumb to powerful corporate interests and appearing to give in to the politically savvy, well-to-do residents from Fox Ridge. Mayor Miller characterized it as "one of the toughest decisions this council has made."[35] The apparent end came in September when Les Copeland informed the *Daily News* that Wal-Mart was no longer trying to put a store in West Bend.[36]

THE ANTI-PR MAN

An account of the Valley Avenue controversy would be incomplete without a special mention of Todd Murphy, the public relations specialist hired by Wal-Mart. Murphy's name came up repeatedly during my interviews and almost everyone who mentioned him, regardless of the position they had taken during the dispute, said he had made such a bad impression that he had actually hurt Wal-Mart's chances. Murphy came across as a self-important, big-city, public relations consultant who treated the people in West Bend like a bunch of hicks. Murphy's attitude and demeanor alienated nearly everybody, especially the alders. Many described him as "slick" and several mentioned his expensive suits and frequent cell phone conversations. In fact, Murphy's actions and statements were not substantially different from those of Wal-Mart's own public relations representatives during other siting controversies or those of the private developers who often do the local public relations work. The problem was that his condescending manner and "slick" style were anathema to the people of West Bend. His overall effect was to undermine Wal-Mart's chances of securing the rezoning that it needed.

THE REST OF THE STORY: WAL-MART RETURNS

Two years later, in October 1997, the residents of West Bend found out that Wal-Mart was coming to town after all. Continental Properties, a real estate development company based in nearby Menomonee Falls, announced that it had secured Wal-Mart as one of the first tenants for a commercial park that it planned to build on the southwestern edge of the city. Later in the month ground was broken for the project, to be known as the West Bend Corporate Center. This site had been suggested earlier by many as superior to the Valley Avenue site. The West Bend Corporate Center is a 145-acre development containing a mixture of retail, office, and light industrial uses. The largest structure in the center, a 205,000-square-foot building, now houses a Wal-Mart Supercenter. The Supercenter, which opened in 1998, includes a pharmacy, a photography studio, a nursery, a bank branch, a pretzel vendor, a nail salon, a hair cutting business, a "Vision Center," and an automobile lubrication and tire operation. Mayor Miller and Betty Pearson were extremely pleased with the West Bend Corporate Center and Wal-Mart's decision to put a store there. At the Center's groundbreaking ceremony Miller said, "This will probably be the most wonderful project in the state of Wisconsin."[37] The Common Council also supported the project and approved a tax incremental financing (TIF) district to help pay for the necessary infrastructure such as roads and sewerage.[38]

Wal-Mart's entry into the city via the West Bend Corporate Center was accompanied by almost no vocal protest. This appears to be explained by two factors. First, Wal-Mart and the developer were secretive about the retailer's interest in the site. The land was annexed and zoned without any official mention of Wal-Mart and only after the project was well under way did Continental announce that Wal-Mart would lease the largest building and open a Supercenter.[39] Second, there were few homes in the area, so the kind of protest that occurred over the Valley Avenue site was unlikely. The half dozen residents who had homes near the Corporate Center were seriously affected by the development, but their homes were in the town of West Bend and they had no control over what the city of West Bend did.[40]

OTTAWA, OHIO

"We have to have a place for commercial, for residential, and for industrial."

—An opponent

The village of Ottawa (population 4,352) is in northwestern Ohio and serves as the county seat for Putnam County (population 34,785). The largest major city in this part of the state is Toledo, about fifty miles to the northeast. Two smaller cities, Findlay and Lima, are located about twenty miles from Ottawa, to the east and south, respectively. Ottawa itself is surrounded by Ottawa Township, which consists mostly of farmland. Ottawa's downtown consists of half a dozen blocks of well-maintained brick buildings, including the handsome county building, which dates from the turn of the century. Although there are a number of stores, downtown is clearly not the retail center of the village. The village, in fact, does not have an area that could properly be called the central business district. Retail and other commercial establishments are found in various parts of the village, mostly in the form of strip development. Despite Putnam County's status as the number two producer of wheat in the state, the largest percentage of jobs in the county (35 percent) is found in manufacturing.[41] A large Philips picture-tube plant is located not far from downtown. Several other large manufacturing plants are found out among the fields in the southeastern portion of the village. Ottawa has many nice older homes spreading out around downtown as well as newer homes in various residential districts in other parts of the village. The village appears prosperous and well maintained and has relatively few chains except fast food restaurants.

In 1994 Wal-Mart proposed to build a store near the edge of the village on North Perry Street, about one and half miles from downtown. The western side of North Perry Street consisted of residential areas, separated by farmland. These residential areas contained attractive, well-maintained, single-family homes. The eastern side of the street consisted of unplanned commercial strip development and undeveloped land. The commercial development included a two-story office building, an optometrist's office, an independent restaurant called the Red Pig Inn, a small mobile home park, and the Pamida Discount Center, a discount department store chain similar to Wal-Mart but with smaller stores and only a regional presence. It was on the *western* side of North Perry Street, on a piece of farmland in between two of the residential areas, that Wal-Mart wanted to build a store of approximately 100,000 square feet. The store, to include a garden center, a tire facility, and an oil-change facility, would have been the largest retail establishment in the village.

LAND ISSUES

The land that Wal-Mart wanted consisted of two adjacent parcels, a smaller parcel of 2.44 acres that bordered North Perry Street and a much larger parcel of 36.06 acres that extended to the west beyond the smaller parcel. The smaller parcel was inside the village limits (known as the corporation line) and was zoned R–1 (residential). The larger parcel was outside the corporation line and was unzoned because it was undeveloped land located in Ottawa Township. Both parcels were owned by local landowners. For Wal-Mart to build on the site the smaller parcel had to be rezoned from R–1 to B–3 (commercial) and the larger parcel had to be annexed by the village and then zoned B–3.[42]

Wal-Mart had been pursuing this site, which I call the Perry Street site, for several years. Local events commenced in October of 1994 when Marie Heitmeyer, one of the landowners and the principal agent for the other landowners, submitted to the village a "notice of petition for annexation" for the larger parcel. The annexation had to be approved by both Putnam County and the Ottawa Village Council. The county approved the annexation without incident. In accordance with the village ordinance, the petition for annexation had to be "read" before the council on three separate occasions and a thirty-day period for public comment had to elapse. The three readings took place during February 1995. On 13 March 1995, the council approved the annexation. At that time Marie Heitmeyer confirmed that "a real estate firm representing

Wal-Mart of America has signed an option to possibly purchase the 36-acre site."[43] On 4 May 1995, Heitmeyer submitted a request to the council to have all 38.5 acres (the 2.44 acres plus the 36.06 acres) zoned B-3.[44] Before the council voted on the matter, however, it would become the subject of a major local controversy.

SUPPORTERS OF THE PERRY STREET SITE

The Perry Street site had various supporters:

The Landowners

The land was owned by several local families who had a direct pecuniary interest in having the land zoned commercial as it would increase the value of their property. Richard Niese, one of the landowners, told the village council that his father had once owned the land and that it had been his wish that a discount store might locate there someday.[45]

The Attorney and The Engineer

Robert Albright, an attorney from Columbus, Ohio, who had worked with Wal-Mart on other sitings, represented the company at various official meetings. The site plans were prepared by David Oakes of CESO, a professional engineering company from Dayton, Ohio. It was the task of Albright and Oakes to convince the village council and the village at large that the site was appropriate for a Wal-Mart store and that Wal-Mart would be good for Ottawa. They devoted most of their energy to making the case that Wal-Mart would be good for the community.

The County

Economic development in Putnam County is overseen by the Putnam County Community Improvement Corporation (CIC). Martin Kuhlman, director of the CIC, supported having a Wal-Mart in Ottawa, whether at the Perry Street site or elsewhere. In his view the jobs and tax revenue generated by a Wal-Mart would constitute an economic boost for the county.[46] He emphasized that it was important to consider what was good for the entire county and not just for a particular community. Kuhlman did not address the question of how much Wal-Mart would hurt the sales of existing businesses in Ottawa and other nearby communities.

A Local Employer and Its Employees

The largest employer in Ottawa is the Philips Display Components Company, which employs about two thousand workers. Wal-Mart purchases products from Philips and took advantage of this fact to induce Philips and its employees to appeal to the village council and the community at large to approve the Perry Street site. Employees of Philips collected approximately 900 signatures on a petition that read, "Please sign if you would like Wal-Mart to come to Ottawa. Help keep Philip's [sic] product in Wall-Mart [sic] stores."[47]

Other Supporters

The prospect of having Wal-Mart come to Ottawa was supported by many other people, as evidenced by signatures on petitions, form letters, and letters to the editor. These other supporters had various interests. Some were simply interested in being able to have a local Wal-Mart instead of having to drive twenty miles to Findlay or Lima, the closest cities with a Wal-Mart. For this group, the convenience, low prices, and wide selection outweighed all other considerations. One supporter wrote to the council to say that she had "heard rumors that Wal-Mart was coming to Ottawa. . . . [and] couldn't wait."[48] Another wrote, ". . . how soon can it open[?] The thought of not having to drive 45 miles to get a decent price on shampoo and to have every household item available at a low price is outstanding."[49] Part of what motivated these proponents was the feeling that their opportunity to have a local Wal-Mart was being thwarted by two small minorities: the nearby homeowners and local small retailers. The proponents argued that the homeowners were being overly protective of their residential neighborhoods and really should not object to B–3 zoning because there was already commercial development on the other side of Perry Street. The local small retailers, they argued, were trying to keep all the local business for themselves. Although the merchants in Ottawa were quite muted in their publicly expressed opposition, the possibility that a Wal-Mart might not get built in Ottawa elicited strong anti-small-business sentiment from some quarters. For example, an unsigned letter submitted to the council and written in response to a flyer distributed by the opponents, included the following:

> What about the hardworking TAXPAYING residents who would LOVE to see WAL-MART come to Ottawa?? Nobody wants to hear from US! . . . Don't just give this opportunity to the small business owners who THINK they own the entire town because they own a business. . . . The local small businesses employ mainly family and friends. . . . "Getting Rich At the Expense of Others"—What have ALL of the local businesses been doing for YEARS?? They Know that you

will either pay their price, or you HAVE to go elsewhere. . . . I would think that since there are A LOT of people who pay Ottawa City Taxes, that we should have the right to vote, and not let the small business owners run the town.[50]

Other supporters espoused classic growth machine ideology and equated a new Wal-Mart with growth and progress. In their view, not to approve the request for commercial zoning would be interpreted as being antibusiness. Moreover, the tax revenue that the Wal-Mart would bring could be used to help finance other things that Ottawa needed, such as a college or a medical center. They argued that it was foolish for Ottowans to contribute sales dollars and tax revenue to other cities when the money could stay in Ottawa. The proponents did not, for the most part, put their energy into arguing that Perry Street was a good site for a Wal-Mart store. Instead, they emphasized the presumed benefits of Wal-Mart itself and framed the issue as a matter of bringing Wal-Mart to Ottawa and not allowing a "small minority" to keep Wal-Mart out.

OPPONENTS OF THE PERRY STREET SITE

Wal-Mart's proposed siting of a store at the Perry Street site aroused opposition from three categories of Ottawans: residents who lived near the site; owners of local stores; and other people opposed to the site, to Wal-Mart, or to both.

The Nearby Homeowners

The homeowners who lived near the site, along with citizens from other parts of the community, organized themselves into the Concerned Citizens Coalition (CCC) and obtained legal counsel from a law firm in Findlay.[51] The CCC provided the only sustained and organized opposition to the proposed siting. In the view of the CCC, a superstore at the proposed site would be completely out of character with the residential areas on both sides of the site. They felt that their peaceful, well-maintained residential districts were being invaded by large-scale commercial development. They objected to the increased noise and lights, as well as the design of the store itself (a "metal building," in the words of one opponent).[52] Some opponents were concerned that the store would be poorly maintained and would become an eyesore after a few years; others feared that it would lead to decreased property values. One problem they stressed repeatedly was the increased traffic, which they argued would pose a danger to the many children who were on foot in the area, not only because it was a residential area, but also because the local high school and municipal pool were near and many children walked to these destinations. As one opponent argued,

> I'm sure there is a place for Wal-Mart. Just not in a residential area. The village needs to grow, but it needs to have planned growth for what benefits all the community. This area, especially with the school, is already very congested with traffic.[53]

The CCC framed the issue mainly as a matter of proper zoning and well-planned growth. In particular, they emphasized the necessity of keeping commercial development apart from residential areas. One resident commented, "We have to have a place for commercial, for residential, and for industrial,"[54] while another stressed that people living in a residential subdivision should be afforded some "protection" from commercial development.[55] Besides objecting to commercial development next to their homes, the opponents also argued that the site should be zoned residential because it was one of the village's prime housing sites and would be needed for future residential development.

These homeowners were concerned not only with the negative effects of a Wal-Mart but also with the possibility that *other* types of commercial establishments might locate at the site. They argued that B–3 zoning would allow a wide range of businesses, some of which they considered distinctly undesirable, to locate there in addition to, or in place, of Wal-Mart. What were these other types of businesses? In a letter to the editor of the local newspaper, Thomas Schmiedebusch specified the types of commercial establishments allowed by B–3 zoning:

> A review of Ottawa's zoning ordinances will show you that voting for this zoning change will permit any of the following uses: hotels and motels, hospitals, clinics (i.e., abortion clinics?) and nursing homes, drive-in eating and drinking places, summer gardens and road houses, bakeries, billiard parlors and bowling alleys, retail sales and services, trade schools including shops, testing laboratories and studios, automotive service stations, automotive sales including sales lots, used car lots, trailer lots, repair garages, body and fender shops, paint shops, laundry, dry cleaning and dying shops, wholesale distributors of merchandise, warehouses and storage facilities, display rooms and show rooms, laboratories, including experimental, film or testing laboratories, bus terminals, animal hospitals and veterinary clinics, commercial recreation, building material yards, retail lumber yards, storage and sales of grain, livestock feeds or fuels, public utilities storage yards, and crematories.[56]

Schmiedebusch was clear about which of these he considered most undesirable:

Certainly, none of us want to see crematories, abortion clinics, experimental laboratories, or other such non-desirable projects located within our community, let alone within the middle of a residential subdivision located so closely to our public schools.

In sum, the basic stance taken by the CCC was that the village council had a duty to protect and safeguard residential districts, and that to allow the Perry Street site to be zoned commercial would be a dereliction of that duty.

The residents claimed to be opposed to commercial zoning, not to Wal-Mart per se, and the CCC was careful not to criticize the company directly for fear of being sued. However, many of those opposed to commercial zoning were also critical of Wal-Mart or, as often happens, developed a critique of Wal-Mart in the course of the controversy. The company's mode of operation struck them as aggressive and highhanded. One resident said she felt that Wal-Mart had just "barged into their neighborhood."[57] Another was irritated by the attorneys representing Wal-Mart, who "make you feel you don't have a choice."[58] It seemed to them that Wal-Mart got preferential treatment, as no local business would have even considered trying to get the Perry Street site zoned commercial. Some of their materials criticized Wal-Mart directly, such as a flyer titled *Is the Wal-Mart Way of Business Good for America?* which offered a negative view of Wal-Mart's business practices, including its use of "economic clout to squeeze out competing local businesses," its propensity to sell foreign-made goods while claiming to be all-American, and its "lower wages" and "inferior benefits." The CCC also showed two videos that present Wal-Mart in an unfavorable light: the *60 Minutes* segment used to advantage by the opponents in Gig Harbor and an independently produced video called *The Wal-Mess*.[59] Both graphically depict the negative effect that Wal-Mart has had on small towns and present the view that the long-term effect of a Wal-Mart store is to undermine a community's vitality.

Owners of Local Stores

The exact reaction of local small businesses to the proposed Wal-Mart was difficult to ascertain. Many of the small business owners I contacted declined to be interviewed. With few exceptions, their views were not reported in the local press and they did not present their views at the various meetings of the village council. David Laudick, president of the village council, said that few local merchants came to see him about the Wal-Mart matter.[60] Does this mean that they were unconcerned? Probably not. A local observer and former village official speculated that some merchants may have been reluctant to talk about it because they feared being sued by Wal-Mart. In his view, just about "all the merchants were against it."[61] Other commentators judged the reaction of local businesses to be more mixed. An interviewee familiar with the local merchants explained that a small minority were "vocally opposed," but that the "general reaction [among the merchants] was concern, not panic."[62] Timothy Macke, a member of the village council, observed that most merchants were not upset because they offered products that differed from those sold by Wal-Mart and thus were able to avoid direct competition.[63] He noted, however, that the hardware stores and pharmacies were concerned. S. Scott McDowell, the safety-service director (the village's planner), acknowledged that some downtown businesses had been concerned.[64] Jack Williams, the municipal director, recalled that the reaction of local business owners was mixed, with some downtown businesses and retailers opposed, but some restaurant owners and other retailers in favor.[65]

The business most directly threatened by Wal-Mart, however, was not a locally owned small business, but Pamida, the discount department store located directly across the street from the site. The management of Pamida was undoubtedly aware that Wal-Mart usually prevailed when pitted directly against other discount merchandisers. In spite of this threat, I encountered no mention of special pleading by Pamida.

Other Opponents

While the CCC maintained that it was only concerned about the site, some Ottawans took a stronger position and held that the village did not need a superstore anywhere. In their view, Ottawa had a friendly small-town atmosphere, was quite nice as it was, and Wal-Mart could only have a negative impact on the village. Some conceded that items were cheaper at Wal-Mart, but felt that saving a little money was not worth the negative effects, especially the loss of family-owned businesses.[66] One letter expressed these views in the following way:

> First of all, Ottawa has a reputation to uphold. We have a beautiful community with successful businesses providing for its people. Our merchants are community oriented. . . .
> If we allow Wal-Mart to come to Ottawa, we are inviting may unforeseen business foreclosures, bankruptcies, and other tragedies to our community. . . .
> Wal-Mart will take away from us what we have worked so hard to achieve, namely individual attention, personal care, loyalty, and added service that can only be provided by small town merchants.[67]

Another objection involved the delicate issue of social class. A Wal-Mart, it was feared, would attract a certain type of customer: people who were looking for a bargain, those "with a different buying mentality," in the words of one opponent.[68] A store that specializes in offering goods at the lowest possible price will inevitably attract a disproportionate number of people from both Ottawa and the surrounding area for whom low price is the paramount consideration. From this perspective, the overall attractiveness of the village would be diminished by Wal-Mart; a discount superstore that attracted a lot of bargain hunters would not necessarily be a bargain for the village.

The opponents used several tactics to advance their cause: they spoke at official meetings, wrote letters to the editor, displayed signs in their front yards, showed people the videos mentioned above, and sent out flyers. The general strategy of the nearby homeowners at the heart of the opposition was to gain the sympathy (and empathy) of residents in other parts of the village.

NEUTRAL ACTORS

Three organizations that could have put their considerable clout into supporting or opposing a Wal-Mart at the Perry Street site were the Ottawa Area Chamber of Commerce, the *Putnam County Sentinel*, and the village government. Instead, these organizations remained neutral throughout the controversy.

The Chamber of Commerce

The possibility of Wal-Mart coming to Ottawa was definitely a matter of interest to the chamber and was discussed frequently at meetings of the chamber's retail merchants committee. Although a Wal-Mart located near the edge of town posed a threat to some downtown merchants, the chamber was an organization that existed to represent all business interests in Ottawa, not just those located on Main Street. The chamber "has to be for all businesses," as one observer put it,[69] and could not single out a particular business, even if it was the world's largest retailer, and say that it was not welcome. In response to concerns about Wal-Mart's effects on existing businesses, the chamber took the stance that Ottawa retailers simply had to learn to compete with Wal-Mart.

The Newspaper

The weekly *Putnam County Sentinel* covered the dispute extensively. In the middle of the controversy the paper used its editorial privilege to remind citizens that the issue was being debated at council meetings and exhorted them to "Let your elected village officials know what you think."[70]

Village Government

During the controversy the members of the council did not voice strong opinions either for or against the site. They took the position, furthermore, that it was strictly a zoning issue and thus they were not going to get involved in the question of whether or not Wal-Mart would be good or bad for the community. Councilman J. Dean Meyer explained that "they were never trying to keep Wal-Mart from locating in Ottawa . . . [and] the entire issue was location."[71] Village officials emphasized that Wal-Mart had not received any special treatment.

ATTITUDES TOWARD GROWTH

The dispute over Wal-Mart brought up the question of growth, an ongoing concern in Ottawa. The members of local government were in favor of growth, but they were cautious and felt that the village should be selective. The village had attracted and kept a number of major manufacturers, including Philips, W.C. Wood (a manufacturer of freezers), and Lousiana-Pacific (a manufacturer of aluminum and wood products). They attributed this success, in part, to careful planning, which included setting aside land for industrial use and building infrastructure to meet the needs of manufacturers. Attracting big *retailers* was not a high priority.

Others did not question the type of growth and simply thought that Ottawa needed to grow. They felt that growth was necessary in order to enlarge the tax base, which would allow the village to bring in needed amenities such as a medical facility or college. They argued that a Wal-Mart would contribute to growth by keeping local shoppers in the village, pulling in shoppers from the surrounding area, and providing jobs and tax revenue. By contrast, there were others who valued the small-town atmosphere in Ottawa and simply did not want the kind of growth that a superstore represented. They liked and supported the local merchants, even though they knew that certain items would be cheaper at a Wal-Mart. If they wanted to shop at a large discount department store, they were quite willing to make the occasional trip to Findlay or Lima.

TWO PUBLIC HEARINGS AND A VOTE BY THE VILLAGE COUNCIL

By May of 1995 the matter was set squarely before the village council, but before deciding the council convened two public hearings, both of which were held in the cafeteria of Ottawa Elementary School in order to accommodate the large number of interested parties. At the first hearing, on 22 May, Mayor Maag began the proceedings by emphasizing that the issue was zoning, not Wal-Mart.[72] The proponents and opponents then made their arguments. David Oakes, the engineer, explained how the site plan could be modified to make the proposed store more acceptable to the nearby residents. This involved plans for landscaping, fencing, and constructing a grassy mound as a buffer, none of which mollified the nearby residents. Robert Albright, the attorney representing Wal-Mart, showed a video about a Wal-Mart store that had been built in a residential district in Delaware, Ohio, that was similar to Perry Street. According to Albright, there had been no resistance from the homeowners. Albright, however, had interviewed only the developers, not the homeowners. Martin Kuhlman of the CIC spoke in favor of having a Wal-Mart and stated that the village would gain $200,000 in tax revenue from the store and additional revenue from the income taxes paid by the store's employees. Michael Gilb, attorney for the CCC, insisted that the issue was zoning, not Wal-Mart, and argued that the residents he represented were not opposed to commercial development in Ottawa, but felt that it should not take place next to a residential neighborhood. At the second public hearing, held 26 June, the topics discussed and the parties giving their views were essentially the same as before.[73] The proponents brought in the manager of the Wal-Mart in Findlay to speak about the community benefits of having a Wal-Mart. Albright signed a document "guaranteeing" that Wal-Mart would adhere to the provisions of the site plan regarding fencing, landscaping, setbacks, and other similar matters. The CCC reiterated its concerns and emphasized that if this land were allowed to be zoned commercial, then residents in other parts of the village could find themselves confronted with unwanted commercial development next to *their* homes.

Throughout the controversy the various interested parties submitted an assortment of petitions, form letters, and individualized letters to the council. The final tally for these is as follows:

- 600 form letters in support of Wal-Mart.
- 900 signatures on a petition supporting Wal-Mart because it buys products from Philips.
- fifteen individualized letters, most opposing Wal-Mart.
- 100 signatures on a petition drawn up by CCC against commercial zoning.
- ninety signatures in favor of commercial zoning collected by an employee of Louisiana-Pacific.

At the end of the second public hearing the village council voted (5–1) to deny the landowners' request for commercial zoning.

"IT'S UP TO THE VOTERS"

A council vote against a request for a zoning change would normally be the end of the matter. Some local Wal-Mart supporters, however, decided to persevere in their efforts to get a Wal-Mart in Ottawa. During the following month they collected enough signatures on an initiative petition to compel a proposed ordinance to be placed on the ballot of the next general election. In Amy Sealt's article, "Signatures, Place Zoning Isue, on November Ballot," Albright explained, "We want to put the question to the people, it's up to the voters. That's what government is all about, isn't it?" (August 2, 1995) The proposed ordinance specified a zoning change for the Perry Street site, but the real intent of the petition drive was to get a Wal-Mart in Ottawa. The petition was motivated, in part, by the feeling that a discount department store was needed in Ottawa and those who opposed it "didn't show much concern for the little guy," in the words of a supporter who was active in gathering signatures on the petition.[74]

Less than a month after the initiative petition had been submitted to the village clerk, Michael Gilb and several of the nearby homeowners filed a challenge to the petition before the Putnam County Board of Elections. They maintained that the petition should be disqualified because the signers had been misled into thinking that it involved support for having a Wal-Mart store in Ottawa, when in fact it involved a narrowly written zoning change. The Board of Elections convened a meeting of all interested parties, dismissed the objections of the homeowners, and ruled that the petition was valid. The proposed ordinance was placed on the ballot. On 7 November 1995, the voters rejected the proposed ordinance 818 to 776.

THE REST OF THE STORY: THE SECOND SITE

Despite being defeated at the Perry Street site, Wal-Mart continued to show interest in Putnam County and less than a month after the popular vote the CIC was helping Wal-Mart find another local site.[75] Among the sites of interest was one located on the *eastern* side of Perry Street, about a quarter of a mile north of the original site (I will refer to this as the "second site"). The land in question was undeveloped except for a small office complex owned by Annandale Development Corporation, a local real estate company. The rest of the land was owned by New Creation Lutheran Church, which had recently acquired it and planned to build a church on the site. Although the land was undeveloped, most of it was zoned commercial. Annandale Development was eager to sell to Wal-Mart and New Creation came aboard soon too. In January 1996 the church voted to option their land to Engelhart Realty, a

Michigan-based realtor working on behalf of Wal-Mart. In April 1996 Wal-Mart submitted preliminary site plans to the village. The plans were drawn up by CESO, the same engineering firm that had worked on the Perry Street site, and called for a 190,000-square-foot Wal-Mart Supercenter consisting of a regular Wal-Mart and a full-sized grocery store.

The second site presented the same problems as the original site: noise, traffic, lights, and the presence of a large commercial development in close proximity to residential areas. And, of course, it was still a Wal-Mart; in fact, it was an even bigger Wal-Mart. Still, it was not quite in the backyard of the nearby homeowners, as the Perry Street site had been. In spite of the similarities between the two sites, there was almost no public controversy or debate regarding the second site. There are two explanations for this. First, the bulk of the land was already zoned commercial and thus as long as the site plans conformed to village requirements for traffic mitigation, utilities, parking, lighting, and other related factors, Wal-Mart could not be prevented from proceeding with its plans. And second, the homeowners who had fought the Perry Street site were simply tired of fighting. Although the council was by now fully aware of the strong feelings associated with the siting of a Wal-Mart, it did not have to make any hard decisions because most of the land was already zoned commercial and thus there was not much they could do, even if they wanted to.[76] As one council member commented, "[Wal-Mart] couldn't be stopped."[77]

In May CESO submitted a modified site plan that had been developed in response to concerns regarding traffic and other site design issues. The next month the planning commission and the council approved a replatting of the land, allowing Wal-Mart to acquire the exact parcels it wanted. In August Wal-Mart purchased 15.5 acres, about six from Annandale Development and about nine from New Creation. There were some hard feelings on the part of those who felt that Annandale Development and New Creation had sold out the community for the sake of a windfall profit.

In October of 1996, when it became clear that Wal-Mart was finally coming to Ottawa, the chamber of commerce put on a one-day seminar designed to help area merchants compete with retail giants such as Wal-Mart. This seminar, led by Professor Kenneth Stone (mentioned in chapter 3), attracted several hundred persons.

The Wal-Mart Supercenter opened in May of 1997. The opening was attended by local dignitaries with musical fanfare provided by the Ottawa-Glandorf High School Titan Marching Brass Band. Wal-Mart sponsored appearances by such advertising characters as the Keebler Elf and the Energizer Bunny. The Pamida Discount Center soon ceased operations and converted to Heartland Home Furnishings, a discount furniture store.[78] New Creation eventually built its church in a different part of the village. A Wendy's was later built in front of the Wal-Mart.

A NOTE ON GATHERING DATA IN OTTAWA

In all the case studies, I encountered persons on various sides of the issue who were reluctant or unwilling to discuss the events surrounding the controversy. In Ottawa, however, this reluctance was greater than elsewhere. It may reflect the self-contained nature of the village, but there seemed to be another reason. Some interviewees mentioned that people were afraid of being sued by Wal-Mart if they made damaging remarks about the company. This fear seemed to stem, at least in part, from their recollections that Kmart had sued some local merchants for actions they took that damaged an unsuccessful attempt by Kmart to site a store in the area. According to Timothy Macke, a member of the Ottawa Village Council who was familiar with the case, the suit was in fact not brought by Kmart and did not involve a reprisal by Kmart against local merchants for speaking ill of the company, although the case did derive from a business deal that involved Kmart.[79] What is important in the context of the Wal-Mart controversy, however, is not the details of the Kmart case, but the fact that Ottawans felt unable to express their views for fear of being slapped with a lawsuit by a large corporation.

The cases in West Bend and Ottawa turned out to have more in common than I suspected when I chose them. Not only was the threat posed by the stores similar, but the general strategy taken by the opponents was similar too and led to similar results. In both cases the proposed site threatened a residential district and the opposition was coordinated by an organization formed by residents. In both places the site was within the city limits and the key land use issue was zoning. CAAP, in West Bend, and CCC, in Ottawa framed the issue as a matter of proper land use and the protection of residential neighborhoods. In contrast to the mobilization efforts of the opponents in Gig Harbor and Petoskey, the efforts of CAAP and CCC seem quite moderate: no town meetings intended to stir people up, no presentations by experts, no marching in the local Fourth of July parade, and no petitions with more signatures than residents. In spite of their moderate level of mobilization the opponents in these two places did have some local supporters to contend with. In West Bend much of the growth machine was solidly behind Wal-Mart, including the landowner, the mayor, the planning department, the chamber of commerce, and several major local employers. In Ottawa there was a counter social movement in the form of a group of shoppers that organized, collected signatures, and forced the rezoning to be put to a popular vote after it had been denied by the city council.

The outcome in these cases appears to be the result of several key factors: an adequate level of mobilization; effective framing; and the fact that the final decision was made locally, that is, by the officials or residents of the affected municipality. These cases suggest that threats to residential areas can be framed in such a way that elected legislators and the public at large can be persuaded to be more responsive to the plight of residents than to the influence of a large corporate retailer, the growth machine, or the arguments of those who seek improved shopping options.

NOTES

1. West Bend's population increased 10.6 percent between 1990 and 1994. Southeastern Wisconsin Regional Planning Commission, *Economic Profile: City of West Bend, Wisconsin,* 1994. The county grew 12.2 percent between 1990 and 1995 and was the fastest growing county in the state in the early 1990s. "It's official: Washington is state's growth leader," *West Bend Daily News* (WI), 11 August 1995.

2. Barry Gantenbein, "Neighbors don't buy sales pitch," *West Bend Daily News,* 14 December 1994.

3. Minutes of West Bend Common Council meeting, 19 December 1994.

4. Interview with Michael Miller, mayor, City of West Bend.

5. Quoted in Barry Gantenbein, "Council Balances Wal-Mart Plans," *West Bend Daily News,* 15 December 1994.

6. The *West Bend Daily News* changed its name to the *Daily News* sometime in 1995.

7. Editorial, "Wal-Mart announcement good news for West Bend," *West Bend Daily News,* 8 November 1994.

8. Interview with Betty Pearson, executive vice president, West Bend Area Chamber of Commerce.

9. Betty Pearson, "Growth Makes West Bend Strong," *West Bend Daily News,* 22 March 1995.

10. Barry Gantenbein, "Wal-Mart Submits Westside Store Plan," *West Bend Daily News,* 9 December 1994.

11. Manufacturing is the city's most important industrial sector and accounted for approximately one-third of all employment in 1993. Southeastern Wisconsin Regional Planning Commission, *Economic Profile: City of West Bend, Wisconsin,* 1994.

12. Statement by John Capelle, director, West Bend Department of Community Development, minutes of West Bend Plan Commission meeting, 26 April 1995.

13. Quoted in Geralyn McBride, "Wal-Mart Protest Suffers Setback," *Milwaukee Journal*, 23 February 1995.
14. Video of West Bend Common Council meeting, 8 May 1995.
15. "Rezone for Wal-Mart? Appropriate? . . . Announcing the Formation of CAAP, Inc." May 1995.
16. Southeastern Wisconsin Regional Planning Commission, *A Land Use Plan for the City of West Bend: 2010,* 1992, 190.
17. Tom Ross and Ken Kaplan, "Wal-Mart is OK, but the Valley Avenue site is inappropriate," *Daily News*, 24 April 1995.
18. Comments of anonymous contributor to "Sound Off," *Daily News*, 26 April 1995.
19. Kenneth Kaplan, letter to the editor, *West Bend Daily News*, 17 February 1995.
20. Interview with Tom O'Meara III, West Bend Common Council.
21. Anonymous telephone interview.
22. Anonymous interview, West Bend.
23. Barry Gantenbein, "Store's Economic Impact Uncertain," *West Bend Daily News,* 3 March 1995.
24. Miller interview.
25. *West Bend Daily News,* "'2010' plan maintains status quo in the city," 9 January 1995.
26. Comment made by Tom O'Meara III at meeting of West Bend Common Council, 8 May 1995.
27. Jill Badzinski, "Wal-Mart: Group says store would change area's 'character,'" *Daily News*, 5 May 1995.
28. Letters in file ZA-94-18, Department of Community Development, City Hall, West Bend, Wisconsin.
29. Comments of anonymous contributor to "Sound Off," *Daily News*, 25 April 1995.
30. *Daily News*, "Wal-Mart tops local '95 stories," 30 December 1995.
31. Editorial, "Sam's (Zoning) Club," *Daily News*, 7 April 1995.
32. Barry Gantenbein, "Wal-Mart: Valley, Highway 33 site the best," *Daily News,* 21 April 1995.
33. Wal-Mart Stores, Inc., "An Open Letter From Wal-Mart," *Daily News*, 24 April 1995.
34. Barry Gantenbein, "Wal-Mart concept plan cleared," *Daily News*, 27 April 1995.
35. Quoted in Jill Badzinski, "Council Struggle with 'Hottest Issue,'" *Daily News*, 9 May 1995.
36. Barry Gantenbein, "Wal-Mart Drops West Bend," *Daily News*, 14 September 1995.
37. Quoted in Jill Badzinski, "Ground Broken for 'City Gateway,'" *Daily News*, 28 October 1997.
38. Tax incremental financing (TIF) uses potential future tax revenue to fund current development.
39. This does not mean, however, that it was impossible to guess that a Wal-Mart store was being planned. The size of the building and the name of the developer, a known developer of Wal-Mart stores, were good clues to the intended occupant. Robert Motl, personal communication.

40. As the Corporate Center took shape these six homeowners found themselves almost enclosed by commercial development. Finding that their properties were no longer viable or valuable as residences, they had no option but to try to convince town officials to rezone *their* land to commercial, thereby enabling them to sell and move.

41. Office of Strategic Research, Ohio Department of Development, *Ohio County Profiles*. Columbus, Ohio: 1995.

42. The exact name for B-3 zoning was "highway-oriented business district."

43. Amy Sealts, "Annexation may become Wal-Mart site," *Putnam County Sentinel* (OH), 15 March 1995.

44. For the smaller parcel it was technically a *re*zoning.

45. Minutes of Village of Ottawa Council meeting, 22 May 1995.

46. Minutes of Village of Ottawa Council meeting, 22 May 1995.

47. Wal-Mart Project files, Ottawa Municipal Building, Ottawa, Ohio.

48. Letter to the council president and members of the council, n.d., Wal-Mart Project files, Ottawa Municipal Building, Ottawa, Ohio.

49. Letter to the editor, *Putnam County Sentinel*, 15 February 1995.

50. Letter (n.d.) in the Wal-Mart Project files, Ottawa Municipal Building, Ottawa, Ohio.

51. The law firm was Oxley, Malone, Fitzgerald and Hollister.

52. Anonymous interview, Ottawa, Ohio.

53. Quoted in Nancy Kline, "Ottawa Rejects Zoning Ordinance," *Putnam County Sentinel*, 8 November 1995.

54. Anonymous interview, Ottawa, Ohio.

55. Anonymous interview, Ottawa, Ohio.

56. Letter to the editor, *Putnam County Sentinel*, 25 October 1995.

57. Anonymous telephone interview.

58. Anonymous interview, Ottawa, Ohio.

59. *The Wal-Mess* (video), produced by Glenn and Angela Falgoust, Donaldsville, Louisiana, n.d.

60. Telephone interview with David Laudick, president, Ottawa Village Council.

61. Anonymous interview, Ottawa, Ohio.

62. Anonymous interview, Ottawa, Ohio.

63. Interview with Timothy Macke, Ottawa Village Council.

64. Interview with S. Scott McDowell, safety-service director, Ottawa.

65. Telephone interview with Jack Williams, municipal director.

66. Anonymous interview, Ottawa, Ohio.

67. Letter to the editor, *Putnam County Sentinel*, 8 February 1995.

68. Anonymous interview, Ottawa, Ohio.

69. Anonymous interview, Ottawa, Ohio.

70. Editorial, "Wal-Mart issue debated," *Putnam County Sentinel,* 24 May 1995.

71. Interview with J. Dean Meyer, Ottawa Village Council.

72. Minutes of Village of Ottawa Council meeting, 22 May 1995.

73. Minutes of Village of Ottawa Council meeting, 26 June 1995.

74. Anonymous interview, Ottawa, Ohio.

75. Amy Sealts, "Wal-Mart seeking other store sites," *Putnam County Sentinel*, 29 November 1995.

76. A small part of the land acquired by Wal-Mart had to be annexed. It was annexed without incident and then zoned commercial.

77. Meyer interview

78. Heartland is a subsidiary of the company that owns Pamida.

79. Macke interview.

6

Ashland, Wisconsin, and Eureka, California

Economic Benefit for Whom?

The last pair of case studies, like the first two, involves cities located on the water: Ashland, on the shore of Lake Superior in northern Wisconsin, and Eureka, on the Pacific Coast in northern California. Unlike Gig Harbor and Petoskey, however, Ashland and Eureka are overwhelmingly middle and working class. Also, in both cities much of the controversy involved the threat that the proposed superstore posed to local merchants. In spite of these similarities the two controversies unfolded differently and had different outcomes.

ASHLAND, WISCONSIN

"Ashland needed modernizing."

—A supporter

"Some of them act as if the Holy Grail is coming to town."

—An opponent

"It was a nasty, nasty time."

—A city employee

The city of Ashland (population 8,744) is located in northwestern Wisconsin on the shore of Lake Superior and serves as the county seat for Ashland

County (population 16,307). The only larger city in this part of the state is Superior, sixty-five miles to the west. During the first half of the twentieth century Ashland was an important Great Lakes port and much of the lumber and ore that came from the Lake Superior region passed through the city. As the shipping industry declined Ashland became home to a number of manufacturing and service industries. The city is currently making an effort to become a resort and tourist center.[1] Ashland has a relatively intact downtown that serves as the civic and retail center of the city and many of the independent merchants are still located downtown.

The story begins with a section of land near downtown known as the central rail yard. During Ashland's industrial heyday this area served as the turning yard for the Soo Line, but it was no longer used by the railroad and had become an undeveloped eyesore. Although located near downtown, the land had remained undeveloped because of industrial contamination accumulated over many years of use by the railroad. The city was very interested in finding a party that would invest in cleaning up and developing this area. In the late 1980s the city was economically depressed, with an unemployment rate nearly twice that of the state.[2] Munsingwear, a major local employer, had closed recently and city officials had not had much success at attracting new employers. In September of 1988 mayor Fran Ante announced that a mall developer had signed a six-month option to purchase the central rail yard.[3] The developer was soon revealed to be Centres Inc., a Milwaukee-area developer with plans to build a 86,000-square-foot Kmart. The city wanted to encourage commercial development downtown and was pleased that Centres Inc. and Kmart were considering taking on the job of cleaning up the rail yard.

Vic Alfsen, of the Northwest Regional Planning Commission (NWRPC), which did city planning for Ashland, spoke to the city planning commission the next month. As part of his presentation, which was intended to help the commission prepare for the Kmart project, he went over the comprehensive plan that the NWRPC had prepared for the city in 1984. Major provisions of the plan included providing support to the strong central business district, encouraging and planning for redevelopment of the downtown area as the prime location for commercial services, and discouraging strip commercial development.[4]

In November another developer, Pointer Development Corporation, based in New York, informed the city that it was interested in building a mall on U.S. Highway 2 on the eastern side of the city, about one and half miles from downtown. The mall would include a 70,000-square-foot Wal-Mart, a grocery store, and as many as a dozen smaller stores. I will refer to this site as the Highway 2 site. In January 1990, John "Berry" King, president of Pointer Development, presented his plans to the planning commission. The local merchants were alarmed by the prospect of a big Wal-Mart situated a mile and a half from downtown and immediately expressed their concerns. In the words of one retailer: "We're scared and don't want to see the downtown come to an end."[5] King, however, dismissed such fears:

> We're not here to try and empty the downtown. You're painting a very bleak picture of Ashland, that it will dry up and blow away, and that's not what we want. We want the city to grow and progress.[6]

TWO STORES AND FOUR SITES

The city was now presented with the possibility of two superstores coming to Ashland in the near future. City officials offered to initiate a tax incremental financing (TIF) district to help Centres Inc. finance the necessary infrastructure for its downtown site for Kmart. Meanwhile, city officials informed King of their desire to maintain the downtown as a viable retailing area and proposed two locations for Wal-Mart that they felt were superior to the Highway 2 site: one was downtown and right across from the proposed Kmart; the other was south of downtown, on State Highway 13.[7] City officials preferred to see Wal-Mart go downtown. Barring that possibility, they favored the Highway 13 site over the Highway 2 site because it would at least attract some people to downtown. The trouble with the Highway 2 site, aside from the fact that it was not downtown, was that people could drive in from the east, shop at the Wal-Mart, and then simply turn around and drive back home without ever getting near downtown. Pointer Development, however, never seriously considered either the downtown site or the Highway 13 site. The Highway 13 site was unattractive to King's client, Wal-Mart, because the traffic level was far below that of Highway 2.

The Highway 2 site had been platted for residential development and was laid out with streets and alleys. The site contained several homes that were owned by local residents, as were the various parcels of undeveloped land. To the east was a small residential neighborhood; to the west was undeveloped land and some industrial buildings; to the south was undeveloped land; and to the north, across the highway, was a small independent motel and a few homes. The entire site was zoned residential ("single-family homes") and had to be rezoned to commercial ("highway commercial") to allow the construction of a Wal-Mart.[8] The site also contained some wetlands that required special consideration. Pointer Development's proposal would have to be considered by three official bodies: the Ashland Physical Improvements Committee, the Ashland Planning Commission, and the Ashland City Council. The first two of these were charged with making recommendations to the council, which would then approve or deny the request for rezoning. In January 1990 Jeff Birtch of Benchmark Group, which worked with Pointer Development, notified the city that he had options to purchase all the property on the Highway 2 site. On this basis he then requested that the city rezone the land from residential to commercial.

Plans for large-scale retail development in the city were now going in several directions. In February the planning commission unanimously recommended to the council that the rezoning of the Highway 2 site be approved. At about the same time the council, responding to the advice of Vic Alfsen, asked Pointer Development for a site plan for the Highway 13 site. King, however, reaffirmed Wal-Mart's intention to build at the Highway 2 site. Meanwhile, the council approved Centres's site plan for the downtown Kmart and approved the TIF funding that Centres wanted. Kmart, however, was not happy about the possibility of Wal-Mart also coming to Ashland, especially if a Wal-Mart store were to be located on Highway 2. Centres's representative commented, "If retail moved from the central business district to the east, west or south it would make us reassess the situation."[9]

The Wal-Mart/Kmart issue had by now gathered a lot of steam and had become a major local controversy. The opponents of the Highway 2 site, especially the downtown merchants, continued to voice their objections. Also, the residents who lived near the Highway 2 site objected to having such a large commercial development located near their homes. Seven of the abutters signed an official "petition of protest." These seven represented at least 20 percent of the homeowners who lived adjacent to or within one hundred feet of the site, which meant that the rezoning would have to be approved by a supermajority (three-fourths) vote of the council.

On 1 March 1990, the physical improvements committee, after hearing from many of the opponents, denied Pointer Development's request for street discontinuances and vacations of the Highway 2 site. (This was a request to "discontinue" the existing street grid and was a necessary prerequisite to large-scale commercial development on the site.) Two weeks later the city council, which included several local merchants, took up the zoning issue. At a well-attended meeting on 13 March 1990, the council heard from the supporters and opponents, and then denied the rezoning request on a 5–5 vote.

Before continuing with the sequence of events, I will describe the various supporters and opponents of the Highway 2 site, consider the issues they raised, examine their tactics, and discuss the local political issues that became entangled with the Wal-Mart controversy.

SUPPORTERS

The proposed Wal-Mart superstore and the Highway 2 site found substantial support in Ashland among the following groups:

The Developers and The Real Estate Agent

Pointer Development and Benchmark Group were major supporters. Pointer Development's president, "Berry" King, emphasized various economic benefits associated with the store. According to a demographic report that he distributed, the store would pull in customers from a trade area with 91,000 potential customers.[10] He asserted that some of the people who came to Wal-Mart would go downtown also and therefore the store would benefit other merchants as well. Furthermore, per King, the store would help Ashland retain some of the sales dollars that were being spent outside the city. The entire project, including Wal-Mart and the other stores, would "create approximately 150-160 full-time jobs, and between 200-250 jobs overall," according to King.[11] In response to concerns about the property values of nearby homeowners, King said that "historically property values surrounding these developments rise astronomically." He did not produce any evidence to support this statement.[12] In response to concerns about the store's appearance—whether it would be attractive and in keeping with local architectural style—King's project engineer said that Wal-Mart was mindful of the importance of appearance and had become "pro-landscape" in recent years.[13] Lastly, King said that the mall would be a six million dollar construction project and Pointer Development would hire local contractors and subcontractors where possible. The Larson Agency, a local real estate broker, handled transactions between Pointer Development and the Highway 2 property owners.

The Homeowners and Landowners

About twenty people owned property or inexpensive homes on the site and most of them seized on the opportunity to sell their property at above-market prices; some became vociferous supporters of Wal-Mart, but only at the Highway 2 site.

Other Supporters

The Highway 2 site was supported by a variety of other local residents, most of whom seemed more interested in having a Wal-Mart than in where it was located. The possibility of Wal-Mart coming to Ashland seemed to them a golden opportunity for the city and one that city officials should not let slip away. They expected a Wal-Mart superstore to provide economic benefits, improve local shopping options, and generally contribute to the growth and modernization of Ashland. The promise of 200-250 new jobs was persuasive to many because of the poor state of the local economy. The supporters claimed also that a Wal-Mart would contribute $200,000 annually in tax revenue, an important consideration for those who claimed that Ashland had inordinately high taxes and thus desperately needed more tax revenue. They also maintained that a Wal-Mart store would improve local shopping options with its wide selection and low prices. Some supporters said that they were tired of driving sixty-five miles to Superior or Duluth to find a mall or large department stores. To many, Wal-Mart's biggest advantage was its low prices. One woman, for example, explained that:

> From the time my son was born, I have been making regular trips to Duluth to purchase diapers and baby formula since I can get a can of formula for $5.88 in Duluth as opposed to $8.83 per can in Ashland. Diapers are also approximately $2.00 more per package in Ashland than in Duluth. I am tired of hearing the downtown Ashland merchants complain about Ashland residents shopping outside the Ashland area.[14]

Furthermore, they looked forward to a store that was open Sundays and had longer hours than the local shops.

For others, having a Wal-Mart store was associated with growth and progress: "The addition of Wal-Mart to our stellar city is in keeping with progress."[15] The supporters hoped that having a Wal-Mart would attract other businesses to Ashland—some even talked of Ashland becoming a major regional shopping center. To keep out Wal-Mart seemed provincial, an attitude they associated with the downtown merchants, whom they portrayed as a minority that was selfishly holding back growth that the city desperately needed. These comments are typical:

> Need a job? Concerned about your real estate tax bill? Simply interested in Ashland as a good place to live and raise a family?
> Tonight at 7 pm the Ashland City Council will decide if this city is really interested in growing—providing jobs and tax base or if they represent the very small minority who have become rich and complacent and do not want growth in Ashland because they are afraid of "competition."
> . . .
> We have the opportunity to see a modern Wal-Mart shopping complex—new and clean—lots of close parking—real competitive prices—over 200 jobs—a big taxpayer.[16]

The local proponents wrote letters to the editor, spoke at official meetings, and engaged in several "spontaneous" boycotts of downtown businesses. Although they raised numerous issues, they focused on the downtown merchants, whom they attached mercilessly. They also made Wal-Mart an election issue in the 1990 election (see below). King promoted the store at various city meetings and sent a promotional flyer to all residents. At one point he intimated that Pointer Development might consider finding a site for Wal-Mart in one of the nearby towns if Ashland did not approve the rezoning.[17] It seems likely that King encouraged the Highway 2 property owners to be vocal about their support for Wal-Mart, but only at the Highway 2 site.

OPPONENTS

The Wal-Mart superstore and the Highway 2 site were opposed by a wide range of Ashlanders, led by the downtown merchants.

The Downtown Merchants

Many of the city's small merchants were located downtown and they were the most vocal opponents. They claimed to be more opposed to the Highway 2 site than to having a Wal-Mart store in Ashland. It was not always possible, however, to distinguish the effects of a Wal-Mart store from the effects of a Wal-Mart store at the Highway 2 site. The downtown merchants felt that the project posed a serious threat to the viability of downtown Ashland and thus to the future of their businesses and the investments they had made over the years. They researched the effects of Wal-Mart on other small towns around the country and were distressed by what they learned. They regarded Rice Lake, a city about 100 miles to the southwest and approximately the same size as Ashland, as an example of the fate they wanted to avoid. Rice Lake, according to the opponents, had a thriving downtown until a mall was built. Now "you can shoot a cannon down Main Street,"[18] in the words of a Rice Lake resident who tried to warn Ashlanders about the effects of a Wal-Mart. The opponents derided the supporters for being more interested in buying cheap goods than in the overall well-being of the community.

The merchants did not form an organization to coordinate their response to Wal-Mart, although there were a couple of organizations that promoted the downtown area. One organization, the Main Street committee, issued a statement that strongly supported keeping retail development in the downtown area:

> We have very strong reasons for believing that development of a retail nature should be in the central rail yard area of the city. We have over the past years had developers and community development specialists, on numerous occasions, look at the city and come back to us with their recommendations. They all come to the same conclusion: Development of a retail nature should occur in the central rail yard. . . .[19]

Another organization, the Downtown Development Corporation (DDC), opposed the Highway 2 site on the grounds that it was incompatible with the city's comprehensive plan. In response to arguments about increased tax revenue, a DDC spokesman noted that "strip growth or sprawl growth does not increase the tax base but only shifts it to a different area."[20]

The controversy was very personal and emotional for the merchants because, as one council member put it, they "had their whole lives tied up in their businesses."[21] They also found it somewhat confusing. Several held part-time positions in local government, which gave the supporters the opportunity to accuse them of using their political position to thwart Wal-Mart merely to protect themselves. The merchants, by contrast, viewed their participation in local government as an indication of their desire to be involved in the community, not as an attempt to run local government for their own ends. One merchant stated:

> I am proud to be in business, every morning I turn the key in the door, every woman, man and child that has been in my store turns the key with me in my mind. I refuse to be made to feel ashamed that I am in business. I am not rich, I am not greedy, I am not controlling this city.[22]

They felt that they were promoting land use policies that were in the long-term interest of the whole community, not trying to favor downtown to the detriment of the rest of the city. They were disappointed that so many of their fellow citizens seemed more interested in a large out-of-state corporation than in the merchants who had contributed to the city for many years. One downtown retailer described the relationship between herself and other members of the community in these terms: "When you invest in a [local] business you are investing in them . . . and when they shop at your store . . . they are investing in themselves."[23] It seemed to this retailer that it was Wal-Mart, Pointer Development, and Benchmark Group who were taking advantage of the city, not the downtown merchants. In the words of a downtown hardware store owner, "We live here, we have made our investments in this city. We have more of an interest in this city than they do."[24]

The merchants in Ashland, unlike those in some of the other towns, were not reluctant to express their views publicly. They spoke at the official meetings, wrote letters to the editor, and placed an advertisement in the *Daily Press*, the city's major newspaper. They studied the effect that Wal-Mart had had on other towns such as Rice Lake and tried to disseminate relevant "facts and figures" to the council members and the public. In response to a flyer distributed by Pointer Development some of the opponents made up their own flyer, which they printed on pink paper and distributed around town at night by placing it under car windshields. This small piece of activism caused a brouhaha. The distributors were referred to as the "pink panthers" and their method of distribution was criticized as being cowardly[25] (because the flyer was unsigned) and illegal.[26] The flyer itself used a question-and-answer format to discuss the problems posed by a Wal-Mart—especially one at the Highway 2 site.

The Mayor

Mayor Ante had originally been favorable to both the Wal-Mart and the Kmart projects, although she preferred to see Wal-Mart go downtown. In March 1990, however, she announced that she was opposed to the Wal-Mart at the Highway 2 site as a result of having becoming familiar with a study by Professor Kenneth Stone that showed that Wal-Mart stores have a significant negative effect on central business districts in small towns.

The Nearby Homeowners

There were homeowners on both sides of Highway 2 who objected to the site because they feared that a Wal-Mart superstore would degrade their residential neighborhoods. They argued, moreover, that it was unfair to change the zoning from residential to commercial simply to please a corporation. Their concerns, however, never predominated and they were never able to successfully frame the issue as a matter of maintaining the integrity of residential neighborhoods, as had the homeowners in West Bend and Ottawa. The position taken by these homeowners was exactly opposite to that taken by their neighbors who owned property *on* the site and who had options to sell to Wal-Mart; these two groups were "at each others' throats."[27]

An important concern throughout the controversy was the infrastructure costs, mainly for street and highway improvements for the Highway 2 site. There were competing claims about how much the necessary infrastructure would cost and who should pay for it. The opponents were afraid that the taxpayers would end up paying for most of it. King was reluctant to commit to spending much on infrastructure, but as the dispute dragged on and he encountered difficulties in getting the rezoning he needed, he became more willing to spend money and eventually stated that he did "not need one penny from the city."[28] Some merchants objected to the city spending money on Wal-Mart, which clearly did not need it, when the city had not spent any money to help them get their businesses going.

Some opponents raised a more general objection to Wal-Mart. They asked pointedly how a discount merchandiser would affect the overall quality of life in the area:

> How would another nationwide discount complex on U.S. Highway 2 east of Ashland affect the quality of life here in the northland?
> For me, another discount giant on U.S. 2 would do absolutely nothing to enhance the beauty or economic good of this area.
> Will our lives be enhanced because we can buy goods at discount prices? Well, maybe for a couple of years—until all of our local resident small business owners are underpriced out of existence. . . .
> . . .
> . . . I, for one, don't need a Walmart [sic] or a Kmart.[29]

This type of criticism, however, never became a major issue during the controversy.

NEUTRAL ACTORS

The Ashland Area Chamber of Commerce remained neutral throughout the controversy.

The *Daily Press* gave extensive coverage to the Kmart/Wal-Mart affair but did not take a stand regarding the Highway 2 site. Most of the opponents of the Highway 2 site, however, felt that the paper was against them.[30] The letters to the editor section of the paper, known as the "People's Forum," served as a principal method for interested parties to communicate their views to each other. This included all local politicians, up to and including the mayor. If a council member, for example, wanted his or her views on an issue to be known, he or she would write a letter to the editor. The letter, when published, functioned as an open letter to the entire community. Much of the exchange of views that took place during the controversy occurred in the People's Forum.

LOCAL POLITICS

The superstore controversy in Ashland revealed some of the existing cleavages in the city and became entangled with a divisive local political issue, the city administrator question, that was already being disputed when the superstore controversy began.

There was a latent territorial divide in the city between the east side and the west side. Downtown was on the west side, as were the hospital and the country club. The residential district adjacent to downtown contained many of the city's nicest homes, including many restored Victorian buildings. "All the prominent people lived on the west side," according to a council member who supported the Highway 2 site.[31] It seemed to some on the east side that the west side had received more than its share of business development and public improvements. As a result, the city's efforts to have Wal-Mart sited south of the city on Highway 13, or sited downtown, or not sited at all, struck them as unfair. This antagonism was inadvertently inflamed by a remark made by Vic Alfsen at a meeting of the physical improvements committee. The *Daily Press* gave the following account:

> "I see the south end of town as prime for development," Alfsen said. "I feel the eastern site is incorrect."
> Alfsen used the analogy of adding a family room to a house to illustrate the difference in impact of the two locations.
> "Putting . . . [the Wal-Mart] on Highway 2 is like building a family room in the basement next to the water heater," he said. "[Whereas,] if you build the family room at the back of the house [on Highway 13] then visitors walk through the living room first."[32]

This analogy was intended simply to illustrate that the Highway 13 site was more likely to draw people downtown. Some east side residents, however, seized on the analogy and took it as a personal insult. An east side supporter of the Highway 2 site responded:

> Vic Alfsen must be new in town. He described the proposed site for Wal-Mart on Highway 2 like putting their store in the basement next to the water heater. We who live in the east side say, "Thank you very much!" . . .
> We who presumably live in the basement area of town feel our taxes are equivalent to the taxes paid by residents of Ashland who are fortunate enough to live in the living room.[33]

This east/west antagonism, although not a big issue for most people, did exist beneath the surface, and just as some people felt that they were being denied the shopping options that Wal-Mart represented, some east side residents felt that they were being denied commercial development in their part of town. As one commented, "it's not fair to always talk downtown."[34] The city administrator issue also became entwined with the Wal-Mart controversy.

Before June of 1989 the city was run by a full-time elected mayor and an elected city council. In June the council reduced the mayoral position to part-time and hired a full-time city administrator, who would have substantial responsibility for the city's business, although the mayor and council would retain final authority over policymaking. The mayor and council members would continue to be elected; the city administrator would be appointed by the council. The council made this change because they felt that city government had become so complicated that a full-time professional administrator was needed. Mayor Fran Ante was herself in favor of the change,[35] which had been discussed extensively at council meetings before it was implemented and, according to the city's attorney, did not have to be approved by the voters because it did not constitute a change in the form of government. In spite of the apparent legality of the change, an uproar ensued as soon as it was publicized. The change was criticized for being undemocratic in two ways: first, it was extremely high-handed for the council to institute such an important change without putting it to a popular vote; and second, the new arrangement created a powerful, full-time position that was not accountable to the people (because the city administrator was not elected). The council, according to its critics, was taking power away from the people of Ashland.

A group of disgruntled citizens formed an organization called Citizens for the Right to Vote (CRV), which collected nearly one thousand signatures on a petition protesting the council's action and requesting that the matter be put to a popular vote. The CRV demanded that the city council "discontinue this practice of pursuing the wishes of the minority of the Ashland voters and themselves and start pursuing the wishes, and indeed the demands of the majority of the people who entrust them to hold the office of city council members."[36] The referendum desired by the CRV would itself have to be approved by the council. In late 1989 the council voted 7–3 not to have a referendum on the matter, a decision the critics took as further proof of the council's unwillingness to be accountable to the public. The city administrator issue and the Wal-Mart issue, in the view of the critics, were similar. In their eyes the council represented a small minority that had refused to let the public vote on the city administrator position and now was trying to keep out a store that would provide discount shopping as well as bring jobs and tax revenue. This disenchantment with the council would have important consequences.

THE TONE OF THE CONTROVERSY

Of the six controversies, the one in Ashland was the most intense. A longtime city employee who observed the events closely described it as a "nasty, nasty time."[37] One downtown merchant characterized it as "an actual battle;"[38] another said that "there were husbands and wives fighting."[39] One council member depicted it as an "ominous time;"[40] another said the whole affair was "traumatic."[41] Things got so bad that Mayor Ante had to have the police present at some of the meetings to keep order. Part of this intensity could be traced to the pecuniary interests of the people who owned land or homes on the Highway 2 site. This group had a rare opportunity to sell their property above market value and did not want to let it slip away. It seems probable that they, either directly or through friends and relatives, were responsible for much of the publicly expressed support for siting a Wal-Mart on Highway 2. They did not mention the financial gain they expected to reap; instead, they advanced all sorts of other arguments in favor of Wal-Mart and the Highway 2 site, and simultaneously attacked the downtown merchants and minimized the advantages of all other locations.

THE ELECTION AND ITS AFTERMATH

I return now to the story. To review, in March 1990, after extensive discussion and public input, the council voted down the commercial zoning that Pointer Development needed for the Highway 2 site.

A city council and mayoral election, which had been scheduled before any of the current controversies arose, was set for April 3. Council members in seven of the city's eleven wards faced challengers. The seven challengers were a loosely organized group motivated by dissatisfaction with the current council. Aside from the city administrator position and the Wal-Mart issue, they had various complaints about the city's finances, the handling of various public works projects, and local taxes. Although the challengers had filed their applications for candidacy before the council denied the rezoning request, the Wal-Mart issue fit well with their other grievances and became a major campaign issue.[42] The members of this group, most of whom had not been involved in local politics before, ran political advertisements in which they presented themselves as a slate and promised, if elected, to investigate

High property taxes
Lack of opportunity to vote on major issues
Financial responsibility
Nepotism
Favourtism [sic]
Protectionism

Special interest influence
Closed meetings
Distain [sic] for the average citizen
Distrust and dissatisfaction with city government[43]

The election was a stunning triumph for the challengers, who prevailed in six of the seven races and unseated three council members who had voted against the rezoning. The newly elected challengers now dominated the council. The opponents called it "the council from hell"[44] and contended that the new members, most of whom left local politics after a couple of years, were uneducated and poorly equipped to run the city.

Less than a week after the election Pointer Development submitted a request to have the Highway 2 rezoning reconsidered. In late April the planning commission held a special two-day public hearing at which all the interested parties once again expressed their views. The matter was then submitted to the council and failed narrowly by a vote of 8–3. (A vote of 8–3 constituted a *defeat* because a supermajority [three-fourths] vote was required.) This outcome keenly disappointed the supporters, who put much of the blame on council member Ed Melin, who had voted against the rezoning. Melin was roundly denounced in the People's Forum and received threatening phone calls. King announced disgustedly that Pointer Development was through with Ashland and said he would be looking for another city in which to build the store. He threatened to sue the "pink panthers" and said he might ask the city to reimburse him for the money he had spent preparing site plans. At this point several local leaders, including representatives from the power company, the hospital, and a local manufacturing firm, called for an end to the internecine fighting and urged the citizens of Ashland to try to work together and compromise.

The supporters, however, still wanted Wal-Mart and they still wanted it on Highway 2. A small group studied the planning map showing the various property owners who abutted the site. They figured out how the site could be reduced slightly and its perimeter redrawn in such a way that fewer of the nearby homeowners would be abutters, thus eliminating the requirement for a supermajority vote by the council. They shared this analysis with Pointer Development, which prepared a revised site plan and requested once again that the land be rezoned. On 31 May 1990, the issue was put before the planning commission and the council for the third time. The opposing sides once again gave their views. It was a raucous affair during which the supporters heckled the merchants who spoke against the rezoning.[45] The planning commission voted to recommend approving the rezoning, which the council then approved on a vote of 9–1.

In August Pointer Development completed its purchase of the site on behalf of Wal-Mart. Twenty-three separate pieces of property were involved in the transaction.[46] Construction began in October and the store opened in July 1991. The grocery store and the other smaller stores that would have comprised the "mall" were never built, with the exception of a Payless Shoe Source. Adjacent to the parking lot is a grassy area fenced in with a chain link fence. This area, approximately one-third the size of the parking lot, is the "wetlands." There is no landscaping and the store is a standard-design Wal-Mart. Centres Inc. eventually abandoned its plans to build a Kmart in downtown Ashland.

EUREKA, CALIFORNIA

"[We don't want to be] just one of 10,000 big box profit centers."

—An opponent

"Prices at some local places are so ridiculous it's outrageous. I need to watch out for my family. Viva Wal-Mart!"

—A supporter

Eureka (population 25,429) is located on the Pacific Coast in California, about 275 miles north of San Francisco. It is the largest city in Humboldt County (population 122,163) and serves as the county seat. Humboldt County is known for its scenic beauty and has a number of state and national parks, including Redwood National Park. Fishing, lumber, and dairy were the region's dominant industries for many years. Fishing and lumber, however, have declined over the last forty years and have not been replaced by other industries. As a result, the city has experienced moderate economic distress on an ongoing basis. Unemployment in the city averaged 7.3 percent in 1998 (when the controversy began), compared with 5.9 percent for the state.[47] The city's economic malaise is reflected in U.S. Census data, which show that between 1960 and 1990 the population of the city declined 4 percent, compared with an increase of 89 percent for the state as a whole.[48] To improve the local economy the city has been engaged in a long-term effort to attract industry and stimulate investment. Eureka has the only deep-draft harbor with commercial potential between the San Francisco Bay Area and Coos Bay, Oregon, 250 miles to the north, and hopes to incorporate the harbor into its future development plans. The city is also aggressively promoting itself as a tourist destination, based on its image as a "Victorian seaport."

Eureka's downtown, once the retail hub of the city, now contains a combination of thriving businesses, underutilized retail space, and vacant storefronts. Adjacent to the northern edge of downtown is an area near the waterfront known as Old Town, home to a large number of old Victorian buildings, many of which have been restored in recent years. Old Town also contains a variety of retail establishments and is an important part of the Victorian seaport image that the city seeks to project. Another area containing retail development is along Highway 101 (known locally as Broadway) as it enters the city from the south. Broadway is lined with strip development, including an assortment of chain stores and motel chains, some of which had once been located downtown.

In September of 1998 Union Pacific Railroad announced its intention to sell a 34.4-acre parcel of land near the waterfront to Wal-Mart, which planned to build a 130,000-square-foot store. The site, when fully developed, would include other stores, restaurants, and a small park. The store would be the largest retail establishment in Eureka, although not the city's first or only department store, as it already had a Kmart, a J.C. Penney's, a Mervyn's, a Sears, a Montgomery Ward, and a Costco.

THE SITE

The site that Wal-Mart wanted was known variously as the balloon track, the balloon tract, the railroad property, and the railroad yard; I will refer to it as the balloon track, or simply, the site. Located in a part of the city known as the Westside Industrial Area, the site is shaped like a balloon, a result of its former use as a maintenance yard and turnaround area for the Northwestern Pacific Railroad. Rail cars would enter the area, go around the perimeter, and then exit heading in the other direction. In 1998 it was owned by Union Pacific Railroad, based in Omaha, Nebraska. The site had not been used for turning around rail cars, or for any other productive purpose, for at least twenty years and had become an eyesore, with overgrown weeds, dilapidated buildings, old rail cars, and rusting rail parts. The land was contaminated from many years of use as a rail yard, with cleanup costs estimated at half a million dollars.[49] The existing rail track running along the western edge of the site was still usable, but had not been used since 1998, when rail operations in Eureka had ceased because of severe damage to the tracks in Eel River Canyon south of the city. The site was located near Humboldt Bay but was actually several hundred feet from the waterfront. Although the site was part of the Westside Industrial Area, it was also adjacent to a new public marina and about four blocks from Old Town. The site was zoned "public," a classification that allows public facilities such as schools, sewage treatment plants, and hospitals, but not commercial development. The exact location of the site, its former and current status, and its relationship to the waterfront and the harbor, would all play important roles in the ensuing controversy.

THE CALIFORNIA COASTAL COMMISSION AND AN EARLY SKIRMISH

The California Coastal Commission (CCC) has extensive authority over development in the "coastal zone," that portion of the California coast which extends from roughly the Pacific Ocean inland to the first major public road. Any changes to a city's general plan that affects the coastal zone must be approved by the CCC. Approximately one-third of Eureka, including the balloon track, is within the coastal zone, which meant that any change in the status of the site had to be approved by the CCC. In February 1997 the Eureka City Council approved a major revision of the city's General Plan. Part of the revised plan involved the coastal zone and thus had to be approved by the CCC. As part of the revision the city council approved changing the designation of the balloon track from "public" to "industrial," a change intended to promote industrial development on the waterfront. In Eureka designation of "industrial" can include commercial uses, although a separate rezoning is still necessary for commercial development.

In September 1998, just two weeks after Union Pacific had announced its intention to sell the balloon track to Wal-Mart, the CCC convened in Eureka to review, and presumably approve, the city's updated General Plan. This sequence of events made it appear to many that city officials were trying to "sneak in" Wal-Mart. According to Kevin Hamblin, the city's director of community development and chief planner, this interpretation was erroneous because the council had changed the site's designation back in 1997 before anybody knew about Wal-Mart's plans.[50] At the CCC hearing, the change was opposed by a wide range of people and organizations, including the Greater Eureka Chamber of Commerce, the Humboldt Taxpayers' League, the Northcoast Environmental Center, Citizens for Port Development, the city of Arcata (located five miles north of Eureka), the harbor district, and various business owners.[51] The CCC voted to approve all of the revisions to Eureka's General Plan except those that pertained to the balloon track. The results of this somewhat confusing course of events were that the site retained a designation of "public," which meant that Wal-Mart would have to seek a change in the General Plan designation and a rezoning in order to proceed with its plans, and many Wal-Mart opponents felt that they were up against a concerted effort by the city to bring in Wal-Mart.

THE CONTROVERSY HEATS UP

By this time Wal-Mart's intentions were well-known and the controversy heated up. The owner of a local independent book and video store began selling at cost a recently published anti-Wal-Mart book titled *How Wal-Mart is Destroying America and What You Can Do About It*.[52] Written by Bill Quinn, a Texas journalist, the book contains a vigorous critique of all aspects of Wal-Mart's operations, especially its impact on small towns. Quinn's book, however, was more than an extended op-ed piece. It contained many examples from around the country and suggested courses of action for those fighting the company. Inexpensive and accessible, *How Wal-Mart is Destroying America* provided ammunition for the merchants and others who opposed the store.

In October 1998 Wal-Mart announced the results of a telephone survey conducted by a professional research firm that it had hired. Based on a sample of 500 registered voters, the survey found that 61 percent of Eureka voters and 63 percent of county voters supported building a Wal-Mart in Eureka.[53] At a news conference held to publicize these findings, Wal-Mart spokeswoman Cynthia Lin said, "It's awful that the vocal minority is drowning out the silent majority."[54]

The following month Wal-Mart made what was to be the first of several well-publicized blunders during the dispute. A nonlocal firm hired by Wal-Mart was doing some preliminary drilling on the site one morning when an employee of the county health department happened to be out jogging in the vicinity. The employee inquired as to what they were doing and for whom, and then informed them that such procedures were illegal without a permit, which they did not have. The firm doing the drilling was fined by the county and Wal-Mart promised to obtain all necessary permits before proceeding with further drilling. These events were reported prominently in the *Times-Standard*.[55]

In March 1999, Friends of Humboldt County ("Friends"), a newly formed group dedicated to maintaining the quality of life in the county and averse to superstores, sponsored a town hall meeting on the Wal-Mart issue. The event was held at the Eureka Municipal Auditorium and drew a crowd of nearly one thousand, an indication of the high level of interest in the issue. Daphne Davis, another Wal-Mart official, spoke first and described the benefits associated with having a Wal-Mart in Eureka: jobs, tax revenue, and bringing more shoppers to the area. The opposing position was presented by Al Norman, the nation's leading anti-big-box activist, who vigorously disputed the "myths" presented by Davis.[56] In response to Davis' claim that a Wal-Mart in Eureka would attract more shoppers to the city, Norman observed that there were already Wal-Marts to the north (in Crescent City), to the east (in Redding), and to the south (in Ukiah), and asked sarcastically if she expected customers to come overseas from Japan.

AN ACT KNOWN AS "THE CITIZENS' RIGHT TO VOTE ON A WAL-MART IN EUREKA"

The city's normal rezoning procedure required proposed changes to be reviewed by the Eureka Planning Commission and then approved or denied by the city council. In March 1999, without ever having submitted a rezoning request to the city, Wal-Mart decided to bypass the normal procedure and take its case directly to the voters. In California a proposed change to a local ordinance (i.e., a rezoning) can be placed on the ballot through the initiative process. Wal-Mart's proposed ballot measure, if passed, would change the zoning of the balloon track from "public" to "commercial." A rezoning, however, would not be sufficient to allow Wal-Mart to proceed with its plans. The CCC would still need to approve the change and Wal-Mart would still have to go through the city's environmental impact review. It is not clear why Wal-Mart decided to take this route in Eureka, although it seems likely that the company figured that the voters were more likely than the city council to grant the rezoning it needed. Wal-Mart hired people to gather signatures and soon had enough to qualify the measure. The initiative proposed an act to be known as the "Citizens' Right to Vote on a Wal-Mart in Eureka." In spite of the act's title, the question to be put to the voters was not whether a Wal-Mart should be allowed on the balloon track, but whether the site should be rezoned to "commercial." Known as Measure J, it would be the only item on the ballot at a special election to be held 24 August 1999. Wal-Mart offered to pay for the election but the city council declined the offer.

Wal-Mart's decision to use the initiative process instead of following the normal rezoning procedure was criticized immediately and became an issue itself. Opponents asserted that Wal-Mart was pursuing a course of action that was generally unavailable, because of cost, to other businesses and average citizens. The *Times-Standard* editorialized that Wal-Mart "ought to jump through the same bureaucratic hoops as every other business seeking variances from the city's zoning codes"[57] and objected on the grounds that "it's a matter of a wealthy corporation finding a way to rewrite the process and [it] sets a bad precedent."[58] Wal-Mart responded that it wanted to give the people in Eureka a chance to vote on an issue of such importance.

SUPPORTERS

The principal supporters were Wal-Mart itself and various unorganized residents. There were only a few local businesses that supported Wal-Mart and they were not very vocal.

Wal-Mart

Early in the controversy Cynthia Lin offered the standard list of reasons why the store should be welcomed: it would create between 250 and 300 jobs ("quality jobs, not minimum-wage jobs," 70 percent of them full-time), generate tax revenue, and enhance shopping options by providing good merchandise at low prices.[59] Responding to fears from local merchants, Lin said the store would not offer the same merchandise as the Old Town shops; rather, it would compete with other local discount stores. Moreover, the store would benefit existing retailers by attracting more shoppers to the city. Also, Wal-Mart would be involved with the community and the store would have its own "charity committee." Lastly, putting a store on the site meant that the balloon track would finally get cleaned up and returned to productive use. Wal-Mart formed a political action committee (PAC) known as Eureka Citizens, Businesses and Wal-Mart Stores for Responsible Economic Planning. Despite its name, it was funded entirely by the company, which promoted Measure J through television advertisements, political advertisements in the newspaper, press conferences, several mailings, telephone polling, and a website.[60]

Residents

It was the residents who would ultimately decide the fate of Measure J and Wal-Mart definitely had supporters, although they were not organized. As there was no organization to speak for the resident-supporters, it is difficult to characterize their views. An examination of the letters to the editor of the *Times-Standard*, however, revealed some frequently expressed sentiments. Many asserted that the city needed a Wal-Mart because it would offer lower prices and a wide selection of merchandise, especially as compared with local merchants. According to one:

Now, it looks like we might finally be getting a Wal-Mart. Local business, with the help of county government, has fought long and hard to keep big business out. Price fixing is so much more difficult when you have to compete.

Wal-Mart won't hurt tourist or specialty shops, and if it cuts into the profits of other local businesses, well, frankly, too bad. Prices at some local places are so ridiculous it's outrageous. I need to watch out for my family. Viva Wal-Mart![61]

Other letters mentioned jobs and tax revenue. A more general argument was that Wal-Mart represented modernization and those who were trying to keep out the store were portrayed as backward. One supporter, alluding to the north coast's reputation as a haven for old hippies, warned, "Wake up, Eureka. The millennium is around the corner, not 'The '60s by the Sea.'"[62]

Some supporters took issue with the opponents' contention that commercial development was an inappropriate use of the balloon track. While all parties agreed that developing the port would be important for Eureka's future, the supporters argued that it was highly improbable that the *particular* site chosen by Wal-Mart would ever be used for the sort of purposes envisioned by the opponents, who wanted to see it developed as an intermodal rail–sea transportation facility or industrial facility requiring proximity to the rail line and/or the harbor. The supporters saw several problems with this vision. First, the site was not actually on the waterfront, which made waterfront uses problematic. It was, however, close to Old Town, which already had some stores. Furthermore, the site was across the street from an attractive public marina that had been completed recently. To put a cargo handling or industrial facility across the street from a recreation-oriented, small-boat marina seemed incongruous and unlikely. In their view, if Wal-Mart was interested in buying the site, cleaning it up, and developing it in an attractive manner, then it should be allowed to proceed with its plans.

OPPONENTS

Opposition to the site and to Wal-Mart was extensive and came from various segments of the community, including the following:

Local Businesses

Many local businesses opposed Measure J. They were represented by the chamber of commerce, Friends, and Think Twice (see below).

Residents

Many local residents opposed Measure J. They were also represented by Friends and Think Twice (see below).

Friends of Humboldt County

Early in the controversy a diverse group of concerned citizens formed a nonprofit organization called Friends of Humboldt County ("Friends"), which was concerned with:

> ... the quality of life and economic well-being of Humboldt County's residents. In those interests we oppose the introduction of big box retailers into our community. Through our opposition to these big box retailers and our support of local business and light industry development, we hope to ensure the long-term health, safety, and welfare of our county's citizens, and maintain a sensible balance in Humboldt County's growth and development policies.[63]

Friends construed its purpose as mainly educational, although it was clearly opposed to having a Wal-Mart on the balloon track and was concerned about the well-being of local merchants. The group sent letters to the editor, posted signs, placed political advertisements in the newspaper, and organized the town hall meeting mentioned above. Members of Friends also spoke to other groups in the county and tried to explain the disadvantages of big box stores in general and Wal-Mart in particular.

Think Twice

In June 1999, two months after Measure J was placed on the ballot, a number of residents and community leaders announced the formation of a PAC called Think Twice Campaign/No on Measure J ("Think Twice") to coordinate opposition to the measure. Unlike Friends, Think Twice was overtly political. It was headed by two experienced political campaigners, Bonnie Neely, a Humboldt County Supervisor, and Patty Berg, a community activist. Relying on volunteers, Neely and Berg put together a campaign that was regarded by everybody, including their opponents, as extremely effective. Think Twice raised over $66,000 at an auction of donated merchandise and artwork. Over the course of the campaign several hundred individuals contributed to Think Twice.[64]

Neely, Berg, and the other activists researched the effects of Wal-Mart superstores on communities. Collecting this information was facilitated by Berg's contact with Al Norman, who advised Think Twice but did not direct their campaign. Having this information helped them to counter Wal-Mart's arguments. Armed with the best information and data available, Think Twice held press conferences, handed out literature, ran a television advertisement, ran radio spots, sent out a mailing, created a website, and placed political advertisements in the newspaper. They lobbied the members of the city council and spoke to a wide range of groups in Eureka and Humboldt County, including unions, political clubs (Democrats and Republicans), womens' clubs, teachers, nonprofits, professional organizations, and service organizations. As the special election approached, they organized a phone bank to call potential "no" voters and encourage them to vote. The campaign literature and advertisements created by Think Twice emphasized the large number of individuals and organizations that opposed Measure J. A full-page advertisement listed the following organizations that had taken a stand against Measure J:

> Eureka City Council
> Humboldt County Board of Supervisors
> City of Eureka Harbor Commission
> Redwood Region Economic Development Commission
> Humboldt Bay Harbor and Recreation District
> Humboldt Taxpayers' League
> Humboldt/Del Norte Central Labor Council
> Citizens for Port Development
> Greater Eureka Chamber of Commerce
> Friends of Humboldt County
> American Federation of State, County and Local Municipal Employees, Local 1684
> United Food and Commercial Workers Union, Local 101
> Fortuna Chamber of Commerce
> Eureka Business Leaders Roundtable
> Democratic Central Committee
> Henderson Center Merchants Association[65]

Think Twice made a strategic decision to frame the issue as a matter of land use and economic development. In their view the balloon track represented a key to the eventual revitalization of the harbor and thus to the reinvigoration of the Eureka economy. They argued that it would be imprudent and shortsighted to take more than thirty acres of prime waterfront property and use it for a discount store.[66] In the words of Patty Berg:

> What we need is industrial and manufacturing growth. This is the only piece of land that not only has harbor access, but rail access. That's the key to our economic

future. It's harbor development and reactivating the railroad. This is an absolutely pivotal piece of land for these purposes.[67]

This argument was all the more compelling, in their view, because recent activity suggested that progress was being made toward the long-sought harbor revitalization. One major obstacle to the commercial viability of the harbor was its relative shallowness, which prevented it from accommodating large modern ships. Plans were in the works, however, to dredge the harbor. Another obstacle was the lack of rail service between Eureka and the San Francisco Bay area. As noted above, the rail line was out of operation because of extensive storm damage to a section of the line south of the city. However, a public agency was working on restoring the railroad to service and efforts were being made to obtain state and federal funds to repair the line. Think Twice contrasted the economic stimulus provided by new manufacturing companies (such as might locate on or near the site), which would bring money into the local economy, with new retailing, which would only redistribute existing sales dollars; and it contrasted the medium to high wages of potential manufacturing jobs with the low wages offered by Wal-Mart and other retailers.

While careful not to let the merchants become the issue, Think Twice noted the effect Wal-Mart would have on them. They argued that both the city and the county were already saturated with retail development and thus another big department store such as Wal-Mart would inevitably hurt existing businesses. Similarly, they insisted that the new jobs created by Wal-Mart would be offset by the loss of jobs at existing businesses, and they maintained that the sales tax revenue generated by Wal-Mart would be countered by a decrease in tax revenue from existing merchants.

There was also some general criticism directed toward Wal-Mart itself. Some of this criticism involved Wal-Mart's decision to have the question placed on the ballot. The strategy here was to portray Wal-Mart as a special interest that was using its financial clout to avoid having to submit to the oversight that would normally accompany a rezoning request. One advertisement, for example, featured the chairman of the Eureka Harbor Commission, who declared:

> Measure J guts our zoning process. . . . [It] circumvents the established zoning procedures of the City of Eureka. You and I have to follow these procedures, but apparently large corporations don't.[68]

Some opponents complained that Wal-Mart was a large, nonlocal corporation that lacked any genuine interest in local welfare and siphoned money out of the local economy. One resident put it this way:

> Big companies from outside Humboldt County periodically invade Eureka, bringing ambitious plans for sprawling retail developments touted to be the cure for our economic woes and a solution to many of our social problems as well. Their well-rehearsed representatives all dance to the same old broken record rendition of pie in the sky promises, hundreds of new jobs, big new tax revenues and wonderful social benefits. Blah, blah, blah.
> We've heard it all before. Kmart, Bayshore Mall, Costco, and now Wal-Mart. And once again, the same old song.
> What these outside corporations actually do for us is ship our hard-earned dollars off to places like Los Angeles, Troy, Mich., and Wall Street.[69]

Others disliked the size and appearance of Wal-Mart stores, feared that such a store would undermine the city's uniqueness, and felt that it was incompatible with the quality of life they wanted to maintain or enhance: "Eureka is unique. The bay is unique. Why put something as common as Wal-Mart on our coastline?"[70] It is difficult to assess the degree of animosity toward Wal-Mart itself, separate from the land use/economic development issue, although it seems to have been substantial. Purely anti-Wal-Mart sentiments, however, were downplayed in favor of the land use/economic development framing. The framing strategy of Think Twice, then, was to tie Eureka's economic future to the outcome of the vote on Measure J. Given the economic stagnation of the area, this framing resonated well with many residents. It also served to shift attention away from the merchants, who were accused, as in Ashland, of opposing Wal-Mart for purely selfish reasons.

City Council

Most members of the city council eventually opposed Measure J.

The Chamber of Commerce

The Greater Eureka Chamber of Commerce took a public stand against Measure J. The chamber was not against Wal-Mart per se, but objected to its chosen site. In the chamber's view, the balloon track should be reserved for a more appropriate use, such as industrial development, a high-tech facility, or something that required proximity to the waterfront.

The County Board of Supervisors

The Humboldt County Board of Supervisors had no jurisdiction over the balloon track, but took an active interest in the controversy and formed a committee to study the issues that it raised. The board had several concerns: What would be the economic impact of big box development on the county? Would a big box store in Eureka simply benefit the city at the expense of other communities in the county? What could be done to mitigate the negative effects of big box development? There was thus a keen awareness of possible negative effects at the regional level. The majority of supervisors eventually opposed Measure J.

Regional Economic Development Organization

The Redwood Region Economic Development Commission (RREDC) is a regional organization that includes representatives from the county, the cities, and the various service districts (e.g., water districts). Its purpose is to facilitate economic development throughout the county. The RREDC opposed Measure J because it was concerned that land that should be used for industrial uses might be taken for retail development instead.[71]

The Newspaper

The *Times-Standard* covered the controversy extensively and devoted more than a dozen front-page stories to it. The paper ran several editorials that were critical of the balloon track site and Wal-Mart's campaign tactics. The main issue, in the editor's view, was the potential squandering of waterfront property that was vital for the city's economic development.

NEUTRAL ACTORS

Some parties stayed neutral throughout the issue:

City Officials

The mayor, the city manager, and the director of community development were perceived as advocates of Wal-Mart and the balloon track site. However, according to Kevin Hamblin, the director of community development, the city in fact never took a position on the Wal-Mart issue. The city did not solicit Wal-Mart, although city officials did meet with Wal-Mart to discuss its plans, as the city would meet with any developer, especially if a large project were being proposed. Mayor Nancy Flemming and city manager Harvey Rose presented statistics on the sales tax revenue that a Wal-Mart would generate and described favorably the experiences that some other cities had had with Wal-Mart. As a result of presenting this information, they were pegged by the media and the anti-Wal-Mart activists as supporters, when in fact they were "desperately trying to stay neutral," according to Rose.[72] Flemming and Rose, however, were definitely not opposed to having a Wal-Mart in Eureka or to large-scale commercial development on the balloon track. Mayor Flemming considered it important to treat all businesses fairly and to not be "prejudiced" against Wal-Mart or other big box retailers.[73]

Other Cities in Humboldt County

The other cities in Humboldt County showed relatively little interest in trying to entice Wal-Mart to locate within their municipal boundaries. There are several explanations for this lack of intercity competition. First, there was simply a dearth of large commercial sites available anywhere in the county.[74] Second, some of the other cities did not want Wal-Mart. Arcata, for example, which was just north of Eureka, was a college town with a strong presence by the Green Party and widespread anti-Wal-Mart sentiment. Third, Think Twice and Friends spoke to the officials and residents in other cities and explained that a Wal-Mart, whether in Eureka or elsewhere, would not lead to a net increase in either jobs or tax revenue. Finally, some cities, including Eureka, were willing to share with other cities a portion of the sales tax revenue generated by big box stores located within their municipal boundaries.[75] By agreeing, at least in principle, to a sort of nonaggression pact, the cities in Humboldt County undercut Wal-Mart's ability to play them off against each other.

THE CAMPAIGN

By mid-April 1999 Wal-Mart had collected enough signatures to qualify the measure for the ballot. With the measure officially slated for a special election in August the campaigns for and against Measure J began in earnest. They were remarkably similar to other political campaigns and featured PACs, political consultants, political advertisements, fund-raising (by the opponents only), window and lawn signs, slogans, extensive media coverage, polls, telephone banks, and allegations of campaign improprieties.

Early in the campaign, before Think Twice was established, the pro-Wal-Mart PAC filed a complaint with the state Fair Political Practices Commission claiming that Friends was illegally engaged in political campaigning. Wal-Mart argued that if Friends, which was registered as a nonprofit organization, was going to conduct a political campaign, then it should be registered as a PAC, just like the pro–Measure J PAC.[76] The commission exonerated

Friends of any wrongdoing in June; Think Twice announced its formation later the same month.

In May 1999 the Federal Emergency Management Agency (FEMA) agreed to release funds to repair certain badly damaged sections of the rail line. The funds would not be enough to restore service on the entire line and there would still be no service into or out of Eureka. The opponents, however, took the action by FEMA as evidence that rail operations were indeed viable and that the balloon track should be reserved as a possible site for such uses.

In June Wal-Mart conducted a telephone poll in which people were asked to respond to a lengthy list of questions. In addition to asking interviewees typical campaign questions, such as whether they favored having a Wal-Mart and how they intended to vote, the pollsters asked a series of questions about the interviewees' opinions of various local politicians, appointed officials, activists (e.g., Al Norman), organizations (e.g., Friends), and the media (i.e., the *Times-Standard*). Although this type of "push" polling is not unusual in political campaigns, it sparked a denunciation by the *Times-Standard*, which made an analogy to the infamous "enemies" list of the Watergate scandal.[77]

The next month another Wal-Mart-sponsored telephone operation resulted in more bad publicity for the company. A number of Eureka residents complained that a polling firm representing Wal-Mart had called them early on Saturday or Sunday morning and, in some cases, had called them repeatedly. The *Times-Standard* put the story on its front page, "Wal-Mart hits city with calls," and described the travails of one unfortunate woman who was waiting for a phone call about her sick father, but instead received eleven calls from the polling firm.[78] Apparently the polling firm used by Wal-Mart was located in a different time zone and did not realize how early it was on the west coast.[79]

Another incident involved a bulk mailing about to be sent out by the pro-Wal-Mart PAC. This mailing included literature in support of Wal-Mart and an application for an absentee ballot. Upon examining the mailing, U.S. Postal Service officials noticed that the return address did not match that of the PAC, but was in fact that of the Humboldt County Elections Office, thus making it appear that the county endorsed Measure J. Wal-Mart agreed to change the mailer. Once again, however, the *Times-Standard* put Wal-Mart's misdeeds on the front-page story and editorialized about the "disturbing pattern" that these various incidents seemed to reveal.[80]

In July the county supervisors passed a resolution opposing Measure J. Although not binding, the resolution did constitute a formal statement of their position.

In early August a specialized dredging vessel arrived in Humboldt Bay and began the long-awaited job of deepening the channel. The dredging was taken as further evidence of the viability of port development.

During the runup to the election the city, the county, and Wal-Mart all released reports. First came the report of the Humboldt County Ad Hoc Committee on Big Box Development, which found that the overall impact of a superstore on the region would be negative:

> The siting of a big box retail store . . . will result in negligible impact on the generation of sales, and therefore the generation of sales tax revenue, within Humboldt County.
> A big box retail store sited in Humboldt County will generate a substantial majority of its business by drawing customers away from existing businesses, resulting in a significant negative impact on the viability of its competitors.
> . . . The jurisdiction in which a big box retail store is located will have incremental sales tax revenues flow to it from surrounding communities . . . .
> The opening of a new big box retail store will not result in an increase in overall full or part-time jobs because there is not an overall increase in retail activity, but instead a shift of retail activity within the County.[81]

Shortly thereafter Wal-Mart issued the results of a study that addressed one of the opponents' principal claims: that the balloon track was unsuitable for commercial use, but was essential for waterfront-related uses. The report, commissioned by Wal-Mart and prepared by J. Laurence Mintier & Associates, a Sacramento-based consulting firm, concluded that:

> The Eureka Railyard Property is an appropriate location for large-format commercial uses since:
> 1) As an urban-infill project, it would restore a blighted, abandoned site to productive commercial use.
> 2) The project would help revitalize Old Town and Downtown by attracting shoppers from throughout the region to Central Eureka.
> 3) The site is not needed for other uses.[82]

The report noted that "over the last 35 years, the city had planned and zoned the Railyard Property for commercial, light industrial or public use—never for coastal-dependent or port-related use."[83] The report referred to recent studies that found that "containerized cargo handling is an unlikely prospect for Humboldt Bay because of a small regional population base, unreliable rail service, and competition from well-equipped west coast ports."[84] The balloon track was not a good candidate for port-related development because it did not have bay frontage and there were other parcels available that were more suitable for break bulk and other cargo handling activities. In an addendum to the report Mintier minimized the importance of the recent harbor dredging and the recent release of funds by FEMA for rail line improvements. He described these actions as "important, but relatively small steps along the path to making Humboldt Bay a viable multi-cargo port."[85] The opponents dismissed the Mintier's findings on the grounds that Wal-Mart had paid for the study and noted, furthermore, that Mintier himself had come to a different conclusion in a previous study.[86] Finally, the city council released a report that it had commissioned from Bay Area Economics (BAE), based in Sacramento. The BAE report, which came to conclusions similar to those reached by the county, found that "the slow population growth in Eureka and Humboldt County, combined with relatively low median income levels and sluggish employment growth, may limit the ability of the trade area to support new retail development."[87] A new Wal-Mart superstore, according to BAE, would simply take business away from existing retailers.

One week before the election the city council approved a nonbinding resolution that stated that "the city of Eureka publicly expresses its firm opposition to Measure J because it jeopardizes the successful revitalization of Eureka's harbor and industrial development as envisioned in the 1998 general plan."[88] Mayor Flemming did not support the resolution.[89]

THE SPECIAL ELECTION

On 24 August 1999, Eureka voters went to the polls to cast their votes in this one-issue special election. By a vote of 61 to 39 percent they rejected the proposed rezoning of the balloon track and thereby ended Wal-Mart's bid to locate in Eureka at its chosen site. Al Norman characterized the outcome as "a big setback for the biggest retailer in the world" and a "colossal waste" of money by Wal-Mart.[90] Wal-Mart Community Affairs Director Daphne Davis said, "We still believe this is a great place for a Wal-Mart store."[91] Campaign spending reports showed that Think Twice had spent $41,572, compared with $235,000 by Wal-Mart.[92]

While the controversies in Ashland and Eureka may appear similar, a closer look reveals some important differences. One difference that must be acknowledged at the outset is that the opponents in Eureka faced Wal-Mart almost ten years after their counterparts in Ashland. During that period Wal-Mart's modus operandi, as well as the basic issues, remained unchanged; however, scores of superstore conflicts occurred throughout the United States, which constituted a source of experience and knowledge for other opponents. Also, dozens of articles were published, a few books were written, reports were issued, websites were set up, videos were produced, and Al Norman established his antisuperstore consulting service. The opponents in Eureka made good use of this accumulated knowledge and it contributed to their success.

The opponents in both Ashland and Eureka faced considerable opposition, although of different types. In Ashland, they faced a loose coalition of local shoppers, local landowners, and individuals with preexisting complaints about the merchants, while in Eureka, they faced a PAC organized and funded by Wal-Mart. The support for Wal-Mart in Ashland was more organic and appeared to reflect the views of a significant segment of the public, although it was probably dominated by the landowners.

The two sets of opponents employed different framings. In Ashland the issue was clearly about "saving" downtown and the local merchants. The supporters, however, were able to portray the opponents as a small minority that was interested only in its own welfare. The fate of the local merchants was of considerable importance to the opponents in Eureka also, but they were very careful not to allow it to become the central issue. Instead, they emphasized land use and economic development. Concern with local economic malaise and unemployment was a concern in both disputes, but it worked more to the detriment of the opponents in Ashland. The opponents in Eureka were able to counteract Wal-Mart's claims to bring jobs and money to town by arguing that a superstore on scarce waterfront land would actually hinder economic development. Lastly, the opponents in Eureka were better organized, more sophisticated, and had more resources than the opponents in Ashland or in any of the other cities, except possibly Gig Harbor.

NOTES

1. Northwest Regional Planning Commission, *City of Ashland Land Use Plan and Comprehensive Plan*, 1992; Discovery Group, Ltd., *Ashland Waterfront Development Plan*, n.d.

2. In 1989 the city's unemployment rate was 10.2 percent; statewide it was 5.2 percent. U.S. Census Bureau, *1990 Census of Population and Housing, Summary of Social, Economic and Housing Characteristics*, Table 5.

3. Fran Ante was serving as interim mayor. The previous mayor had resigned to take a job in state government and Ante had been appointed interim mayor by the council.

4. Minutes of Ashland Planning Commission meeting, 11 October 1989.

5. Quoted in Evan Sasman, "Mall will help downtown: developer," *Daily Press* (WI), 25 January 1990.

6. Quoted in Evan Sasman, "Mall will help downtown: developer," *Daily Press*, 25 January 1990.

7. I will refer to the Highway 13 location as a "site," although no specific site on Highway 13 was specified.

8. The developer also had to obtain street discontinuances and vacations. I will focus on the rezoning because it was the central requirement.

9. Jerry Severson of Centres Inc., quoted in Mary Thompson, "Council denies Wal-Mart rezoning," *Daily Press*, 14 March 1990.

10. Reported in Evan Sasman, "Mall will help downtown: developer," *Daily Press*, 25 January 1990.

11. Reported in Evan Sasman, "Mall will help downtown: developer," *Daily Press*, 25 January 1990.

12. Quoted in Evan Sasman, "Commission tables zoning change for mall development," *Daily Press*, 25 January 1990.

13. Minutes of the joint meeting of the Ashland Planning Commission and Ashland Physical Improvements Committee, 24 January 1990.

14. Letter to the editor, *Daily Press*, 21 March 1990.

15. Letter to the editor, *Daily Press*, 21 April 1990.

16. Letter to the editor, *Daily Press*, 13 March 1990.

17. Evan Sasman, "Bayfield County contacts developer about Wal-Mart." *Daily Press*, 20 March 1990.

18. Minutes of meeting of the Ashland Planning Commission, 25 April 1990.

19. Press release of the Ashland Main Street Committee Board of Directors, published in the *Daily Press*, 18 March 1990.

20. Minutes of combined meeting of Ashland Planning Commission and Ashland Physical Improvements Committee, 13 March 1990.

21. Interview with anonymous council member, Ashland, Wisconsin.

22. Letter to the editor, *Daily Press*, 31 March 1990.

23. Interview with anonymous downtown retailer, Ashland, Wisconsin.

24. Quoted in Mary Thompson, "Wal-Mart plans draw protest of store owners," *Daily Press*, 2 March 1990.

25. Editorial, "Those who distributed the anonymous bulletin demonstrated a cowardice akin to a rooftop sniper wreaking havoc in the street," *Daily Press*, 28 April 1990.

26. *Daily Press*, "Pamphlets can draw penalties," 26 April 1990.

27. Interview with anonymous opponent, Ashland, Wisconsin.

28. Minutes of Ashland Planning Commission meeting, 25 April 1990.

29. Letter to the editor, *Daily Press*, 10 March 1990.

30. Interview with anonymous downtown merchant, Ashland, Wisconsin.

31. Interview with anonymous council member, Bayfield County, Wisconsin.

32. Mary Thompson, "Wal-Mart plans draw protest of store owners," *Daily Press*, 2 March 1990.

33. Letter to the editor, *Daily Press*, 6 March 1990.

34. Frank Myott, quoted in Evan Sasman, "Malls take another step," *Daily Press*, 22 February 1990.

35. Interview with Fran Ante, mayor, City of Ashland.

36. Quoted in Evan Sasman, "Petitioners want administrator plan abolished," *Daily Press*, 31 October 1989.

37. Interview with anonymous city employee, Ashland, Wisconsin.

38. Interview with anonymous downtown merchant, Ashland, Wisconsin.

39. Interview with anonymous downtown merchant, Ashland, Wisconsin.

40. Interview with anonymous council member, Ashland, Wisconsin.

41. Interview with anonymous council member, Ashland, Wisconsin.

42. There is another possible explanation for the actions of the challengers. According to some interviewees, all seven council challengers ran for office for one reason only: to get elected so they could approve the Highway 2 rezoning. According to this view, they did this because they owned property at the site (or had friends or relatives who did). In this view, the challengers were not really interested in the city administrator issue, or any other issue except the Wal-Mart issue, but used it as a means of turning the voters against the incumbents. This view assumes that the challengers decided to run for office *before* the planning commission or the council voted on the rezoning. It is also possible that some of the challengers ran for office to get the site rezoned and others ran because of other reasons. At least two of the challengers appear to have had reasons other than the Highway 2 site to run for office: one had ongoing disputes with the council concerning his taxi business and another was deeply involved in the city administrator controversy. In the final analysis, it probably does not matter which scenario is correct. What is important is the feature that is common to all accounts: the presence of a group of local property owners who for reasons of narrow pecuniary self-interest were very active and extremely vocal in promoting a particular superstore at a particular site.

43. Political advertisement placed by Edward J. Kay, *Daily Press*, 22 March 1990.

44. Interview with anonymous opponent, Ashland, Wisconsin.

45. Mary Thompson, "Wal-Mart rezoning passes," *Daily Press*, 1 June 1990.

46. "Wal-Mart developer completes purchases," *Daily Press*, 22 August 1990.

47. U.S. Department of Labor, Bureau of Labor Statistics, "Local Area Unemployment Statistics." http://www.bls.gov/lau.

48. Based on *City of Eureka General Plan, adopted February 27, 1997, as amended through February 23, 1999*, p. 4-2, Table 4-1.

49. Kevin Hamblin, director of community development, City of Eureka, personal communication.

50. Interview with Kevin Hamblin, director of community development, City of Eureka.

51. David Anderson, "Coastal panel won't switch land-use rule," *Times-Standard* (CA), 10 September 1998.

52. Bill Quinn, *How Wal-Mart Is Destroying America*.

53. Evans/McDonough Company Inc., "Research Report: Wal-Mart Proposal, Eureka and Humboldt County." Wal-Mart file, Eureka Department of Community Development, Eureka, California, n.d.

54. Quoted in Barbara Henry, "Poll favors Wal-Mart," *Times-Standard*, 6 October 1998.

55. Jason Kennedy Steele, "Wal-Mart contractor cited for illegal testing," *Times-Standard*, 9 December 1998.
56. *The Arcata Eye* (CA), "Wal-Mart's friends, foes debate," 9 March 1999.
57. Editorial, "Ballot proposal has many holes," *Times-Standard*, 7 March 1999.
58. Editorial, "Zoning not an issue for voters," *Times-Standard*, 25 May 1999.
59. Quoted in Jonathan Jeisel, "Big Debate Over Wal-Mart," *Humboldt Beacon* (CA), 27 August 1998.
60. Nate Ferguson, "Wal-Mart group targets foes," *Times-Standard*, 27 May 1999.
61. Letter to the editor, *Times-Standard*, 23 September 1998.
62. Letter to the editor, *Times-Standard*, 2 November 1998.
63. Friends of Humboldt County. http://humboldt1.com/friends/mission.htm.
64. Interview with Bonnie Neely, County Supervisor, Humboldt County, Eureka, California.
65. "No on Meausure J." Political advertisement paid for by Think Twice Campaign/No on Measure J, published in the *Times-Standard*, August 1999.
66. The balloon track was referred to often as a waterfront location, although strictly speaking it was not on the waterfront, as noted earlier.
67. Quoted in Mark Tide, "Measure J: Set to Pop 'Balloon Track' of Region's Economic Dreams," *Arcata Journal* (CA), 17 August 1999.
68. "Measure J guts our zoning process." Political advertisement paid for by Think Twice Campaign/No on Measure J, published in the *Times-Standard*, 23 August 1999.
69. Letter to the editor, *Times-Standard*, 24 October 1998.
70. Laura Reneau, quoted in Eric Malnic, "Eureka Voters Reject Plan for Wal-Mart," *Los Angeles Times*, 25 August 1999.
71. *Times-Standard*, "Wal-Mart faces more opposition," 2 August 1999.
72. Interview with Harvey Rose, city manager, City of Eureka.
73. Telephone interview with Nancy Flemming, mayor, City of Eureka.
74. Telephone interview with Kirk Girard, director of community development services, Humboldt County.
75. Proposition 11, passed by California voters in 1998, was specifically intended to make it easier for cities and counties to enter into local sales tax sharing agreements and thereby eliminate costly bidding wars for retail establishments. *Los Angeles Times*, "The California Elections," 1 November 1998.
76. Nate Ferguson, "Wal-Mart group targets foes," *Times-Standard*, 27 May 1999.
77. Editorial, "Wal-Mart targeting honest brokers," *Times-Standard*, 24 June 1999.
78. Nate Ferguson, "Wal-Mart hits city with calls," *Times-Standard*, 29 July 1999.
79. Nate Ferguson, "Wal-Mart dumps phone poll firm," *Times-Standard*, 30 July 1999.
80. Editorial, "No Thanks–to Wal-Mart and yet another foul-up in its efforts to locate a store in Eureka," *Times-Standard*, 7 August 1999.
81. *Report of the Humboldt County Ad Hoc Committee on Big Box Development*, July 1999.
82. J. Laurence Mintier & Associates, *Eureka Railyard Property Land Use Study*.
83. J. Laurence Mintier & Associates, *Eureka Railyard Property Land Use Study*.

84. J. Laurence Mintier & Associates, *Eureka Railyard Property Land Use Study*, 1–2.

85. "Addendum to the Eureka Railyard Property Land Use Study," J. Laurence Mintier & Associates, 28 July 1999.

86. Nate Ferguson, "Land-use study firm takes heat," *Times-Standard*, 7 August 1999.

87. Quoted in Nate Ferguson, "Big-box bad for retailers, study says," *Times-Standard*, 6 August 1999.

88. Quoted in Nate Ferguson, "Wal-Mart loses key backing," *Times-Standard*, 18 August 1999.

89. Quoted in Nate Ferguson, "Wal-Mart loses key backing," *Times-Standard*, 18 August 1999.

90. Quoted in Nate Ferguson, "Measure J fails to win approval," *Times-Standard*, 25 August 1999.

91. Quoted in Nate Ferguson, "Measure J fails to win approval," *Times-Standard*, 25 August 1999.

92. Nate Ferguson, "Voters 'think twice.'" *Times-Standard*, 25 August 1999.

7

Explaining Success

After completing the case studies I had nearly twenty variables that seemed to have some potential to explain the different outcomes (see Table 7.1). Some variables, such as whether the social movement organization took legal action and whether the various growth machine actors supported the store, came from previous research. Others, such as whether a prosuperstore group mobilized and whether there was evidence of widespread opposition, only became apparent in the course of the fieldwork. Only four of the variables (numbers 1–4) represent actions that were under the control of the antisuperstore social movement organization; the others (numbers 5–19) are environmental variables and refer to actions taken by other parties, the nature of the threat posed by the superstore, and miscellaneous other actions and conditions. Social movement research has generally found that outcomes cannot be explained fully on the basis of action taken by a social movement organization; other factors must be invoked also. Likewise with these controversies: the outcomes are best understood as resulting from a combination of action by the opponents, action by the supporters, and the local context.

In comparing the cases I looked for variables that took the same value for both of the complete successes and took the opposite (or different) value for both of the failures. For example, the local newspaper opposed the store in both of the complete successes *and* supported the store in both of the failures; thus, the stance of the newspaper is one of the key variables. There are five key variables that constitute the heart of the explanation. Before describing these, however, it is useful to look briefly at some of the other variables that turned out to have less explanatory power. These other variables either did not differ among the outcomes, or did not differ systematically and thus, while

Table 7.1. Explanatory Variables

Variables Under the Control of the Social Movement Organization (SMO)

1. SMO mobilized at a high level
2. SMO produced evidence of widespread opposition
3. SMO framed the issue broadly
4. SMO took legal action

Environmental Variables

Growth Machine

5. Chamber of commerce supported the superstore
6. Mayor supported the superstore
7. City council supported the superstore
8. Local real estate interests supported the superstore
9. Local merchants opposed the superstore

Media

10. Local newspaper opposed the superstore

Prosuperstore Efforts

11. Prosuperstore group mobilized
12. Wal-Mart mobilized at a high level
13. Wal-Mart made blunders

Nature of the Threat

14. Superstore was a threat to local scenic appeal
15. Superstore was a threat to the viability of downtown
16. Superstore was a threat to a residential district

Miscellaneous

17. Issue decided by local voters
18. City was economically depressed at time of controversy
19. Affluent segment present in the city

Source: Based on Halebsky, "Explaining the Outcomes," 451, Table 1.

they may have played a role in particular cases, it is difficult to generalize about their effects.

VARIABLES WITH UNCERTAIN EFFECTS[1]

The literature on siting disputes, as well as common sense, suggests that success is more likely when a social movement organization mobilizes at a high level. Although level of mobilization is difficult to measure precisely, there were definite differences among the cases. In Gig Harbor the opponents activated an existing neighborhood organization with a paid director, turned out 350 persons at an official meeting, drew 400 to a town meeting featuring an anti-Wal-Mart video shown on a big screen, wrote letters to the editor, credibly threatened to demonstrate if excluded from a meeting with Wal-Mart, hired their own environmental experts, presented officials with a petition with 14,000 signatures, marched in a local parade, displayed placards, and created a website. In Ashland, by contrast, they appeared in small numbers at official meetings, distributed a flyer, wrote letters to the editor, and placed a political ad in the newspaper. Did these differences matter? The opponents succeeded in Gig Harbor and failed in Ashland, but they also failed in Petoskey, where they had mobilized at a level approaching that of Gig Harbor. While the importance of vigorous mobilization seems likely, it did not vary consistently with the outcomes and thus we cannot conclude much about its effects.

I was curious to see if local groups that used legal tactics were more (or less) likely to succeed. As it turned out, legal tactics were used in only one case (the lawsuit filed by the opponents in Petoskey) and thus no conclusion can be drawn about the effectiveness of such tactics.

Local real estate interests supported the proposed superstore to a greater or lesser extent in every case, but the other growth machine actors opposed (or failed to support) the store in almost every case. The chamber of commerce, in particular, was conspicuous by its lack of support in every case except West Bend. Because the stance of the growth machine varied so little, it cannot explain the different outcomes.

We would expect the likelihood of success to be inversely related to the level of corporate mobilization. Unfortunately, the case studies cannot test this proposition because Wal-Mart's level of mobilization was high in every case. Unlike its opponents, Wal-Mart had ample resources, which it did not hesitate to deploy. Its tactics, furthermore, were remarkably similar in most cases and included the following:

- Staging a media campaign.
- Sending promotional flyers to all residents.
- Making strategic use of surveys and studies that invariably find that residents want the store.
- Framing the issue as a matter of economic benefits and improved shopping options.
- Attempting to divide and conquer the local populace by pitting consumers against the "greedy" small merchants and setting working people against the "snobs."
- Diverting attention from the real question (should the store be allowed in the first place?) by trying to get everybody preoccupied with the details

of the site plan (e.g., should the new stoplight be placed at intersection A or intersection B?).
- Responding to predictable complaints about the ugliness of the store with architectural and landscaping "concessions" that are touted as an indication of its responsiveness to local concerns.
- Pitting one city against another.
- Claiming that its preferred site is the only viable site and threatening to abandon the city altogether if it cannot have the site it wants.

The variables pertaining to the nature of the threat and the miscellaneous variables also have uncertain effects because they either did not differ systematically across the complete successes and failures or were the same in the complete successes and the failures. For example, the successful opponents in Gig Harbor and Eureka were motivated by the threat to local scenic appeal, but so were the unsuccessful opponents in Petoskey. Similarly, Wal-Mart was perceived as a threat to downtown in one complete success (Eureka), but not in the other complete success (Gig Harbor), making it hard to draw any conclusions about the effect of this variable. The superstore did not pose a threat to a residential district in either the two complete successes or the two failures, thus providing no basis on which to evaluate the impact of this variable. In several cases the final decision was taken out of the hands of the local elected legislators and submitted to the voters, which raises the question, is success more likely when "the people" decide? It is difficult to say because there was no systematic relationship between voting and outcomes: a vote was taken in one complete success (Eureka) but not in the other, and a vote was taken in one failure (Ashland) but not in the other.[2] Were the opponents less likely to prevail if their city was suffering from a depressed local economy, a situation in which Wal-Mart's claim to create new jobs might be seductive? Again, it is difficult to say because there were no systematic differences: the opponents succeeded in a depressed economy (Eureka) and failed in a normal economy (Petoskey). Likewise with regard to the presence of an affluent segment in the city: the opponents succeeded in upscale Gig Harbor but failed in Petoskey, which also had an affluent segment and affluent opponents.

The effect of affluence brings up the issue of class. There is a widespread belief that only the upper middle class objects to Wal-Mart, a belief that the company and its supporters strategically encourage by intimating that the opponents are snobs, thereby fomenting class antagonism. This view evinces a certain condescension as it implies that the middle and working classes have an inferior sense of aesthetics and cannot comprehend the adverse effects of corporate retailing. While this may characterize the shoppers, it does not apply to many other groups. In every case, I encountered many Wal-Mart opponents who were solidly middle or working class. While the affluent upper middle class is more likely to oppose Wal-Mart, it does not follow that other groups are unqualified supporters, which suggests that attempts to portray Wal-Mart siting disputes in strict class terms are overstated.

FIVE VARIABLES THAT DID MATTER

So, how did a few small, local groups prevail against the world's biggest retailer and what can their success tell us about the possibilities for resistance to corporate action? In short, they succeeded because they produced evidence of widespread opposition, framed the issue broadly, received backing from the media, did not have to contend with a counter social movement, and benefited from blunders by Wal-Mart. All five of these key variables varied systematically across the complete successes and failures. But there is more to the explanation—the opponents also succeeded because they were able to enlarge themselves and their cause, a result of the combined effect of the first three variables. Let us begin with the individual variables.

Evidence of Widespread Opposition

The opponents mobilized in every city, but in the two failures mobilization alone was not sufficient. While the social movement literature has understandably emphasized the importance of mobilization, I argue that attention should be paid to its effectiveness as well. Although a high level of mobilization will almost invariably help a social movement, it may come to naught if it does not result in tangible *evidence* of widespread opposition. This is part of what seems to have been lacking in the two failures. The opponents in Petoskey, for example, were active, sophisticated, and relatively well funded, but they were not able to offer the kind of evidence that could convince others that they had a wide following. In Eureka and Gig Harbor, by contrast, the opponents could point to petitions overflowing with large numbers of signatures, the presence of large numbers of persons at public meetings and town meetings, and the publication of full-page newspaper advertisements with long lists of sympathetic local organizations and individuals.

Large corporations are rarely influenced by the mere fact that their actions are widely unpopular, even if there is ample evidence of that unpopularity, so this variable does not affect the corporation directly. However, disputes involving corporate action are often mediated by the state and that is where this variable becomes salient. As a concrete manifestation of public opinion, evidence of widespread opposition signals politicians that a local anticorporate movement is *not* a minority interest that can be safely ignored. It demonstrates to local politicians, many of whom have a keen interest in being reelected, that *many* of their constituents oppose a certain corporate action, thereby motivating them to make decisions that are in line with the desires of their constituents. "Evidence that a large number of persons and influential organizations . . . hold[s] a certain view can work to convince decision makers that the costs of opposing the [anticorporate] movement are too high."[3]

Framing

The framings used in the complete successes have a common feature: they construed the proposed superstore as a threat to the interests of a wide swath of the community. Thus, broad framings were more successful than narrow framings. In Gig Harbor the opponents criticized every possible adverse effect of the store—increased traffic, decline of local merchants, degradation of the natural environment, and disintegration of the city's unique character—and thereby appealed to many Gig Harborites. In Eureka the opponents appealed to people throughout the city by stressing how the proposed store would undermine local economic development, an issue of concern to many because of the city's economic stagnation. In Ashland and Petoskey, by contrast, the opponents framed the issue mainly as a matter of preserving downtown and the downtown merchants, an approach that struck many as narrow. The opponents in Petoskey also emphasized the dangers of sprawl, but many people never conceived of sprawl as a problem for them (or never understood the concept). To say that broad framings worked better than narrow ones, however, is insufficient. In fact, all the opponents *tried* to use broad framings. In Ashland and Petoskey they tried to elicit broad support for their position by arguing that the fate of downtown and the downtown merchants was an issue of concern to the whole community. The problem is that their framing did not resonate with the public and local officials. To talk about a common interest is not enough; it must be talked about in a way that is convincing to large numbers of people and taps into something of real concern to them.

Like evidence of widespread opposition, a broad framing does not produce favorable outcomes by affecting the corporation directly; rather, it affects local officials and the public, whose decisions affect the corporation. It affects local officials by indicating that an issue is of concern to many of their constituents and thus should be taken seriously, and it affects the public by compelling people to see an issue as a problem for *them* and not just for somebody else.

The Media

Another difference between the complete successes and the failures is the stance taken by the local newspaper, the dominant medium in many small towns. In Eureka and Gig Harbor the paper editorialized strongly against the store or the site, and gave ample coverage to the views of the opponents. In Petoskey, by contrast, the newspaper never editorialized strongly for or against the project and printed enough positive stories to counter any that were negative. And its curious practice of putting Wal-Mart's logo on the front page in colored ink to accompany stories about the controversy suggests that it was not opposed to the store.

The case studies suggest, then, that the local newspaper can affect the outcomes of community-corporate controversies. While this is perhaps not unexpected, what may be less expected is the direction of that effect: in both of the complete successes (and in one of the partial successes) the newspaper actively opposed Wal-Mart's plans. These results raise doubts about the presumed conservatism of the media and suggest that local anticorporate groups may find support from this source. This variable, like the previous two, affects outcomes principally by influencing local officials and local voters rather than by affecting the corporation directly. The corporation, however, can suffer directly from bad press if it is sufficiently negative to affect sales.

Counter Social Movement Organizations

It is striking that an indigenous pro-Wal-Mart counter social movement organization was active in both of the failures but in neither of the successes. The pro-Wal-Mart groups "touted Wal-Mart's shopping options, played upon latent local antagonisms, and attacked the local merchants and downtown."[4] While not large, they seem to have been feisty enough to have influenced the outcomes. In Petoskey they rallied for the "many, many average working people" who could not afford to shop downtown,[5] while in Ashland they raised a torrent of protest against the downtown merchants, whom they portrayed as a self-interested minority that had "denied our entire community jobs and tax dollars."[6] Local counter social movement organizations affect outcomes by challenging the framing put forth by the (original) social movement organization, forcing it to spend time and energy refuting assertions, and diverting media attention.

Indigenous procorporate groups are most likely to arise when corporate action can be construed as beneficial to the community. Suppose a nonlocal company wants to build and operate a bad-smelling waste incinerator, using nonlocal labor, on land that is not locally owned. And suppose further that the proposed incinerator will burn nonlocal waste and generate minimal tax revenue for the local municipality. Given these conditions, there would be little basis for an organized procorporate effort. But suppose the company intends to hire local workers. If there is substantial local unemployment many residents may feel that the incinerator will be beneficial to the community, in spite of its adverse effects. Of course, what is "beneficial to the community" is itself subject to debate, as we saw in the superstore controversies. But even if a corporate action is widely seen as not beneficial to the community it may still have a few local beneficiaries. Because our economy is so thoroughly dominated by large corporations, and because large corporations are involved in so many areas of life, it often turns out that there are connections between a corporation, even one headquartered far away, and at least a few local persons. For example, they may own the land the company wants, or they may stand to make money from brokering the sale of the land, or they may hope to make money by providing advertising or consulting services to the company, or they may hope to sell their manufactured goods to the company, or the company may produce or sell a product or service that has personal significance for them, or the nonprofit organization for which they work may be funded by the company. It is also possible for a corporation to strategically create local beneficiaries by deliberately doing business with some local actors. Consequently, even if there is general agreement that a corporate action is not in the interest of most of the community, there may still be some local actors who stand to benefit from it and who organize to promote it because it serves their interests, which they are likely to disguise as the community interest.

Corporate Blunders

Wal-Mart made a series of embarrassing blunders in Gig Harbor and Eureka but not in Petoskey or Ashland, suggesting that this may have contributed to success. These blunders were disseminated widely because they appeared prominently in the local newspapers. In Eureka, for example, the newspaper broadcast Wal-Mart's blunders on the front page (e.g., "Wal-Mart hits city with calls" and "Big-box bad for retailers, study says"). Blunders can undercut a corporation's public relations efforts and undermine support among the public as well as public officials. To the extent a corporate action depends on approval from these groups, blunders can cause serious problems for a corporation. It should be evident that local opponents can capitalize on corporate blunders only if they are aware of them and are able to publicize them.

THE PARTIAL SUCCESSES[7]

An analysis of the partial successes provides further support for the importance of a broad framing and suggests the weaknesses that may have resulted in only *partial* success. The opponents in West Bend and Ottawa did not mobilize at a high level and failed to produce evidence of widespread opposition. This combination, however, was not fatal and effective framing is probably why. In both cities the opponents framed the issue as a matter of protecting their homes from unwanted large-scale commercial invasion and, by extension, protecting the residential environment of *all* homeowners in the city. As the opponents in West Bend argued, "If Wal-Mart gets the city to make an exception at the Valley Avenue site, it may not be long before other large corporations get exceptions to plan in *your* neighborhood."[8] This broad framing appealed to many and perhaps mitigated the need to visibly demonstrate widespread opposition.

The presence of a counter social movement organization appears to have weakened the opposition in Ottawa, as evidenced by the closeness of the final popular vote on the original site (818 to 776 against). In West Bend there was no counter social movement, but heavyweight growth machine actors such as the mayor and the chamber of commerce pushed vigorously for the superstore. Thus, effective framing can help to offset weak mobilization, but a social movement organization may still not attain complete success if it has to contend with an active adversary, whether in the form of a countergroup or organized growth-machine elites.

COMBINING VARIABLES[9]

Community-corporate controversies typically involve parties of unequal size and resources. To have a fighting chance a small anticorporate social movement organization needs to somehow enlarge itself, figuratively speaking. It is probably not a coincidence that the preceding analysis identified evidence of widespread opposition, framing, and the media as three of the five "causal" factors associated with success. I suggest that the reason these factors are so important is because they enable a small organization to increase its influence and reach, thereby increasing the likelihood of success against a corporation. These factors are important singly, and we would expect a straightforward additive combined effect when all are present. Beyond that, however, there is a combined effect that results from mutual reinforcement that works as follows: Supportive media can help a small organization to project its framing beyond what it could otherwise do and can help to publicize whatever evidence of widespread opposition the opponents have generated. Supportive media can also help a small organization to capitalize on blunders by a corporation. A broad framing enlarges the range of potential constituents and allies (some of whom may help provide evidence of widespread opposition and uncover corporate blunders) as well as the size of the bystander public. Such a framing may also increase the salience of the issue for the local media. And evidence of widespread opposition serves to convince others, including the media, that this enlargement is valid, while simultaneously giving credence to the broad framing proffered by the opponents. The magnification that results from this mutually reinforcing combination is often crucial because it enables a "puny" local social movement organization to "bulk up" and confront a corporation on more equal terms.

While an anticorporate group would like to orchestrate matters to achieve this sort of influence, we should note that only framing and evidence of widespread opposition are under the control of the social movement organization; the media remain part of the environment. Thus, this mutually reinforcing combination is similar to the models proposed by other writers insofar as efforts by a social movement organization are not sufficient to produce positive outcomes, but must take place in a favorable context. Last, an active counter social movement organization can undermine this combination by presenting a competing framing, offering its own evidence of widespread support, and changing the extent and nature of coverage by the media.

SOME CORPORATE WEAKNESSES

In addition to specific variables this research also suggests some general corporate weaknesses that can be exploited by local opponents. These weaknesses are not unique to Wal-Mart but are related to the nature of big companies, so we would expect them to apply to other companies as well. First, even big companies make blunders, as we saw above. If a company as sophisticated as Wal-Mart can make the blunders described earlier, we can expect other big companies to make blunders that are similar or worse. Blunders can take various forms: getting caught doing something illegal, disseminating advertising or public relations material that has unintended negative consequences, framing the issue in a way that fails to resonate with the public, and taking actions that are perceived as heavy-handed or bullying, to name a few. Of course, local opponents can capitalize on corporate blunders only if they become aware of them. Second, the tactics of big companies are very predictable, an inevitable manifestation of the rationalization that characterizes the modern corporation. Predictability is a weakness because it means that opponents can anticipate a company's moves and prepare countermeasures. Wal-Mart's predictability was evident in its repeated use of the same tactics, promises, and rhetoric in town after town. Third, big companies have a narrow view of the world, which can lead to blunders, faux pas, and ineffective tactics. As with predictability, this is an inherent feature of the corporation and derives from its narrow focus on maximizing shareholder return. As an example, one of Wal-Mart's (predictable) tactics was to commission and then tout a study that invariably found that a town was "underserved" by existing retailers and thus "needed" a new superstore. It never occurred to the company that many local residents might not care about being "undeserved"; that this was not the basis on which they evaluated the desirability of additional retail development; that they preferred to be "underserved" because they did not want the traffic, noise, litter, and general blight of more chain stores; and that, in fact, being "underserved" did not detract from, but contributed to, their quality of life. While corporate cynicism and manipulation are encountered frequently, it is also possible for a corporation to believe, as Wal-Mart did apparently in some instances, that its interests coincide with those of local residents. Such a belief can lead to unsuccessful rhetoric and tactics. To anthropomorphize a little, the corporation, by its very nature, sometimes cannot see beyond its own nose. Fourth, large corporations with local establishments typically have an incomplete understanding of local politics and culture, a result of one or more of the following: the corporation is not headquartered locally; its local operations may represent a small fraction of its total business, which may be spread around the world; the managers of the local establishment hail from outside the local area; and the corporation is uninvolved in local affairs and culture, putting it at a disadvantage compared with local social movement organizations. This can be seen, for example, in Eureka, where Wal-Mart either miscalculated or was unaware of several key aspects of the local scene, such as the economic and cultural importance of the waterfront, the extent of local support for independent merchants, and the antipathy toward big box stores in general and Wal-Mart in particular. A corporation can hire local representatives (e.g., local real estate agents) to help it reconnoiter local affairs, but it would still have to depend on a limited number of representatives and probably would not have the thorough understanding of local affairs that an organic local social movement organization would have. Fifth, large corporations, by virtue of their size and complexity, present many targets to their opponents. This is a weakness because it gives their opponents many opportunities to attack. Wal-Mart, like many companies, could be criticized for its labor policies, its treatment of its vendors (and *their* labor policies), its environmental record, its treatment of women, its impact on towns and cities, its use of government subsidies, and a host of other issues. Moreover, the case studies showed that the opponents were usually more successful when they attacked Wal-Mart on as many fronts as possible. Local opponents can build a case against a corporation by criticizing a wide range of past and current behavior, and if one line of attack does not succeed, they can try another.

A final corporate weakness, and one that requires more explanation, involves the disjuncture between economic and symbolic power. The idea here is that success may be more likely if anticorporate activists are able to shift the terrain of battle from the market, where economic power is usually decisive, to a field defined by media images, public opinion, and impressions, where symbolic power may be more important. This approach has been developed by Haridimos Tsoukas in a study of a dispute that pitted Greenpeace, a nonprofit environmental organization, against Shell, a major multinational oil company.[10] The dispute centered on Shell's plan to sink a defunct oil platform in the North Sea rather than tow it back to shore. Tsoukas argues that in contemporary society the "organizational environment increasingly consists of *signs*, namely mediated images, symbols and knowledge claims."[11] A consequence of this change in the organizational environment is that "the traditional competitive advantage afforded by superior size and resources does not have the same value as before."[12] "The more the contest between organizations is carried out in the symbolic field of interaction, the less important conventional business advantages, such as size, market share and financial resources, are, and the more important symbolic capital is."[13] A corporation may find that it cannot prevail unless it wins in this symbolic field, and that requires winning the hearts and minds of various parties such as the public, politicians, and regulators. Here a small organization may be on a more equal basis with a large corporation. The role of the media is crucial, because it is via the media that images and symbols are conveyed to the public and decision makers. According to Tsoukas, today corporations get drawn into debates with other organizations over issues that cannot be readily settled through normal business means and often involve competing claims of a sort that do not automatically favor the corporation. Shell, for example, had to publicly defend its claim that scuttling a defunct oil drilling platform in the North Sea was environmentally sound. Shell spent money to influence public opinion, but that did not assure it of success, as Greenpeace was able to garner significant media coverage by staging various dramatic and "newsworthy" direct actions. The problem for Shell was that its market power did not translate directly to symbolic power. Moreover, Shell's symbolic capital was suspect to begin with because of its status as a profit-oriented multinational, while Greenpeace, a well-known nonprofit organization that does not accept funding from corporations or governments, was viewed more favorably. Shell eventually capitulated and agreed to tow the platform back to shore. While Tsoukas fails to acknowledge adequately the extent to which economic resources can be used to buy symbolic capital through public relations, advertising, and lobbying, his approach offers insight into the dynamics of disputes involving corporations, including those at the local level.

This analysis can be applied to antisuperstore disputes and to community-corporate conflicts in general. In the two successes, the media publicized various blunders by Wal-Mart, casting doubt on the company's truthfulness and public mindedness, and diminishing its already weak symbolic capital. The opponents in these two cases also produced evidence of widespread opposition, which was subsequently broadcast by the media, thereby undermining Wal-Mart's claims to represent the vast majority of people and raising the question, who really represents the people? Wal-Mart used its financial resources to carry out surveys that predictably found that a majority of local residents wanted a new superstore, but such findings were subject to steep discounting because of the company's low symbolic capital. Meanwhile, local individuals and organizations with more symbolic capital produced competing surveys and advanced counterarguments. Wal-Mart also found itself drawn into debates about community welfare and local quality of life. These sorts of debates involve (relatively) subjective and intangible concerns and cannot be won easily through flexing economic muscle. Furthermore, if a company spends too much money and is too aggressive it may be seen as a bully and alienate local residents and politicians. On this terrain, where symbols and impressions are paramount, a small group of opponents may outflank a corporate adversary, especially if they have the assistance of the media.

A MODEL OF THE CONDITIONS THAT MAKE SUCCESS POSSIBLE

The comparative analysis identified the variables that explain why some antisuperstore groups succeeded and generalized those variables to other local anticorporate efforts. There remains, however, a prior question: why are such groups able to succeed *in the first place?* In the present set of cases the opponents were, after all, attempting to prevent one of the biggest and most determined companies in the world from implementing its carefully planned expansion program. Other instances of community-corporate conflict, while perhaps not involving companies as formidable as Wal-Mart, involve similarly striking mismatches of size and resources. To understand why it is possible for local opponents to succeed we must move beyond specific variables and local contingencies and consider the underlying conditions. In what follows I use the superstore controversies as a basis for constructing a model of the conditions under which it may be possible for a local group to effectively counter corporate action. This model draws on the notion of political opportunity structure, which refers to aspects of the state such as governmental structure, scope of jurisdiction, laws, and procedures.[14] The central idea is that these aspects of the state can provide opportunities (or constraints) for social movement organizations and thereby contribute to their success (or failure). Political opportunity structure, in other words, directs our attention to the political environment in which social movements operate.

Corporations prefer to act without constraint, basing investment decisions strictly on their own criteria, pursuing daily operations and expanding or contracting when and where they please, without regard to negative externalities or input from citizens, small businesses, government agencies, and other organizations. And much of the time they are able to act without constraint. Although corporate actions often have consequences for local communities, people at the local level usually do not have the opportunity or the means to offer meaningful input or otherwise influence such actions. Attempts by government at the state and federal level to influence corporate behavior typically involve regulators, legislators, and judges whose limitations are well-known: regulators may be "captured" by the companies and industries they are supposed to regulate, legislators may be seriously compromised because of their dependence on corporations and trade associations for campaign contributions, and judges may have been appointed by politicians who have close ties to industry or they may be ideologically predisposed to favor corporate interests. These parties, moreover, tend to deal exclusively with corporate representatives and are often far removed from their constituents. Furthermore, their discussions and decisions often do not fall under public scrutiny, or if they do, receive little media coverage. There are of course, exceptions to this scenario, especially in the area of environmental protection where public interest organizations such as the Sierra Club are actively involved, usually at the federal level, with legislation and regulation that affect corporate behavior. Also, some states have adopted procedures, based on the National Environmental Protection Act, that allow for public participation in decision--making processes. In general, though, those affected by corporate behavior have very little meaningful say in the matter, while the parties whose ostensible role is to promote the public good are often compromised and operate with little accountability.

One of the striking aspects of the superstore controversies is the extent to which they do not fit this pattern. Consider what happens when Wal-Mart wants to put a superstore in a small town. If the parcel of land that Wal-Mart wants is already zoned "commercial" then Wal-Mart can purchase it and must satisfy minimal planning requirements only; in planning terminology, the company can proceed to build "as of right." If a rezoning or other approval is not needed then there is usually no controversy—not because of a lack of opposition, but because opposition is rendered nearly pointless when a company can build as of right. Quite often, however, the land is not zoned "commercial," which means that before Wal-Mart can proceed it must seek a rezoning and, implicitly, approval for putting a store in the town. By local ordinance, the nearby residents must be notified of the proposed rezoning, the matter must be on the agenda at a meeting of the city council and often the planning commission as well, and the public must be given the opportunity to comment. With appropriate agitation by a local social movement organization and publicity by the local newspaper, the proposed siting can be turned into a public issue, leading to a local debate that inevitably expands from rezoning to larger questions concerning the costs and benefits to the community of allowing a multinational retail chain to come to town. As part of that debate Wal-Mart or its representatives must appear at the town hall, appeal to local officials, and face the people who will be affected by its store. Local officials themselves can be expected to be confronted with some portion of their constituents, who will express their approval or disapproval of the officials' actions at the next election. The local newspaper carries a lively exchange of views, with op-ed pieces from both Wal-Mart and its critics. After discussion and debate the issue is decided by local elected officials or the voters. Because of longstanding legal precedent supporting local control over land use, in most cases the decision makers can be assured that the courts will uphold their decision.[15]

What all this means is that Wal-Mart must engage in a public debate and, furthermore, must appeal to local decision makers and abide by their decisions. Wal-Mart, of course, can devote substantial resources to advertising and public relations and undoubtedly this has proved decisive in some cases, although excessive advertising can also alienate many people. The point is that the combination of regulation, publicity, debate and local decision making creates a situation in which it becomes possible for a small group of opponents to prevail against a much larger corporate target. This analysis can be generalized in terms of four key conditions—regulatory checkpoints, publicity, debate, and local decision making—that reflect the structure of political opportunity. It should be understood that success does not flow directly or only from the structure of political opportunity—a social movement organization has to take advantage of these opportunities to have a chance of success.

These four conditions constitute a rough logical and chronological sequence. Let's consider them in turn. A *regulatory checkpoint* exists when certain corporate actions are subject to approval by the state. A checkpoint is not a form of prescriptive regulation in that it does not specify what a corporation can or cannot do. Rather, it is a means of allowing those affected by a proposed corporate action to approve or disapprove it. It is not an outright barrier to corporate action, but a checkpoint that prevents a corporation from proceeding without any outside input or approval, and as such it is the minimum prerequisite for effective control over corporate behavior. By requiring a regulatory checkpoint the state provides an opportunity for opponents to contest corporate action.

Assuming that the proposed corporate action is subject to a regulatory checkpoint, it must then be publicized. *Publicity* turns the proposed action, which may have proceeded thus far out of the glare of the public spotlight, into a public issue; it also increases interest and raises awareness of what's at stake. Successful publicity is a function of both the structure of political opportunity, in the form of legal requirements for public notice, and the various actions taken by local opponents and the media to publicize the action. Effective framing by local opponents increases the likelihood that the proposed action will come to the attention of the media and resonate with the local populace.

Requiring the proposed action to be on the agenda at one or more official meetings makes possible a public *debate* in which corporate representatives and public officials have to face the local community, both in person and through the media. Public debate can be further stimulated by allowing members of the public to speak at official meetings, requiring the decision-making body to solicit and consider written comments, and requiring the formation of a citizens' advisory council. While these aspects of the state provide the opportunity for public debate, again it is up to the social movement organization (and the media) to take advantage of them. Mobilization by a social movement organization, if effective, should lead to debate in the local media and in the community at large, in addition to that which occurs in official venues. In a genuine debate decision makers and the public are exposed to a range of arguments, pro and con. In such a debate corporate officials are confronted with critiques they must answer carefully; corporate propaganda will not suffice or will be interpreted as an admission of an inability to answer the charges. Of course, this applies to the opponents as well.

Finally, decisions must be made locally and decision makers must be accountable to the public. *Local decision making* is a clear manifestation of political opportunity structure because it is the state that determines which matters are subject to *local* decision making, and how and by whom decisions are to be made. Without local decision making the three previous features will be ineffective because it is local decision making that forces all the interested parties to engage in a debate.

These four features, taken together, constitute a general model of the conditions under which the inherent advantages of corporate size and organization can be partially neutralized. To the extent that regulatory checkpoints, publicity, debate, and local decision making can be extended and strengthened, local social movement organizations may be able to successfully contest corporate action they deem harmful to their communities.

DELIBERATIVE DEMOCRACY

This model has an affinity with the project known as deliberative democracy and, insofar as they share certain key features, it provides a degree of support for the ideas and efforts that constitute deliberative democracy. At the same time, contrasting this model with deliberative democracy highlights some weaknesses of the latter and suggests how it might be improved. What I propose, then, is a short dialog between my model and deliberative democracy. But first, what is deliberative democracy?

Deliberative democracy refers to a series of developments in political theory and practice in the late twentieth and early twenty-first centuries that aim to significantly improve political decision making and democratic institutions. Deliberative democracy is both a topic in political theory and a term used to describe an array of actual reforms, experiments, and initiatives, mostly at the local level, to implement (and study) one or more aspects of deliberative democracy. Deliberative democracy is not totally new; deliberation as part of the political process goes back to the Athenians.[16] Deliberative democracy in its present form represents both a reaction against widely acknowledged shortcomings of representative democracy as currently practiced and an outgrowth of the "public participation revolution" of the 1960s and 1970s.[17] Advocates of deliberative democracy point to several fundamental limitations of representative democracy as it currently functions.[18] To begin, there is a low level of participation (e.g., voting), especially by those who are perceived to be marginalized, and an even lower level of meaningful engagement (e.g., actual involvement in decision making). There is also the failure of elected and appointed representatives to adequately represent the interests of the public, again with special reference to marginalized segments of the population. Problems of participation, engagement, and representation are related to the troubling and endemic issue of power. As Graham Smith puts it, "the democratic nature of . . . pluralism is undermined by the social and economic imbalances inherent within society. Expressions of economic power and social influence undermine, to a large extent, the assumption of political equality on which liberal representative institutions are frequently defended."[19] Another problem involves the seemingly intractable divisions and conflicts that have become such a noticeable feature of the political landscape. Current political processes are faulted for not adequately handling strongly felt divisions involving race, ethnicity, nationality, religion, gender, class, culture, values, and other sources of political cleavage. Earlier, and in some cases ongoing, attempts to improve representative democracy include Chautauquas, visioning, strategic planning, urban neighborhood councils, citizen advisory boards, study groups, and ballot initiatives and referenda.

The Deliberative Democracy Handbook identifies the following as examples of deliberative democracy: National Issues Forums, public journalism, deliberative polling, consensus conferences, citizen juries, on-line dialogues, town meetings, and deliberative city planning.[20] While these examples blur together somewhat with the precursors noted above, deliberative democracy, at least as envisioned by political theorists, has at its core several features that combine to constitute a unique approach to political participation and decision making. The heart of deliberative democracy is the emphasis on arriving at binding decisions through a deliberative process, the essence of which is "face-to-face discussion by which participants conscientiously raise and respond to competing arguments so as to arrive at considered judgements about the solutions to public problems."[21] The idea (and ideal) is to set up a situation where the better argument prevails and there is "no force except that of the better argument."[22] Decisions generated in this way are held to be "more just and rational" and more likely to be viewed as "fair and legitimate."[23] Since participants must offer arguments that resonate with others (with whom they may have serious disagreements), the implication is that the arguments offered, and the decisions based on those arguments, will tend to promote the public good to a greater extent than the usual noisy battle of competing self-interests. For deliberative democracy to function properly all participants should have an equal opportunity to present their views; at the same time, the function of deliberation is to prod participants to offer reasons "that speak to the needs of everyone affected."[24] To accomplish this, deliberative democracy requires participation by a representative cross section of the population (randomly selected if possible) who are able to engage each other on equal terms. Authentic deliberation "rules out domination via the exercise of power, manipulation, indoctrination, propaganda, deception, expressions of mere self-interest, threats . . . , and attempts to impose ideological conformity."[25] Lastly, advocates contend that deliberative democracy produces not only better decisions but also better citizens because the very process of deliberation requires active engagement and tends to increase knowledge of issues and develop political skills.

My model and deliberative democracy are similar insofar as debate is a key aspect of both. Although advocates of deliberative democracy prescribe how debate is to occur, while I simply note that it is a crucial condition to help offset corporate power, what these two approaches have in common is the view that it will lead to better decisions, where "better" means more likely to promote the good of the community. Extensive debate means that those who question or oppose corporate action have an equal opportunity to present their concerns. As a political actor the corporation typically pursues a narrow self-interested agenda, often hidden behind a flurry of public relations or cloaked in a barrage of slogans implying that what is best for the corporation is best for the community. To the extent company representatives are compelled to debate community members face-to-face in a sustained fashion they will feel pressure to back up assertions that their actions serve the common interest. If local opponents oppose a corporation on grounds of narrow self-interest, then that too should become apparent in the course of debate. We cannot assume a priori that debate will always favor local opponents, but if the logic of deliberative democracy holds, then we would expect the outcomes of such debates to tend to favor the community interest more often than corporate interest (where they diverge). An additional and not insignificant benefit of debate is that it can help citizens and their representatives to develop a clearer sense of what exactly is in the interest of the community as a whole.

The other principal similarity involves decision making. Although some of the experiments in deliberative democracy provide participants with the experience of formulating recommendations only, the ideal is for those involved in debate to be charged with arriving at decisions that are binding on all affected parties. My model emphasizes that decision making should occur at the local level, whether it involves all those who have participated in the debate or only their representatives. Models of deliberative democracy emphasize decision making that is binding on those who have deliberated. In both cases there is a close connection between decision making and the interests of those involved in the debate. This close connection is salutary for democracy, as well as for efforts to constrain corporate action at the local level, for the simple reason that it means that those with more power and resources must abide by decisions made by (and perhaps with) those with less power and fewer resources. Furthermore, it provides an impetus for all to participate in the debate and gives a seriousness to the proceedings.

Deliberative democracy, both in theory and in practice, has been conceived as a means of facilitating political interaction among diverse individuals in a way that avoids allowing those with more power take advantage of those with less. This conception is quite reasonable and attractive, but what is missing is a recognition that in the contemporary world, power emanates from organizations as well as from individuals. Indeed, individuals generally only wield substantial power to the extent they are associated with organizations (e.g., heads of state, military commanders, and corporate executives). Setting aside the state, power in most developed countries is incarnated in one particular organizational form more than any other: the corporation. Advocates of deliberative democracy are concerned with improving citizen-citizen and citizen-state relations. Given the power of modern corporations and their deep involvement in almost every realm of life, we must also consider how to improve citizen-corporate and community-corporate relations. While deliberative democracy can, in theory, be implemented at various levels of government, it has most often been tried at the local level, which is to be expected given its emphasis on face-to-face encounters. The emphasis on the local level also reflects the decentralization and devolution of political power authority that has occurred in many Western countries in recent decades. While decentralization and devolution may promise to offer more demo-cratic decision making, and are broadly consonant with the goals of deliberative democracy, there is a countertrend in the form of large corporations that represent a concentration of economic power and to some extent political power as well. And large corporations, as I have noted earlier, can have considerable impact on the welfare of local communities. For all these reasons, we need to consider how to deal with corporations as political actors at the local level.

Deliberative democracy is intended to produce better decisions, but decisions can be made only on matters that are legally subject to decision making. The virtues of deliberative democracy are moot if an important action can be taken without a debate involving all affected parties. In the present context our concern is with the tendency of a corporation to unilaterally take action that may significantly affect a community, perhaps adversely. That corporations should operate this way is understandable, given the fundamental nature of the corporation, but it can be problematic all the same. My model proposes increased use of regulatory checkpoints as a means of avoiding this problem. A regulatory checkpoint prevents a corporation from acting unilaterally and constitutes the minimum condition for a debate. The deliberative democracy model, by contrast, *starts* with debate—how the various parties get there is a question that has not received much attention. But this question must be taken seriously when one of the parties involved is a large corporation that has no inclination to engage in the sort of face-to-face discussions in which "participants conscientiously raise and respond to competing arguments so as to arrive at considered judgements about the solutions to public problems."[26] I argue, then, that it may be necessary to have a regulatory checkpoint in place so that a deliberative decision-making process *can* be used. Deliberative democracy can, of course, be used to establish appropriate regulatory checkpoints as well as to make decisions on particular matters that become the subject of debate because of a regulatory checkpoint.

A related limitation of deliberative democracy is that it neglects publicity. Publicity serves a crucial function by bringing issues to the attention of the public and local officials and raises awareness about known issues. Furthermore, publicity may be necessary to construct a certain situation or intended action *as an issue*. That a proposed corporate action is problematic in regard to its effect on community welfare may not be readily apparent to many people. As noted above, the central feature and primary focus of deliberative democracy is debate, but before a debate can take place there must be a recognition that something is an issue and that it deserves attention from the community. Topics for deliberation don't simply appear; they are preceded by some amount of publicity.

The emphasis in my model on debate and local decision making parallels a similar emphasis in deliberative democracy, while my discussion of regulatory checkpoints and publicity lacks a counterpart in deliberative democracy. In spite of the differences the overall thrust of my model and deliberative democracy is similar and the four conditions of my model may be seen as an attempt to accomplish more or less the same goal as deliberative democracy, which is to improve civic welfare through a decision-making process based on fair and reasoned debate among all interested parties. To conclude, it is democracy that holds the most promise to maximize community well-being, whether in regard to community-corporate conflicts or disputes among community members. To paraphrase Danton, democracy, more democracy, and even more democracy!

NOTES

1. This section and the following section are based on Halebsky, "Explaining the Outcomes," which has a more technical analysis of this data.
2. I consider the matter to have been effectively submitted to the voters in Ashland because it was a key issue in the city council election.
3. Halebsky, "Explaining the Outcomes," 455.
4. Halebsky, "Explaining the Outcomes," 454.
5. Letter to director of Emmet County Office of Planning and Zoning, 14 October 1994.
6. Letter to the editor, *The Daily Press* (WI), 28 April 1990.
7. This section is taken directly from Halebsky, "Explaining the Outcomes," 455.
8. Tom Ross and Ken Kaplan, "Wal-Mart is OK, but the Valley Avenue site is inappropriate," *Daily News* (WI), 24 April 1995 (emphasis added).
9. This section is based on Halebsky, "Explaining the Outcomes."
10. Tsoukas, "David and Goliath."
11. Tsoukas, "David and Goliath," 500.
12. Tsoukas, "David and Goliath," 500.
13. Tsoukas, "David and Goliath," 507.
14. This approach was first elaborated by Eisenger, "Conditions of Protest." See Gamson and Meyer, "Framing Political Opportunity"; and Kriesi, "Political Context" for recent discussions.

15. Briffault, "Our Localism."
16. Fishkin, "Deliberative Democracy."
17. Plein, Green, and Williams, "Organic Planning."
18. See Barber, *Strong Democracy*, for an important early contribution.
19. Smith, *Deliberative Democracy*, 54–55.
20. Gastil and Levine, *Deliberative Democracy Handbook*. Deliberative Polling® is a registered trademark of James S. Fishkin. Citizens Jury® is a registered trademark of the Jefferson Center.
21. Fishkin, "Deliberative Democracy," 223.
22. Habermas, quoted in Cohen, "Deliberation, " 22.
23. Button and Ryfe, "What Can We Learn," 27.
24. Mutz, *Hearing the Other Side*, 4.
25. Dryzek, *Deliberative Democracy*, 2.
26. Fishkin, "Deliberative Democracy," 223.

8

The Local State, Corporate Retailing, McDonaldization, and Local Anticorporate Activism

In addition to what they reveal about the outcomes of local anticorporate social movements, these controversies can be mined for other insights. I begin this chapter by discussing in greater depth the role of the local state in community-corporate conflicts. I then explain why corporate retailing—above and beyond concerns specific to Wal-Mart and superstores—is deeply problematic. This leads to a discussion of McDonaldization and the prospects for resistance. I conclude with a consideration of the significance and effectiveness of local anticorporate activism.

THE CONTINUING IMPORTANCE OF THE LOCAL STATE

I originally conceived of these cases as David-and-Goliath confrontations pitting a big corporation against small groups of local activists. This characterization, while not wrong, proved incomplete because it leaves out a crucial actor: the local state. It has become commonplace to note the increasingly weak control exerted by nation states over multinational corporations, leading to the inference that the *local* state must be truly ineffectual when confronted with such organizations. I do not dispute that satisfactory control over the modern corporation must come from the nation state, or perhaps ultimately from transnational organizations, because the leading corporations are so large and powerful that only another organization of similar or greater reach and power can muster the resources to control them. Fundamental issues such as the legal status of the corporation (e.g., its ability to exist as a legal entity separate from its owners), antitrust, the taxation of corporate income, and the terms on which it deals with employees and unions cannot be dealt with by the local state. However, the local state, in the form of cities, towns, and other municipalities, can still play an important role in community-corporate conflicts and exert at least some influence over corporate actions at the local level. In the previous chapter I used the concept of political opportunity structure to explain how the state may create opportunities (or constraints) for social movements. Here I extend that argument to the relationship of the local state to corporate actions and community-corporate conflicts. Stated generally, the local state can affect corporate behavior directly by *regulating* at least some of what corporations can and cannot do, and indirectly by *structuring* the conflicts that arise between corporations and other parties. While I draw on the superstore controversies for examples, the following points are meant to be applicable to other sorts of corporations and other sorts of community-corporate conflicts too.

Under the doctrine of "police power," cities and towns in the United States are entitled to implement and enforce laws to "promote order and to protect the public safety, health, morals, and general welfare within constitutional limits."[1] This doctrine provides cities and towns with the authority to regulate at least some of what occurs within their borders and thus can be used to influence corporation behavior. Police power has been used as "the basis for enacting a variety of substantive laws in such areas as . . . fire and building codes, gambling, discrimination, parking, crime, licensing of professionals, liquor, motor vehicles, bicycles, nuisances, schooling, and sanitation."[2]

The regulation of land use is one of the most important manifestations of police power. Cities and towns in the United States down to the level of tiny municipalities exercise considerable authority over land use, as prescribed by longstanding tradition and legal precedent.[3] While the extent of local control over land use is greater in the United States than in many other countries, it is to be expected that the state would have this authority as control over what occurs within its territory is an essential part of the very notion of the state.[4] In spite of globalization a corporation still must be physically sited in *some place* and thus is subject to rules regarding land use. Retailers, by definition, provide goods and services directly to consumers, which means that they must operate establishments at many locations. Such businesses do not care about any (particular) place, but have to put their establishments in many places because that is where their customers are, thus making them subject to regulation by the local state. By exercising power over land use local municipalities are able to affect what type of businesses may operate within their boundaries. They may effectively ban certain types of businesses by deliberately failing to include within their borders any land with the necessary zoning; they may also refuse to rezone land to accommodate certain types of businesses, as long as they do not discriminate against specific companies or act arbitrarily. They may also limit the size of certain types of businesses (again, as long as they do not discriminate or act arbitrarily), which can effectively exclude those businesses. While disputes over land use are a common, even banal, feature of local politics, we should not overlook the importance of the decisions made here. The importance of local control over land use can be seen clearly in the superstore disputes where much of the controversy involved efforts by Wal-Mart to have land rezoned. The very fact that Wal-Mart *had* to do this, as opposed to simply building what and where it pleased, is evidence of the authority and power of the local state. While the superstore opponents encountered many difficulties when they challenged Wal-Mart, the weakness of the local state in regard to land use regulation was not one of them. In fact, many of the municipalities seemed to have more power than they were aware of or willing to use.

The local state affects the nature and outcome of community-corporate conflicts by structuring almost everything about them, including the procedures to be followed, the designation of decision makers, the criteria by which decisions are (ostensibly) made, how the media and other parties are to be notified, and the extent of public input. The form taken by the superstore controversies—the fact that most of them were fought out formally as land use disputes and not, say, as disputes over economic impact—illustrates how the local state structures and thereby influences disputes that arise between community groups and corporations. The superstore disputes, of course, were about much more than land use and the opponents brought up other issues and concerns, but the formal disputes revolved around land use (i.e., zoning) because Wal-Mart had to comply with certain land use ordinances and not, for example, with ordinances about the effects of superstores on the local economy. It probably would have been to the advantage of the opponents if local ordinances had required evidence about the impact on downtown and small merchants to be considered too.[5] Thus, the local state can structure conflicts in a way that is more, or less, conducive to corporate interests.

An important aspect of this structuring is the state's role as the venue for disputes that occur within its borders and as the mediator of those disputes. This can be seen clearly in the superstore controversies: the opponents protested about Wal-Mart, but did so *to* the city council. Of course, they also appealed to Wal-Mart, but the outcome in most cases depended very little on their ability to convince the company of anything or make it do anything; in fact, the opponents could not do much to Wal-Mart directly. Most often it was the city council or the voters themselves who eventually decided what Wal-Mart could or could not do. Thus, while Wal-Mart was the target, the dispute was mediated by the state. This example involves the way the local state mediates land use disputes; other types of disputes may be mediated differently. In general, however, since the state is the mediator, the contending parties have to play by its rules, and those rules may be more, or less, conducive to corporate interests.

The implication of these observations is that the local state can exercise some power over corporations that wish to operate within its jurisdiction and has the potential to play a nontrivial role in community-corporate conflicts. But the fact that the local state has this potential certainly does not mean that the outcomes of such disputes can be expected to favor those who represent, or claim to represent, the interests of the community. The limitations of the local state are well known and include the following: it may be in thrall to the local growth machine, which often favors corporations over residents; it is highly susceptible to corporate promises of jobs; it has a limited ability to impose income taxes and thus is highly susceptible to corporate promises of increased tax revenue through sales or property tax; it does not have absolute and final authority over legal matters, which means that dissatisfied corporations can seek to have their cases adjudicated at higher levels; and it cannot match the resources of large corporations.[6] Furthermore, corporations are able to pit towns and cities against each other in their (the corporations') quest to get the best deal on the siting of a new factory, office building, corporate headquarters, or retail establishment. In spite of these limitations, the involvement of the local state can be advantageous because it has the potential to operate in a fashion that reflects bona fide citizen involvement. Simply put, the state has the potential to be democratic, even if that democracy is highly imperfect. Democratic decision making, to the extent that it functions properly, tends to eventually bring state policy more or less in line with the views of the voters.[7] What this means is that the regulations that affect corporations and the structuring of community-corporate conflicts are subject to input from the community. The corporation, by contrast, is profoundly undemocratic and does not have to consider the concerns of its critics, no matter how numerous those critics may be or how cogent their critiques.

WHY CORPORATE RETAILING IS PROBLEMATIC

Suppose Wal-Mart and other superstore retailers were to put their stores downtown and construct smaller and more attractive buildings. Also, suppose they paid better wages and offered decent benefits. And suppose further that we were not concerned about the effect of such establishments on local merchants, employment, and tax revenue. We would be satisfied then? These issues, after all, constitute the main objections raised during local controversies and now debated nationally. But there are other issues, less visible but equally important, that involve corporate retailing in general and do not pertain strictly to superstores. Corporate retailing, as practiced in the twenty-first century, is inherently problematic and poses problems for communities as well as for political and social life in general. I address these problems under the headings of organizational size, control, homogenization, fakery, and hypertrophy of consumption. While public awareness of superstores has increased dramatically in recent years, these problems remain relatively unexplored and have been completely ignored by the defenders of Wal-Mart and other corporate retailers.

Organizational Size

Even if it were made to behave better and even if its stores were smaller, the fact remains that Wal-Mart is a very large corporation, and while it is by far the largest retailer, the other major chains are quite big too. The principal advantage that a corporate retailer can offer a community is to pass on the lower prices that it can achieve through economies of scale and scope.[8] But there are serious offsetting disadvantages. While corporate retailers typically show little interest in community affairs, with the exception of issues that concern them directly, they have the potential to exert considerable influence over local politics as a result of their extensive resources, especially their ability to spend money to support candidates and promote particular issues. The democratic ideal of one person/one vote is undermined when one or more local political actors is a corporation with resources that dwarf those of other actors. A corporation, moreover, is not simply an ordinary citizen writ large or an oversized version of a small business. It is qualitatively different and has interests that differ from those of a real person or a small business. As a legal entity, it exists to maximize return for its shareholders, and while the interests of a corporation are not necessarily opposed to those of the local populace, it does not have an inherent interest in local welfare as local citizens and businesses do. This is especially the case with companies that are headquartered in another city or another state, as is typically the case with corporate retailers. Bigness might not be such a problem if a corporation were structured so that those affected by it had effective control over it. This, at least in the abstract, is how we conceive of state and federal government—they are big but subject to control by means of direct and representative democracy. The corporation, however, is a profoundly undemocratic organization. It is undemocratic for shareholders, who vote for the board of directors and other matters on the basis of one share/one vote, not one shareholder/one vote, thereby giving priority to those who own more shares. It is undemocratic for employees, who are subject to a hierarchy of managers and supervisors, none of whom are selected by the employees. All important decisions concerning work—pay, hours, job assignments, hiring, etc.—are made undemocratically (this is tempered somewhat if a workplace is unionized). Thus, to the extent that retailing is taken over by corporate retailers, large undemocratic organizations will hold sway over an increasing share of the workforce.

Size affects consumers too. Just as the typical employee has little influence over his or her employer, the typical consumer has little influence over a huge retailer. This is not just a matter of store size, because even if a particular superstore were smaller it would still be part of a chain. Consider the difference in power between big chains and individual shoppers. A small number of corporate retailers accounts for the bulk of most markets, which means that shoppers have little choice but to buy what they offer. Any threat by a shopper to discontinue patronizing a chain would be so insignificant as to be almost comical, and while it is possible for shoppers to act together and stage a boycott, in reality this occurs infrequently and is rarely successful. The practical difficulties of organizing and sustaining a consumer boycott involving a large number of consumers have usually proven insurmountable. A chain, because it is a corporation, is *already organized* and can act effectively to overcome an attempted boycott. Its financial resources and numerous establishments allow it to defy concerted action at any particular establishment or in any particular community, even over a long time. Moreover, corporate retailers, because they are chains, do not have to be responsive to the wishes of any particular community.

Also, as big companies replace small businesses, more and more Americans cease to be masters of their fate. Almost half (49 percent) of all Americans now work for firms (mostly corporations) with at least five hundred employees; nearly two-thirds (64 percent) work for firms with at least 100 employees.[9] In retailing 57 percent of all employees work for the one-third of one percent of retailing firms with at least 500 employees.[10] Painful as it is to contemplate, the reality is that most of us have been reduced to the status of mere employees. Instead of identifying ourselves as the proprietor of X, or a partner in Y, or in terms of our occupation or profession, we just say we work for company A, B or C; "I am" has been replaced by "I work for." Also, as independent operators are replaced by large corporations, decisions about the production and distribution of goods and services are made by fewer and fewer persons, with the result that our role in the economy and in society in general has been reduced more and more to that of passive consumers who buy the goods and services that large companies have decided to produce and market to us. Whether as community members, consumers, or workers, our lives are increasingly dominated by large undemocratic corporations, and corporate retailing contributes to this trend.

Control

Like all large corporations, corporate retailers seek to control as much as possible: employees, customers, suppliers, public opinion, and the political environment. This emphasis on control is a direct manifestation of the bureaucratization that is the foundation of modern large-scale business. It is also a function of size because, as Alfred D. Chandler, Jr. explains, with increasing size companies have greater investment at stake and thus must concentrate on ensuring a steady source of supplies and raw materials, a steady demand for products and services, and a stable legal and political environment.[11] Examples of control abound at Wal-Mart, although, again, it is just the exemplar and not the only corporate retailer that operates this way. Wal-Mart controls its employees by, for example, locking graveyard-shift workers in stores overnight, specifying when and how employees are to talk to customers, and using intimidation to dissuade them from exercising their right to unionize.[12] By putting other merchants out of business, Wal-Mart limits and thereby controls consumers' choice of merchants and consequently their choice of goods and services. The company tries to control the demand for its products through heavy advertising, which influences the buying habits of consumers. Wal-Mart controls its suppliers by requiring them to meet stringent demands for design and delivery. Suppliers are also pressured to sell to the company at prices that are dangerously low (although they may make a substantial profit if their product sells well). The desire for control, and the advantages it offers, is what motivates Wal-Mart to try to become a monopoly vis-à-vis consumers and a monopsony vis-à-vis suppliers. Wal-Mart seeks to control public opinion directly through its use of public relations and indirectly through its funding of think tanks. Finally, the company attempts to control, or at least influence, the political environment by making substantial contributions to selected politicians.[13]

It may be argued that control is a normal part of any business, but the control exerted by corporate retailers vastly exceeds that exerted by small merchants. While some small merchants may try to exert control, they lack the technology, expertise, experience, and financial resources to achieve the level of control characteristic of corporate retailers. They may also lack the incentive. Big retailers are subject to the logic of the stock market, which dictates that they do everything possible to increase profits and maximize share price. Small merchants, by contrast, may have several goals, only one of which is to maximize profit. They may also be concerned with maintaining a certain level of service, continuing to offer a certain selection and quality of goods, and having a beneficial effect on the community of which they are a part.

Homogenization

The problems of size and control lead to the problem of homogenization. This is seen most readily in regard to store appearance, as discussed in chapter 3. Not only do the stores in a chain look alike, but the chains themselves look alike: Wal-Mart looks like Kmart, which looks like Target, etc. As chain retailers take over more and more of local shopping, cities and towns come to resemble each other. "A few decades ago, it was still possible to leave home and go somewhere else: the architecture was different, the landscape was different, the language, lifestyle, dress, and values were different. . . . But with economic globalization, diversity is fast disappearing."[14] Corporate retailing contributes to the problem of place by destroying the uniqueness of particular places—it has become increasingly difficult to identify with particular places because so many places now look like everyplace else. Peter Calthorpe refers to this problem when he writes of "a growing sense of frustration and placelessness in our suburban landscape; a homogeneous quality which overlays the unique nature of each place with chain-store architecture, scaleless office parks, and monotonous subdivisions."[15] There is extensive homogenization within chain stores as well. We encounter the same layout, the same procedures, the same products, and even the same "conversations" as workers are forced to utter the same expressions to customers. Furthermore, as noted earlier, when a few chains replace many independent merchants there is a decline in the diversity of stores and in the overall choice of products, a decline that does not reflect local preferences but is essentially imposed by a nonlocal corporation.

Fakery

Another problem with corporate retailing is fakery. I use this term broadly to include misleading statements, appearances that are contradicted by reality, and anything that is inauthentic, including what social theorists refer to as a simulation or a simulacrum. Among forms of corporate retailing, malls have received the most criticism for their inauthenticity.[16] A mall replaces Main Street with a fake version in which private security guards keep out undesirables, free speech is not allowed, and everything shuts down at night. Businesses normally found downtown such as barbershops, hardware stores, locksmiths, bars, liquor stores, laundry mats, art galleries, and pharmacies are typically missing. While a mall is ostensibly open to the public, in reality it is a tightly controlled piece of private property, owned by a corporation and focused on maximizing sales. Superstores, because they are so large and sell so many different goods and services, are subject to many of these same criticisms.

Fakery at Wal-Mart takes various forms. There is the image that it promotes, an image of an unpretentious retailer that still embodies the spirit of its founder, Sam Walton, portrayed as a plainspoken rural Southerner who kept costs down just so he could pass on savings to other ordinary Americans. Given Wal-Mart's aggressive business practices and its status as one of the world's leading multinationals, this image strikes many as fake. The contrast between the wealth of the Walton family and the low wages paid to Wal-Mart workers reinforces this sense of fakery. Another example is the Buy America campaign in which Wal-Mart claimed that it would buy American-made products, even as it rapidly expanded its use of overseas suppliers.[17] Also, there is Wal-Mart's "community development"/Main Street program, which gives small amounts of money to local communities. Given the hundreds of downtowns and Main Streets that have been seriously damaged by Wal-Mart superstores, the company's claim to be interested in Main Street seems inauthentic. Another instance of fakery is Wal-Mart's claim that it gives generously to charitable organizations and needy individuals. This claim, too, is deceptive because much of the giving for which Wal-Mart takes credit actually comes from its employees and customers. Furthermore, the amount given is low, relative to the company's size.[18]

While small merchants also engage in fakery, it is more common among corporate retailers. This is because corporate retailers must *pretend* to be interested in the community, must *pretend* to be public places, and must *pretend* to care about their employees and customers. Their use of fakery also relates to the rationalization that is an inevitable feature of corporate retailing. The reality of highly rationalized operations is not very pretty and must be covered with a simulation of something nicer and more attractive; hence fakery. Instead of seeing the obsession with control that typifies Wal-Mart and other similar retailers, we see images of happy employees and a caring company. Ritzer argues that the unpleasant reality of rationalization always reappears because the simulation itself is rationalized, leading to a cycle in which new simulations must be (re)created continually in the attempt to reenchant a "disenchanted world."[19]

Hypertrophy of Consumption

One purpose of all this fakery is to get us to buy, which leads to the final problem, hypertrophy of consumption, by which I mean excessive consumption and excessive attempts to induce consumption. While a thorough exposition of the various problems associated with the hypertrophy of consumption is beyond the scope of this book, several can be noted quickly.[20] First, high levels of consumption damage the environment by using up resources and producing goods that ultimately end up as garbage. Second, status-oriented consumption, which accounts for much of our buying, is inherently unsatisfying because others soon have what we have (or better), thus canceling any gain in status we may have achieved. Third, excessive consumption is often associated with excessive use of credit, which involves a well-known set of problems. Fourth, money spent on private consumption (all the goods we buy for ourselves) crowds out public consumption (goods, financed through taxes, that are available to all such as public libraries, public parks, and public transportation). Lastly, more consumption requires more income, which is typically earned by working more hours, which means less time devoted to developing and maintaining relationships with friends and family, the real source of happiness for most people.[21]

The argument here is not that consumption is inherently bad, but that it has expanded to such an extent that it negatively affects individuals and communities. Corporate retailing contributes to excessive consumption through advertising and aggressive retail development. Advertising promotes what Leslie Sklair calls the "culture-ideology of consumerism," the "set of beliefs and practices that persuades people that consumption far beyond the satisfaction of physical needs is . . . at the center of meaningful existence."[22] Corporate retailers, along with the media, the manufacturers, and the advertisers are actively engaged in promoting this ideology. While various manufacturers such as Nike, Ford, and Procter & Gamble may come to mind first when we think of advertising, we should not forget that consumerism enriches retailers as well as manufacturers. Of course, small independent retailers benefit from consumerism too, but they simply do not have the resources of corporate retailers and cannot mount the massive advertising and marketing campaigns typical of the latter.

Hypertrophy of consumption occurs when corporate retailers aggressively expand into previously noncommercialized spaces such as airports, schools, museums, and parks. As larger and larger parts of our towns and cities are occupied by retail development it has become increasingly difficult to avoid such establishments. Aggressive retail development, together with the problems of placement, size, and design noted in chapter 3, has transformed large areas into unattractive commercial zones that degrade nearby spaces, both public and private. While some amount of retail development is vital for a city, in many places it has expanded well beyond the optimal level.

Corporate retailing, then, can be criticized for contributing to consumerism and overwhelming towns and cities with retail development. Of all the critiques, this has received the least attention but may be the most important. Wal-Mart's ultimate justification for its practices is that it has the goods and sells them cheaply. But what if people do not need or want those goods, or do not need or want them in large quantity, or do not need or want them frequently? What if people decide that having easy access to a lot of goods, even inexpensive goods, is simply not that important? What if people just do not need or want another chain store?

RESISTING MCDONALDIZATION

An important part of the contemporary corporate model involves the phenomenon known as McDonaldization. As elaborated by George Ritzer, McDonaldization is an updating of Max Weber's emphasis on rationalization as the master dynamic in modern society.[23] Rationalization refers to the various processes by which more and more aspects of life become subject to measurement, control, rules, and procedures. Rationalization, as it appeared to Weber in the early twentieth century, found its ideal expression in bureaucratic organizations, which came to dominate other forms of organization because they embodied the most efficient approach to large-scale administration. He argued that relentless rationalization would lead to a society in which people become trapped in an "iron cage" of rules and procedures, a paradoxical outcome in which rationality is transformed into irrationality.[24] While Weber emphasized bureaucracy, Ritzer argues that the most important and powerful form of rationalization is now McDonaldization, the process whereby the principles used to organize McDonald's restaurants—efficiency, calculability, predictability, and control—are applied to more and more areas of life.[25] While Ritzer chose McDonald's as the prototype, the general process can be seen in dozens of other organizations. Although rationalization has been part of the production process for over a century, Ritzer's concept of McDonaldization extends it to the realm of consumption. The mania for efficiency and control that characterizes the assembly line now appears increasingly in other areas of life, affecting more and more people as both workers and consumers. Chains are perhaps the preeminent sites of McDonaldization, as illustrated by such diverse examples as oil changes (Jiffy Lube instead of an independent mechanic), lodging (Holiday Inn instead of a family-owned motel), tax preparation (H & R Block instead of a self-employed accountant), weight loss (NutriSystem instead of a private dietician), and, of course, restaurants (McDonalds/Burger King/Taco Bell/etc., instead of an independent restaurant). Like Weberian bureaucracy, McDonaldization has its advantages and disadvantages. The principal advantage for employers is that the principles of McDonaldization generally promote increased profitability. It is probably employees who find McDonaldization the least advantageous, as work in a McDonaldized environment often becomes degraded as a result of the relentless attempts by management to control them.[26] The effects are mixed for consumers. On one hand, the predictability, convenience, and low costs associated with McDonaldized establishments have made them popular with many consumers; on the other hand, McDonaldized establishments tend to be homogeneous, artificial, and impersonal. Furthermore, the convenience and low costs may be illusory, as I noted in chapter 3 in regard to Wal-Mart and as Ritzer notes in regard to other McDonaldized businesses.[27] McDonaldization, then, may be seen either as providing a predictable and pleasant means of consumption or as creating its own irrationality of rationality, to the detriment of workers, consumers, and communities.

I agree with Ritzer that McDonaldization is the most important form of rationalization in contemporary society, and I would add that the dominant force behind this phenomenon is the modern corporation. McDonaldization began in the corporate sector and has been developed most vigorously there. Today other major organizations such as universities, nonprofit organizations, and even churches have become McDonaldized, but they have followed, not led, the corporation.

Wal-Mart is a nearly perfect example of McDonaldized retailing, in regard to both its operations and the reactions it elicits from workers and the public. From the appearance of its stores, which are nearly identical, to purchasing, distribution, and sales, all aspects of Wal-Mart's operations are highly rationalized.[28] It has invested heavily in computers and telecommunications to increase efficiency, calculability, and control.[29] McDonaldized retailing has the same two-sided quality as McDonaldization in general. Many consumers find comfort in Wal-Mart's predictability, prefer having so many goods available under one roof, like the low prices, and find no fault with having local retailing dominated by a single chain store. Others feel that a Wal-Mart store degrades community appearance, undermines local identity, and replaces unique independent merchants with a faceless chain. Thus, local opposition to the siting of a Wal-Mart superstore can be seen, at least in part, as a reaction against McDonaldization and one purpose of my research was to explore what happens when people resist McDonaldization.

Just as Weber considered the spread of rationalization inevitable, Ritzer regards the spread of McDonaldization as "inexorable" and is pessimistic about the possibility of successful resistance:

> Time has been kind to the Weberian thesis, if not to the social world. Rationalization has progressed dramatically in the century or so since Weber developed his ideas. The social world does seem to be more of an iron cage and, as a result, there does seem to be less possibility of escape. And, it does appear less likely that any counter-revolution can upset the march toward increasing rationalization. . . .
>
> [The McDonaldization] thesis accepts the basic premises of rationalization as well as Weber's basic theses about the inexorable character of the process.[30]

Using the superstore controversies as evidence, I offer the following propositions about the prospects and problems associated with trying to challenge McDonaldization. First, the occurrence of numerous, organized, antisuperstore protests around the country indicates that some people will make an effort to resist McDonaldization. In the case of Wal-Mart, they acknowledge that it has low prices, offers a wide selection of goods, and provides easy parking, but oppose it all the same. The large number of protests suggests that awareness of, and dissatisfaction with, the negative effects of McDonaldization may be increasing. If the protestors represent a small fraction of the total number of persons with similar sentiments, then we can infer that the dominance of McDonaldized retailing is not matched by its acceptance in the hearts and minds of the consuming public.

Second, and this is to some extent the flip side of the previous point, the two-sided nature of McDonaldization means that a McDonaldized business may have local supporters as well as local opponents, and some of those supporters may even organize to promote a particular establishment, thus setting up a conflict *within* the community in addition to that between the opponents and the corporation. In superstore disputes this typically takes the form of conflicts between the opponents and the group I call the shoppers. Trying to resist McDonaldization can be doubly difficult if it means opposing other community members as well as a large corporation.

The third point can be introduced via an important question: Is the spread of McDonaldization explained by the inherent appeal of McDonald's and other similar businesses, or by the fact that such corporations have aggressively expanded market share at the expense of other, less rationalized businesses? In other words, is it driven by consumer preference or by corporations? While a comprehensive explanation would obviously incorporate aspects of both views, what I want to do here is cast some doubt on the former and argue for the latter. For advocates of the former, the (financial) success of McDonaldization is taken, ipso facto, as incontrovertible evidence of consumer preference. If pressed, they might argue that McDonald's has discovered a way of doing business that connects so directly with human nature or modern life, or both, that McDonaldization and its expansion must be acknowledged as an inevitable phase in social evolution, at least in the rich countries.[31] Now, it is undeniable that many people patronize McDonaldized businesses, *when they become available*, but does that prove that people have a deep-seated preference for them? The Wal-Mart controversies revealed a minority of people who wanted a Wal-Mart badly enough to organize to promote it, but there was little evidence that local people or local officials actively sought to bring Wal-Mart to town. Some officials may look favorably upon a new Wal-Mart superstore as a source of tax revenue, but that is not the same as wanting a Wal-Mart qua Wal-Mart. Moreover, there is no evidence that people leave small towns because of a lack of McDonaldized businesses; indeed, the presence of non-McDonaldized businesses is often a draw of small towns. Also, people in small towns (and elsewhere) managed quite well before McDonaldization. If the case for widespread consumer preference for McDonaldization is overstated, there is little dispute regarding the role of the corporation in aggressively adopting McDonaldization, placing McDonaldized establishments throughout the United States and around the world, and contributing to—if not creating—consumer preference through extensive advertising and public relations. In this view, McDonaldization does not naturally flow from, or respond to, consumer preferences, but results from deliberate corporate action. What this means in the present context is that resisting McDonaldization entails opposing actual corporations as well as confronting the public's "preference" for McDonaldization.

Fourth, opposition can stimulate debate over whether McDonaldized businesses really serve the interests of the community. Debate is useful because it exposes more people to the issue of McDonaldization, introduces them to views they might not otherwise have been aware of, and encourages them to resist McDonaldization. At the very least it offers an alternative to the ubiquitous advertising that underpins McDonaldization. In the superstore controversies the opponents certainly did not convince everybody, but they increased awareness of the undesirable effects of McDonaldized retailing. Perhaps the best example of this sort of consciousness-raising is the so-called McLibel trial in England in which two critics of McDonald's took advantage of the company's decision to put them on trial for libel to publicly criticize its practices.[32] The trial lasted five years and generated enormous bad publicity for McDonald's. The arguments made by those trying to resist McDonaldization, however, should probably not be made using the terminology of McDonaldization. Very few people other than sociologists think in those terms, even if that is what they are reacting to. At some point the concept may become familiar enough that it can be discussed explicitly, but in the meantime, as the superstore controversies suggest, McDonaldized businesses can be opposed more effectively by talking about economic consequences, land use problems, quality of life, wages and benefits, loss of small merchants, and other issues with which people are more familiar.

Fifth, some small degree of success is possible, but trying to change the actual business practices that constitute McDonaldization and trying to stave off McDonaldized businesses over the long term are difficult. The difficulty with changing the practices that constitute McDonaldization is that they fall preponderantly under what is known as management prerogative, which means that they are not subject to oversight or regulation. Illegal practices, of course, are subject to sanction, but it seems doubtful that more than a few McDonaldized practices could be declared illegal. Alternatively, a community might try to bar specific companies (e.g., McDonald's) or certain types of businesses (e.g., "formula" restaurants). The former approach is untenable because it is illegal to discriminate against specific companies; there has been some success with the latter but it remains limited because restrictions that pertain to certain types of businesses may be construed as targeting specific companies. In the eyes of the law all retailers—Wal-Mart and a corner grocery—are the same. Resistance, therefore, may have to be indirect, as in the present cases where the disputes were fought out over land use even though the real issue was, at least in part, the McDonaldization of local retailing. Another problem is that McDonaldized companies, even if rejected once or twice, generally keep trying to enter a community, as we saw in Ottawa and West Bend. This probably has more to do with the profit-seeking nature of corporations than with McDonaldization per se, but it is an important reason for its spread. McDonaldized retailers are always searching for new locations and thus, as a practical matter, opponents must remain vigilant unless they can implement local ordinances that will permanently protect them from such businesses.

The evidence from the superstore controversies indicates some of the difficulties involved in contesting McDonaldization, but also suggests an increasing awareness of the phenomenon and possibly an increasing willingness to resist. McDonaldization is popular, but that should not cause us to minimize the role of the corporations that aggressively site McDonaldized establishments in as many locales as possible without regard to the desires of the local populace.

WHITHER LOCAL ANTICORPORATE ACTIVISM?

Community organizing, understood as political activism organized at the community level and focused on local issues, has proliferated since the 1960s and 1970s.[33] Examples include efforts to control development; increase local control over schools, police, and other local institutions; prevent gentrification; organize ethnic neighborhoods; and obtain better social services.[34] While community organizing is generally considered desirable because it means that citizens are getting involved in political affairs, critical observers have voiced two key concerns: Does this type of activism truly serve the community interest or does it amount to little more than the defense of insular "enclave" interests? And can it truly challenge the status quo or is it too narrow, too ad hoc, and too underfunded?

The first concern has been elaborated by Sidney Plotkin, who argues that much community organizing is often only neighborhood organizing, typically undertaken by reactionary homeowners with an "enclave consciousness" who seek only to protect their narrow interests, often centered on maintaining property value.[35] Enclave politics, for Plotkin, is often about keeping other people and other development out; it is a politics of exclusion, to the detriment of the community as a whole. Seen from this perspective, neighborhood organizing has much in common with NIMBYism, the phenomenon whereby residents oppose socially useful or necessary projects (e.g., low-cost housing or waste incinerators) in their neighborhood but don't object to such projects if they are built elsewhere.

Carl Boggs has written about the second concern, which he calls "localism."[36] He notes that the plethora of community-based groups has "worked to defend the integrity of neighborhoods, win social reforms, and build local institutions," but asks, does it add up to anything?[37] Does it constitute a viable basis for challenging "corporate colonization and state bureaucracy"?[38] In his view such groups are a positive force at the local level, but are inevitably constrained by a lack of resources, the absence of an ideological focus, narrow goals, ad hoc organization, and a tendency toward parochialism (à la Plotkin). These constraints render such groups ineffective at the national and international level, where many local problems originate: "in the world of corporate capitalism, the power necessary to achieve democratic and egalitarian goals exists, if anywhere, only at the level of the bureaucratic national state."[39]

Local protests against the siting of superstores and other unwanted forms of corporate action clearly fit the definition of community organizing given above, and thus it is pertinent to evaluate such protests in terms of these two concerns. Let's consider antisuperstore activism first. Is it just another instance of enclave consciousness? Partly yes, but mostly no. It is true that some of the opponents I encountered were only interested in preventing a superstore from being built near them, but many others opposed the store even though it did not affect them directly. Some (i.e., the merchants) opposed the store because it affected them *and* because it affected the rest of the community. While the supporters often tried to tar the opponents with allegations of NIMBYism, those allegations do not apply well to superstores. Whereas low-income housing can be justified on the grounds that persons with low incomes have to live some place, and a waste incinerator can be justified on the grounds that garbage has to be incinerated or otherwise disposed of, a superstore can not be justified on the grounds that a community *has* to have such an establishment. Furthermore, the evidence and analysis presented in chapter 3 indicate that superstores are generally not in the long-term interest of most communities. Of course, the community interest itself is debatable and some will argue that Wal-Mart's low prices represent the real community interest. But even if this were so, it does not follow that the opponents are narrow and insular; they simply have a different conception of the community interest.

Local antisuperstore efforts, then, represent a form of local activism that extends beyond enclave consciousness. But can they challenge the status quo? Before answering this let us briefly consider what has happened to antisuperstore and anti-Wal-Mart activism since the 1990s. Most of the controversies recounted here took place during the 1990s and, for the most part, each was a self-contained event with little connection to other movements or other parts of the country, although there was some sharing of information as opponents in the latter part of the decade tried to benefit from the experience of earlier opponents. This situation changed in the early years of the new century as Wal-Mart became—rather quickly—a national issue. Controversial actions by Wal-Mart are no longer confined to small towns but have become a staple of national news. Economists, political commentators, social critics, labor leaders, and others prominently debate the question posed by a public television report, "Is Wal-Mart Good for America?"[40] The output of Wal-Mart-related books, videos, reports, and journalistic coverage has increased significantly during the last five years. This widespread concern and debate has been accompanied, and stimulated, by a national anti-Wal-Mart movement spearheaded by professional organizers and labor unions.[41] While the national movement has incorporated many of the concerns of the local movements, its central issues are related to labor, not to the siting of superstores in small towns. It is concerned primarily with low wages, inadequate benefits, unsatisfactory working conditions, the lack of unionization, and the burden placed on taxpayers who must compensate for these shortcomings.[42]

It is not entirely clear why concern about Wal-Mart moved so quickly from small towns to the national stage. One reason, it seems, is that Wal-Mart began trying to put Supercenters in urban areas, a course of action that has led to bigger and more highly charged siting conflicts, especially in the Northeast, the Midwest, and California, where urban areas are more likely to be union strongholds. Two large unions, the Service Employees International Union (SEIU) and the United Food and Commercial Workers (UFCW) have responded by trying to prevent Wal-Mart from entering urban areas and generally pressuring the company to become a better employer. Also, some urban siting controversies, unlike those in small towns, have received national media coverage. A prime example, and the biggest controversy yet, is the 2004 dispute that arose over Wal-Mart's plan to build a Supercenter in Inglewood, a Los Angeles suburb. This dispute was a major story throughout Los Angeles and was covered by the media nationwide.[43] Although the company spent more than one million dollars promoting a ballot box initiative, it was eventually thwarted by a coalition of unions, churches, and community groups. A series of high-profile news stories exposing Wal-Mart's illegal and unethical labor practices also contributed to making the company a topic of national concern. These practices include locking employees in stores overnight,[44] failing to pay for all hours worked,[45] hiring illegal immigrants to clean stores,[46] not providing meal breaks,[47] and not complying with child labor laws.[48] Since 2001 Wal-Mart has been the defendant in a class action lawsuit involving approximately 1.5 million current and former female employees.[49] The company also began to be criticized heavily for buying merchandise from overseas and domestic suppliers who run sweatshops, a practice that received wide exposure when talk-show host Kathie Lee Gifford weepily responded on national television to claims that her line of designer clothes, sold at Wal-Mart, was made by sweatshop labor.[50]

If Wal-Mart represents the prototypical model of the twenty-first century corporation, then the national anti–Wal-Mart movement represents an explicit challenge to that model and thus can be said to constitute a challenge to the corporate status quo. To what extent have all the local antisuperstore social movements contributed to this movement? Given Wal-Mart's continued expansion, its labor practices, and its uncompromising antiunionism, it seems likely that a national anti-Wal-Mart movement would have developed eventually. However, it also seems likely that the hundreds of local antisuperstore controversies contributed to the emergence of the national movement by promoting awareness of the adverse consequences of superstores in general and Wal-Mart in particular. They also enlarged and deepened the national movement by raising other issues to complement the labor issues. While most of the small-town controversies have taken place in relative isolation, they did eventually lead to several nationally televised documentaries that provided an enormous amount of publicity. Have local superstore opponents changed the fundamental way Wal-Mart and other corporate retailers do business? No, but they have contributed to a larger national movement that seeks such changes, and in some instances they have succeeded in keeping out superstores, which is a significant achievement at the local level.

How about other local anticorporate movements, are they engaged in mere enclave politics? It depends on the specific corporate action being protested. Let's consider the four types of community-corporate conflicts identified in chapter 1. The first involves protests against decisions by corporations to shut down their local operations and move elsewhere. Given the extent to which most communities rely on corporations for employment, it seems clear that such protests would normally be in the interest of the entire community and thus should not be seen as enclave politics. The second involves opposition to the subsidies that cities offer to corporations as part of the intercity competition to attract new factories, offices, and other establishments. Local protests against a particular subsidy are usually based on the expectation that the cost of the subsidy will outweigh the benefits or the benefits will accrue only to a particular segment of the community. There may also be opposition to the very idea of offering subsidies on the grounds that it is inappropriate for tax revenue to be used to enrich already-profitable corporations. In any event, it seems difficult to portray such protests as enclave politics. The third involves efforts to deal with actual or potential degradation of the natural environment by corporations. Whether such efforts constitute enclave politics depends primarily on the scope and severity of the problem. To the extent that a particular environmental problem threatens only a small segment of a community or poses only a minimal risk, anticorporate activism might be considered a reflection of enclave consciousness. Determining the actual scope and severity of many environmental problems, however, is notoriously difficult and there can be genuine disagreement regarding the extent to which a particular problem affects the well-being of the whole community. The last type of community-corporate conflict arises in the course of urban development and growth. Here, more than in the three previous types, it all depends. Some development projects may benefit most of a community at the expense of a small enclave, while others may benefit a small number of local citizens and businesses (e.g., landowners and developers) at the expense of the rest of the community. Moreover, a project that is appropriate for one city may be inappropriate for another. Protests against corporate-sponsored development are neither automatically in the interest of the whole community nor automatically instances of enclave politics. This brief review indicates that local anticorporate efforts, considered en masse, cannot be declared a priori to be enclave politics, although some may indeed reflect only the interests of small enclaves.

This brings us to the final question: can local anticorporate efforts challenge the status quo? In other words, are they "agents of structural social change" or only "symptoms of resistance to . . . social domination[?]"[51] If the question is whether such efforts can *effectively* challenge the status quo, then the answer is clearly no, but if the question is whether such efforts can *contribute* to a challenge, then the answer is more positive. I agree with Boggs that the community organizing that has taken place in cities and towns across the United States over the last forty years has not "added up" to a coherent challenge to corporate capitalism. Local anticorporate social movement organizations are hobbled by many of the limitations identified by Boggs; they tend to be ad hoc, temporary, and short on resources, making it difficult for them to coalesce into a movement that can effectively challenge the corporation at a higher level. The fundamental issues concerning corporate power must ultimately be addressed at the state, national, and perhaps international level. Governmental action at the national level is most pertinent because Congress provides the legislation that regulates the corporation, the U.S. Supreme Court interprets that legislation (and in doing so establishes the legal basis of the corporation and specifies the rights that it enjoys), and federal agencies enforce those regulations. To a large extent the power of American corporations reflects the relative lack of power of American workers, as evidenced by the weakness of unions, and that weakness can be traced, in part, to federal legislation (e.g., the Labor Management Relations Act and its amendments), U.S. Supreme Court decisions, and federal agencies (i.e., the National Labor Relations Board) that fail to adequately support labor as a countervailing source of power.[52] Corporate influence over legislators (and, indirectly, over judges and regulators) is made possible through the current system of campaign financing, itself based on corporate campaign contributions at the federal level.[53] Confronting this state of affairs requires a movement that can transcend the myriad local community-corporate conflicts and wield power at the national level. The ever-increasing mobility of capital, along with the ability of corporations to pit municipalities against each, highlights the need for such a movement.

Yet local protests—especially successful ones—against harmful corporate actions are important. The local social movements that lead such protests may be narrow, but not necessarily. Their engagement with corporations that operate at a regional, national, or international level encourages them to expand their perspective and develop an awareness of the extralocal dimensions of these conflicts. More so than most other forms of community organizing, anticorporate activism raises larger issues about the dilemmas of unbridled profit seeking and the role of business at the local level and in society at large. Polls reveal that popular concern about corporate power is widespread, which means that it is often possible to make connections between specific local problems and the larger issue of corporate power.[54] The struggle against corporate domination and McDonaldization is not an all-or-nothing affair. The failure—endemic to American history—to mount a serious challenge to corporate capitalism at the national level does not mean that all attempts to constrain the corporation are unproductive. We live out much of our lives at the community level and thus the outcomes of community-corporate conflicts can affect us profoundly. They have enormous ramifications for the local economy, the local natural environment, the local built environment, local housing options, local fiscal soundness, local public spaces, local transportation options, local scenic appeal, and overall local quality of life. Even when unsuccessful, local anticorporate efforts can raise political consciousness and even induce some degree of radicalism. These efforts do not automatically add up to an effective larger movement, but they contribute to, and probably amplify, widespread concern about the extent and nature of corporate power in the contemporary world.

NOTES

1. Patrick J. Rohan, *Zoning and Land Use Controls*, quoted in Randle, "Professors."
2. *West's Encyclopedia of American Law*.
3. Briffault, "Our Localism."
4. Weber defines the state as, in part, "a compulsory organization with a territorial basis." Weber, *Economy and Society*, 56.
5. Activists in some cities have attempted to pass ordinances that would require new commercial development to meet requirements regarding community character, historical preservation, aesthetics, the environment, and economic impact. Another tactic has been to attempt to expand the range of issues subsumed under land use, such that appropriate land use is taken to include economic impact and other concerns.
6. One consequence of these limitations, at least in regard to the Wal-Mart controversies, was that many local officials were intimidated by Wal-Mart, or so it seemed to me.
7. Brooks and Manza, *Why Welfare States Persist*, argue for this tendency and provide empirical support in regard to the welfare state policies of the Western democracies.
8. While the lower prices of chains vis-à-vis small merchants would seem to be prima facie evidence of this advantage, chains will sell at lower prices only to the extent that competition compels them to do so. This aspect of retailing is often overlooked.
9. U.S. Census Bureau, *Statistical Abstract of the United States: 2004–2005*, Table 732.
10. U.S. Census Bureau, *Statistical Abstract of the United States: 2004–2005*, Table 732.
11. Chandler, *Scale and Scope*.
12. Wal-Mart's night lock-ins are described by Greenhouse, "Workers Assail Night Lock-Ins." Sam Walton required employees to pledge that they would smile and greet every customer that came within ten feet, Vance and Scott, *Wal-Mart*, 107. See Ortega, *In Sam We Trust*, for an account of Wal-Mart's antiunion efforts.
13. Crittenden and Adams, "Mr. Sam." See also Zimmerman and Maher, "Wal-Mart Warns."
14. Turning Point Project, "Global Monoculture."
15. Calthorpe, *Next American Metropolis*, 18. See also Relph, "Place."
16. See, for example, Barber, "Malled"; Goss, "'Magic of the Mall'"; and Kowinski, *Malling of America*.
17. Dority, Letter to the federal Office of Thrift Supervision.
18. *Denver Post* (CO), "Giving till it hurts" November 30, 2002.
19. The title of Ritzer's book is *Enchanting a Disenchanted World*.

20. This brief exposition is based, in part, on Schor, *Do Americans Shop Too Much?*

21. See Robert E. Lane's authoritative analysis in *The Loss of Happiness in Market Democracies.*

22. Sklair, *Transnational Corporate Class*, 4–5.

23. Ritzer, *McDonaldization.*

24. Weber, *Protestant Ethic.*

25. Ritzer, *McDonaldization.*

26. See Leidner, *Fast Food.*

27. See Ritzer, *Enchanting a Disenchanted World.*

28. Abernathy et al., *A Stitch in Time.*

29. See Ortega, *In Sam We Trust.* Wal-Mart operates the country's largest privately-owned telecommunications system, which it uses to monitor its stores from its headquarters in Bentonville, Arkansas. Feldman, "How Big Can It Get?" Another example of rationalization involves the just-in-time supply model, which Wal-Mart has taken to its logical end by having sales data transmitted directly from its stores to its suppliers, who must then produce and deliver more or less of each product in the appropriate sizes and colors to various stores. This arrangement precludes many smaller companies from selling their products to Wal-Mart because they do not have the computing capability that Wal-Mart requires.

30. Ritzer, "The McDonaldization Thesis," 291–92.

31. Ritzer points out that the prospects for McDonaldization are limited in countries where most people simply cannot afford it. Ritzer, "The McDonaldization Thesis."

32. See McSpotlight, "McLibel Trial."

33. Boyte, *Backyard Revolution*; Costonis, "Tinker to Evers"; Fainstein, "Local Mobilization"; Fainstein and Hirst, "Urban Social Movements"; and Fisher, *Let the People Decide* discuss the rise of neighborhood organizing, community organizing, and urban social movements. See also Fisher and Kling, *Mobilizing the Community*; and Kling and Posner, *Dilemmas of Activism.*

34. These examples are drawn from Fainstein and Hirst, "Urban Social Movements," who discuss them as part of the "neighborhood movement," 188.

35. Plotkin, "Enclave Consciousness," 218.

36. Boggs, *End of Politics*, 185. Fainstein, "Local Mobilization"; Fisher and Kling, *Mobilizing the Community*; and Posner, "Introduction" offer related arguments.

37. Boggs, *End of Politics*, 187.

38. Boggs, *End of Politics*, 190.

39. Kling and Posner, cited in Boggs, *End of Politics*, 189.

40. Smith and Young, "Is Wal-Mart Good for America?"

41. Gimbel, "Attack."

42. A report sponsored by George Miller of the U.S. House of Representatives concludes that "Because Wal-Mart fails to pay sufficient wages, U.S. taxpayers are forced to pick up the tab." Miller, *Everyday Low Wages*, 9.

43. Broder, "Voters in Los Angeles."

44. Greenhouse, "Workers Assail Night Lock-Ins."

45. Greenhouse, "U.S. Jury."

46. Greenhouse, "Illegally in U.S."
47. Joyce, "Calif. Jury."
48. Stowe, "Connecticut."
49. Greenhouse, "Court Approves Class-Action Suit." See also Seligman, "Patriarchy."
50. Greenhouse, "Crusader Makes Celebrities Tremble."
51. Manuel Castells, quoted in Fainstein, "Local Mobilization," 334.
52. James Kenneth Galbraith, *American Capitalism*, originated the idea of organized labor as a countervailing force.
53. Clawson, Neustadtl, and Weller, *Dollars and Votes*.
54. According to a 2000 *Business Week*/Harris poll, 72 percent of Americans "agreed strongly" or "somewhat agreed" with the statement, "Business has gained too much power over too many aspects of American life," and 49 percent "disagreed strongly" or disagreed somewhat" with the statement, "In general, what is good for business is good for most Americans." Bernstein et al., "Too Much Corporate Power?"

Appendix

LIST OF INTERVIEWEES

Note: All titles refer to positions held at the time of the controversy, unless otherwise noted. The stance taken by some interviewees has been omitted to preserve anonymity.

Gig Harbor, Washington

In person:

    Lois Eyrse, president, Gig Harbor-Peninsula Chamber of Commerce
    Tom Morfee, president, Peninsula Neighborhood Association
    Hugh Taylor, planner, Pierce County Department of Planning and Land Services
    Gretchen Wilbert, mayor, city of Gig Harbor
    Anonymous real estate industry source
    Anonymous interviewee, an active supporter
    Anonymous interviewee, an active opponent

By telephone:

    Anonymous planner, City of Gig Harbor

Petoskey, Michigan

In person:

Al Foster, chair, Bear Creek Township board of supervisors
Lyn Johnson, controller, Emmet County
Diane Litzenburger (formerly Murray), president, Petoskey-Regional Chamber of Commerce
Pat Mather, Emmet County Board of Supervisors
Max Putters, director, Emmet County Office of Planning and Zoning
Anonymous interviewee, an active supporter
Anonymous interviewee, an active opponent
Anonymous interviewee, downtown merchant and an active opponent
Anonymous interviewee, an active opponent
Anonymous interviewee, an active opponent

West Bend, Wisconsin

In person:

Jud Dolnick, West Bend Plan Commission
Michael Miller, mayor, city of West Bend
Robert Motl, West Bend Common Council
Hope Nelson, West Bend Common Council
Tom O'Meara III, West Bend Common Council
Betty Pearson, executive vice president, West Bend Area Chamber of Commerce
Ken Pesch, city engineer and West Bend Plan Commission
Anonymous interviewee
Anonymous interviewee, nearby resident and an active opponent
Anonymous interviewee, familiar with downtown West Bend

By telephone:

Anonymous interviewee, downtown merchant and an opponent

Ottawa, Ohio

In person:

Stephen Brinkman, Putnam County Commissioner (position held after the controversy)
Timothy Macke, Ottawa Village Council

Appendix 213

S Scott McDowell, safety-service director, Village of Ottawa
J Dean Meyer, Ottawa Village Council
Anonymous interviewee
Anonymous interviewee, an active opponent
Anonymous interviewee, a supporter
Anonymous interviewee, an active opponent
Anonymous interviewee, nearby resident and an active opponent

By telephone:

David Laudick, president, Ottawa Village Council
Jack Williams, municipal director, Village of Ottawa
Anonymous interviewee, nearby resident and an active opponent
Anonymous interviewee, an opponent
Anonymous interviewee, a supporter of second site

Ashland, Wisconsin

In person:

Fran Ante, mayor, city of Ashland
Lowell Miller, mayor, city of Ashland (position held after the controversy)
James Monroe, mayor, city of Ashland
Anonymous interviewee, downtown merchant and an active opponent
Anonymous interviewee, city employee and an active opponent
Anonymous interviewee, an active supporter
Anonymous interviewee, city employee
Anonymous interviewee, downtown merchant and an active opponent
Anonymous interviewee, downtown merchant and an active opponent
Anonymous interviewee, an opponent
Anonymous interviewee, Ashland City Council
Anonymous interviewee, Ashland City Council
Anonymous interviewee, Ashland City Council

Eureka, California

In person:

Cherie Arkley, Eureka City Council
Patty Berg, co-chair, Think Twice Campaign
Kevin Hamblin, director of community development, City of Eureka
Jack McKellar, Eureka City Council

Bonnie Neely, county supervisor, Humboldt County, and co-chair, Think Twice Campaign
Harvey Rose, city manager, City of Eureka
Anonymous interviewee, an active opponent
Anonymous interviewee
Anonymous interviewee, an active supporter
Anonymous interviewee
Anonymous interviewee, merchant and an active opponent

By telephone:

Daphne Davis, Wal-Mart community affairs director
Kirk Girard, director of community development services, Humboldt County
Nancy Flemming, mayor, city of Eureka

Bibliography

Abernathy, Frederick H., John T. Dunlop, Janice H. Hammond, and David Weil. *A Stitch in Time: Lean Retailing and the Transformation of Manufacturing—Lessons From the Apparel and Textile Industries*. New York: Oxford University Press, 1998.
Andreoli, Teresa. "Despite saturation, store counts surge." *Discount Store News*, 1 July 1996.
Bakan, Joel. *The Corporation: The Pathological Pursuit of Profit and Power*. New York: Free Press, 2005.
Barber, Benjamin R. *Strong Democracy: Participatory Politics for a New Age*. Berkeley: University of California Press, 1984.
———. "Malled, Mauled, and Overhauled: Arresting Suburban Sprawl by Transforming Suburban Malls into Usable Civic Space." Pp. 201–20 in *Public Space and Democracy*, edited by Marcel Henaff and Tracy B. Strong. Minneapolis: University of Minnesota Press, 2001.
Basker, Emek. "Job Creation or Destruction? Labor Market Effects of Wal-Mart Expansion." *Review of Economics and Statistics* 87, no. 1 (2005): 174–83.
Baylor, Tim. "Media Framing of Movement Protest: The Case of American Indian Protest." *Social Science Journal* 33, no. 3 (1996): 241–55.
Beaumont, Constance. *How Superstore Sprawl Can Harm Communities, And What Citizens Can Do About It*. Washington, D.C.: National Trust for Historic Preservation, 1994.
———. *Better Models for Superstores: Alternatives to Big-Box Sprawl*. Washington, D.C.: National Trust for Historic Preservation, 1997.
Benford, Robert D. and David A. Snow. "Framing Processes and Social Movements: An Overview and Assessment." *Annual Review of Sociology* 26 (2000): 611–39.
Bernstein, Aaron, Michael Arndt, Wendy Zellner, and Peter Coy. "Too Much Corporate Power?" *Business Week*, 11 September 2000.

Bernstein, Jared, L. Josh Bivens, and Arindrajit Dube. *Wrestling With Wal-Mart: Tradeoffs Between Profits, Prices, and Wages.* EPI Working Paper. Washington, D.C.: Economic Policy Institute, 2006.

Bianco, Anthony. *The Bully of Bentonville: How the High Costs of Wal-Mart's Everyday Low Prices Are Hurting America.* New York: Doubleday, 2006.

Blanchard, Troy, Michael Irwin, Charles Tolbert, Thomas Lyson, and Alfred Nucci. "Suburban Sprawl, Regional Diffusion, and the Fate of Small Retailers in a Large Retail Environment, 1977–1996." *Sociological Focus* 36, no. 4 (2003): 313–31.

Blanchard, Troy and Todd L. Matthews. "The Configuration of Local Economic Power and Civic Participation in the Global Economy." *Social Forces* 84, no. 4 (2006): 2241–57.

Bluestone, Barry, Patricia Hanna, Sarah Kuhn, and Laura Moore. *The Retail Revolution: Market Transformation, Investment, and Labor in the Modern Department Store.* Boston: Auburn House, 1981.

Bluestone, Barry and Bennett Harrison. *The Deindustrialization of America: Plant Closings, Community Abandonment, and the Dismantling of Basic Industry.* New York: Basic Books, 1982.

Boggs, Carl. *The End of Politics: Corporate Power and the Decline of the Public Sphere.* New York: Guilford Press, 2000.

Bonacich, Edna and Richard P. Appelbaum. *Behind the Label: Inequality in the Los Angeles Apparel Industry.* Berkeley and Los Angeles: University of California Press, 2000.

Bonanno, Alessandro and Douglas H. Constance. "Mega Hog Farms in the Texas Panhandle Region: Corporate Actions and Local Resistance." *Research in Social Movements, Conflicts and Change* 22 (2000): 83–110.

Boorstin, Daniel J. "Consumers' Palaces." Pp. 243–53 in *The Daniel J. Boorstin Reader*, edited by Ruth F. Boorstin. New York: Modern Library, 1995.

Boyd, David. W. "From 'Mom and Pop" to Wal-Mart: The Impact of the Consumer Goods Pricing Act of 1975 on the Retail Sector in the United States." *Journal of Economic Issues* 31, no. 1 (1997): 223–31.

Boyte, Harry C. *The Backyard Revolution.* Philadelphia: Temple University Press, 1980.

Briffault, Richard. "Our Localism: Part I—The Structure of Local Government Law." *Columbia Law Review* 90, no. 1 (1990): 1–115.

Broder, John M. "Voters in Los Angeles Suburb Say No to a Big Wal-Mart." *New York Times*, 8 April 2004.

Brooks, Clem and Jeff Manza. *Why Welfare States Persist: The Importance of Public Opinion in Democracies.* Chicago: University of Chicago Press, 2007.

Bruegmann, Robert. *Sprawl: A Compact History.* Chicago: University of Chicago Press, 2005.

Brunn, Stanley D., ed. *Wal-Mart World: The World's Biggest Corporation in the Global Economy.* New York: Routledge, 2006.

Burchell, Robert W., Anthony Downs, Barbara McCann, and Sarah Mukherji. *Sprawl Costs: Economic Impacts of Unchecked Development.* Washington, D.C.: Island Press, 2005.

Burstein, Paul, Rachel L. Einwohner, and Jocelyn A. Hollander. "The Success of Political Movements: A Bargaining Perspective." Pp. 275–95 in *The Politics of Social Protest*, edited by J. Craig Jenkins and Bert Klandermans. Minneapolis: University of Minnesota Press, 1995.

Button, Mark and David Michael Ryfe. "What Can We Learn from the Practice of Deliberative?" Pp. 20–33 in *The Deliberative Democracy Handbook: Strategies of Effective Civic Engagement in the Twenty-First Century*, edited by John Gastil and Peter Levine. San Francisco: Jossey-Bass, 2005.

Cable, Sherry and Beth Degutis. "Movement Outcomes and Dimensions of Social Change: The Multiple Effects of Local Mobilizations." *Current Sociology* 45, no. 3 (1997): 121–35.

Calthorpe, Peter. *The Next American Metropolis: Ecology, Community, and the American Dream*. New York: Princeton Architectural Press, 1993.

Calvani, Terry. "Predatory Pricing and State Below-Cost Sales Statutes in the United States: An Analysis," 1999. http://www.cb-bc.gc.ca (27 June 2004).

Capital Times (WI). "No charges for Woodman in price comparison case." 14 May 1998.

Carroll, William K. and R.S. Ratner. "Media Strategies and Political Protests: A Comparative Study of Social Movements." *Canadian Journal of Sociology* 24, no. 1 (1999): 1–34.

CBS News, "Up Against the Wal-Mart," *60 Minutes*, 3 September 1995.

Chain Store Age Executive. "Retailers Keep Building More Stores." 73, no. 12 (1997): 168.

Chandler, Alfred D. Jr. *Scale and Scope*. Cambridge, Mass.: Harvard University Press, 1990.

Chapman, Jeffrey I. *Proposition 13: Some Unintended Consequences*. San Francisco: Public Policy Institute of California (occasional papers), 1998.

Clawson, Don, Alan Neustadtl, and Mark Weller. *Dollars and Votes: How Business Campaign Contributions Subvert Democracy*. Philadelphia: Temple University Press, 1998.

Clingermayer, James C. "Electoral Representation, Zoning Politics, and the Exclusion of Group Homes." *Political Research Quarterly* 47, no. 4 (1994): 969–84.

Cohen, Joshua. "Deliberation and Democratic Legitimacy." Pp. 17–34 in *The Good Polity: Normative Analysis of the State*, edited by Alan Hamlin and Philip Pettit. Oxford, England: Basil Blackwell, 1989.

Consumer Reports. "Where to Buy Appliances: Big Stores Aren't Necessarily the Best." September 2005.

Consumer Reports. "Computer Stores: Shop Smart, Step by Step." December 2005.

Costonis, John J. "Tinker to Evers to Chance: Community Groups as the Third Player in the Development Game." Pp. 155–66 in *City Deal Making*, edited by Terry Jill Lassar. Washington, D.C.: Urban Land Institute, 1990.

Couch, Stephen R. and Steve Kroll-Smith. "Environmental Controversies, Interactional Resources, and Rural Communities: Siting Versus Exposure Disputes." *Rural Sociology* 59, no. 1 (1994): 25–44.

Court, Jamie. *Corporateering*. New York: Tarcher/Penguin, 2003.

Cowgill, Race. "Case Study: How to Exploit Wal-Mart's Weaknesses." Zenith Management Consulting, 2005. http:// www.zenith-consulting.com (9 March 2008).

Crawford, Margaret. "The World in a Shopping Mall." Pp. 3–30 in *Variations on a Theme Park: The New American City and the End of Public Space*, edited by Michael Sorkin. New York: Hill and Wang, 1992.

Craypo, Charles and Bruce Nissen. *Grand Designs: The Impact of Corporate Strategies on Workers, Unions, and Communities*. Ithaca, N.Y.: ILR Press, 1993.

Crenson, Matthew A. *The Un-Politics of Air Pollution: A Study of Non-Decisionmaking in the Cities*. Baltimore: Johns Hopkins Press, 1971.

Crittenden, Michael and Rebecca Adams. "Mr. Sam Comes to Washington." *CQ Weekly* 7 November 2005, 972–81).

Currie, Neil and Ajay Jain. "Supermarket Pricing Survey." UBS Warburg 25 July 2002.

Davidson, Sharon M. and Amy Rummel. "Retail Changes Associated With Wal-Mart's Entry Into Maine." *International Journal of Retail & Distribution Management* 28, no. 4 & 5 (2000): 162–69.

DeLind, Laura B. "Parma: A Story of Hog Hotels and Local Resistance." Pp. 23–38 in *Pigs, Profits, and Rural Communities*, edited by Kendall M. Thu and E. Paul Durrenberger. Albany, N.Y.: State University of New York Press, 1998.

Denver Post. "Giving till it hurts." 30 November 2002.

Desjardins, Doug. "Brand Basket." *DSN Retailing Today*, 24 October 2005.

Dicker, John. *The United States of Wal-Mart*. New York: Tarcher, 2005.

Dority, Doug (UFCW president). Letter to the federal Office of Thrift Supervision, reprinted in *Sprawl-Busters Alert*, issue 65, November 1999.

Doukas, Dimitra. *Worked Over: The Corporate Sabotage of an American Community*. Ithaca, N.Y.: Cornell University Press, 2003.

Drucker, Peter. "Drucker on Management: The Economy's Power Shift." *Wall Street Journal*, 9 September 1992.

Drutman, Lee and Charlie Cray. *The People's Business*. San Francisco: Berrett-Koehler, 2004.

Dryzek, John S. *Deliberative Democracy and Beyond: Liberals, Critics, Contestations*. Oxford, England: Oxford University Press, 2000.

Dunham-Jones, Ellen. "Temporary Contracts: On the Economy of the Post-Industrial Landscape." *Harvard Design Magazine* (Fall 1997): 5–11.

Eisenger, Peter K. "The Conditions of Protest Behavior in American Cities." *American Political Science Review* 67, no. 1 (1973): 11–28.

Fainstein, Susan S. "Local Mobilization and Economic Discontent," Pp. 323–42 in *The Capitalist City*, edited by Michael Peter Smith and Joe R. Feagin. Oxford, England: Basil Blackwell, 1987.

Fainstein, Susan S. and Clifford Hirst. "Urban Social Movements." Pp. 181–204 in *Theories of Urban Politics*, edited by David Judge, Gerry Stoker, and Harold Wolman. London and Thousand Oaks, Calif.: Sage, 1995.

Falgoust, Glenn and Angela Falgoust. *The Wal-Mess* (video). Donaldsville, La., n.d.

Feldman, Amy. "How Big Can It Get?" *Money*, December 1999.

Fisher, Robert. *Let the People Decide: Neighborhood Organizing in America*. Updated edition. New York: Twayne, 1994.

Fisher, Robert and Joseph Kling, eds. *Mobilizing the Community: Local Politics in the Era of the Global City.* Newbury Park, Calif.: Sage, 1993.

Fishkin, James. "Deliberative Democracy." Pp. 221–38 in *The Blackwell Guide to Social and Political Philosophy*, edited by Robert L. Simon. Malden, Mass.: Blackwell, 2002.

Fishman, Charles. "The Wal-Mart You Don't Know." *Fast Company*, December 2003.

Forbes. "The 400 Richest Americans: Special Report, September 21, 2006." http://www.forbes.com (7 January 2007).

Fortune. "Fortune 500." 18 April 1994.

Fortune. "Fortune 500." 15 April 2002.

Fortune. "Fortune 500." 5 April 2004.

Fortune. "Fortune 500." 5 May 2008.

Freudenberg, Nicholas and Carol Steinsapir. "Not in Our Backyards: The Grassroots Environmental Movement." *Society and Natural Resources* 4, no. 3 (1991): 235–45.

Frumkin, Howard, Lawrence Frank, and Richard Jackson. *Urban Sprawl and Public Health: Designing, Planning, and Building for Healthy Communities.* Washington, D.C.: Island Press, 2004.

Furuseth, Owen J. and Janet O'Callaghan. "Community Response to a Municipal Waste Incinerator: NIMBY or Neighbor?" *Landscape and Urban Planning* 21, no. 3 (1991): 163–71.

Gaffin, Dennis. "Offending and Defending U.S. Rural Place: The Mega-Dump Battle in Western New York." *Human Organization* 56, no. 30 (1997): 275–85.

Galanter, Marc. "Why the 'Haves' Come Out Ahead: Speculations on the Limits of Legal Change." *Law and Society Review* 9 (1974): 95–160.

Galbraith, John Kenneth. *American Capitalism: The Concept of Countervailing Power.* Boston: Houghton Miflin, 1952.

Gamson, William A. *The Strategy of Social Protest.* Homewood, Ill.: Dorsey, 1975.

———. *The Strategy of Social Protest*, 2d ed. Belmont, Calif.: Wadsworth, 1990.

———. "Bystanders, Public Opinion, and the Media." Pp. 242–61 in *The Blackwell Companion to Social Movements*, edited by David A. Snow, Sarah A. Soule, and Hanspeter Kriesi. Malden, Mass.: Blackwell, 2004.

Gamson, William A. and David S. Meyer. "Framing Political Opportunity." Pp. 275–90 in *Comparative Perspectives on Social Movements: Political Opportunities, Mobilizing Structures, and Cultural Framings*, edited by Doug McAdam, John D. McCarthy, and Mayer N. Zald. New York: Cambridge University Press, 1996.

Gamson, William A. and Gadi Wolfsfeld. "Movements and Media as Interacting Systems." *Annals AAPSS* (July 1993): 114–25.

Garreau, Joel. *Edge City: Life on the New Frontier.* New York: Doubleday, 1991.

Gastil, John and Peter Levine, eds. *The Deliberative Democracy Handbook: Strategies of Effective Civic Engagement in the Twenty-First Century.* San Francisco: Jossey-Bass, 2005.

Gaventa, John. *Power and Powerlessness: Quiescence and Rebellion in an Appalachian Valley.* Urbana: University of Illinois Press, 1980.

Gehl, Jan. Translated by Jo Koch. *Life Between Buildings: Using Public Space.* New York: Van Nostrand Reinhold, 1987.

Gibbs, Lois Marie. "The Movement on the Move." *Everyone's Backyard* 7, no. 2 (Summer 1989): 1, 3.

Gillham, Oliver. *The Limitless City: A Primer on the Urban Sprawl Debate.* Washington, D.C.: Island Press, 2002.

Gimbel, Barney. "Attack of the Wal-Martyrs." *Fortune*, 11 December 2006.

Giugni, Marco G. "Was It Worth the Effort? The Outcomes and Consequences of Social Movements." *Annual Review of Sociology* 24 (1998): 371–93.

Giugni, Marco G., Doug McAdam, and Charles Tilly. *How Social Movements Matter.* Minneapolis: University of Minnesota Press, 1999.

Glazer, Kenneth L. "Predatory Pricing After *Brooke Group*." *Antitrust Law Journal* 62 (Spring 1994), no. 3: 605–33.

Global Insight. *The Economic Impact of Wal-Mart.* 2 November 2005.

Goetz, S. and Anil Rupasingha. "Wal-Mart and Social Capital." *American Journal of Agricultural Economics* 88, no. 5 (2006): 1304–10.

Goetz, S. and H. Swaminathan. "Wal-Mart and County-Wide Poverty." *Social Science Quarterly* 87, no. 2 (2006): 211–26.

Goldberger, Paul. "The Store Strikes Back." *New York Times*, 6 April 1997.

Gordon, Cynthia and James M. Jasper. "Overcoming the 'Nimby' Label: Rhetorical and Organizational Links for Local Protestors." *Research in Social Movements, Conflicts and Change* 19 (1996): 159–81.

Goss, Jon. "The 'Magic of the Mall': An Analysis of Form, Function and Meaning in the Contemporary Built Environment." *Annals of the Association of American Geographers* 83, no. 1 (1992): 18–47.

Gratz, Roberta Brandes, with Norman Mintz. *Cities Back from the Edge: New Life for Downtown.* New York: Preservation Press, 1998.

Greenhouse, Steven. "A Crusader Makes Celebrities Tremble." *New York Times*, 18 June 1996.

———. "U.S. Jury Cites Unpaid Work at Wal-Mart." *New York Times*, 20 December 2002.

———. "Illegally in U.S. and Never a Day Off at Wal-Mart." *New York Times*, 5 November 2003.

———. "Workers Assail Night Lock-Ins by Wal-Mart." *New York Times*, 18 January 2004.

———. "Court Approves Class-Action Suit Against Wal-Mart" *New York Times*, 7 February 2007.

Gruidl, John and Steven Kline. "What Happens When a Large Discount Store Comes to Town." *Small Town* (March/April 1992): 20–25.

Gundlach, Gregory T. "Price Predation: Legal Limits and Antitrust Considerations." *Journal of Public Policy & Marketing* 14, no. 2 (1995): 278–89.

Halebsky, Stephen. "Superstores and the Politics of Retail Development." *City & Community* 3, no. 2 (2004): 115–34.

———. "Explaining the Outcomes of Antisuperstore Movements: A Comparative Analysis of Six Communities." *Mobilization* 11, no. 4 (2006): 443–60.

Hall Jr., Kenneth B. and Gerald A. Porterfield. *Community By Design: New Urbanism for Suburbs and Small Communities.* New York: McGraw-Hill, 2001.

Hartmann, Thom. *Unequal Protection: The Rise of Corporate Dominance and the Theft of Human Rights*. Emmaus, Pa.: Rodale, 2002.
Hawker, Norman W. "Wal-Mart and the Divergence of State and Federal Predatory Pricing Law." *Journal of Public Policy & Marketing* 15, no. 1 (1996): 141–47.
Hays, Constance. "Toy Retailers Find Prices At Wal-Mart Tough to Beat." *New York Times*, 23 December 2003.
Heiman, Michael. "From 'Not in My Backyard' to 'Not in Anybody's Backyard!': Grassroots Challenge to Hazardous Waste Facility Siting." *APA Journal* (Summer 1990): 359–62.
Heller, Laura. "Wal-Mart Outprices Atlanta Competition." *DSN Retailing Today* 18 June 2001.
Hendrickson, Robert. *The Grand Emporiums: The Illustrated History of America's Great Department Stores*. New York: Stern and Day, 1979.
Hughes, James W. and George Sternlieb. "Demographics vs. Development." *American Demographics*, May 1990: 40–41.
Huxtable, Ada Louise. *The Unreal America: Architecture and Illusion*. New York: New Press, 1997.
Jacobs, Allan B. *Great Streets*. Cambridge, Mass.: MIT Press, 1995.
Jacobs, Jane. *The Death and Life of Great American Cities*. New York: Vintage Books, 1992 (1961).
Jenkins, J. Craig and Charles Perrow. "Insurgency of the Powerless: Farm Worker Movements (1946–1972)." *American Sociological Review* 42 (1977): 249–68.
Jones, Bryan D. and Lynn W. Bachelor. *The Sustaining Hand: Community Leadership and Corporate Power*. 2nd ed. Lawrence: University Press of Kansas, 1993.
Joyce, Amy. "Calif. Jury Backs Wal-Mart Workers." *Washington Post*, 23 December 2005.
Kaminstein, Dana S. "A Resource Mobilization Analysis of a Failed Environmental Protest." *Journal of Community Practice* 2, no. 2 (1995): 5–32.
Karjanen, D. and M. Baxamusa. *Subsidizing Wal-Mart: A Case Study of the College Grove Redevelopment Project*. San Diego, Calif.: Center on Policy Initiatives, 2003.
Kearney, Richard C. and Ande A. Smith. "The Low-Level Radioactive Waste Siting Process in Connecticut: Anatomy of a Failure." *Policy Studies Journal* 22, no. 4 (1994): 617–30.
Kelly, Marjorie. *The Divine Right of Capital: Dethroning the Corporate Aristocracy*. San Francisco: Berrett-Koehler, 2001.
Klandermans, Bert. "Introduction: Organizational Effectiveness." *International Social Movement Research* 2 (1989): 383–94.
Kling, Joseph M. and Prudence S. Posner, eds. *Dilemmas of Activism: Class, Community, and the Politics of Local Mobilization*. Philadelphia: Temple University Press, 1990.
Kriesi, Hanspeter. "Political Context and Opportunity." Pp. 67–90 in *The Blackwell Companion to Social Movements*, edited by David A. Snow, Sarah A. Soule, and Hanspeter Kriesi. Malden, Mass.: Blackwell, 2004.

Kowinski, William Severini. *The Malling of America: An Inside Look at the Great Consumer Paradise*. New York: William Morrow, 1985.

Kruse, Corwin R. "The Movement and the Media: Framing the Debate Over Animal Experimentation." *Political Communication* 18 (2001): 67–87.

Kumar, Nirmalya. "The Revolution in Retailing: from Market Driven to Market Driving." *Long Range Planning* 30, no. 6 (1997): 830–35.

Kunstler, James Howard. *The Geography of Nowhere: The Rise and Decline of America's Man-made Landscape*. New York: Simon & Schuster, 1993.

———. "Zoning Procedures and Suburban Sprawl: A Cartoon of a Human Habitat." Address, City Club of Cleveland, 31 October 1997.

Kurtz, Hilda E. "The Politics of Environmental Justice as the Politics of Scale: St. James Parish, Louisiana, and the Shintech Siting Controversy." Pp. 249–73 in *Geographies of Power*, edited by Andrew Herod and Melissa W. Wright. Malden, Mass.: Blackwell, 2002.

Lane, Robert E. *The Loss of Happiness in Market Democracies*. New Haven, Conn.: Yale University Press, 2000.

Leach, William. *Land of Desire: Merchants, Power, and the Rise of a New American Culture*. New York: Pantheon, 1993.

Leidner, Robin. *Fast Food, Fast Talk: Service Work and the Routinization of Everyday Life*. Berkeley and Los Angeles: University of California Press, 1993.

Leong, Andrew. "The Struggle over Parcel C: How Boston's Chinatown Won a Victory in the Fight Against Institutional Expansion and Environmental Racism." *Amerasia Journal* 21, no. 3 (1996): 99–119.

Lewis, Paul G. "Retail Politics: Local Sales Taxes and the Fiscalization of Land Use." *Economic Development Quarterly* 15, no. 1 (2001): 21–35.

Lichtenstein, Nelson, ed. *Wal-Mart: The Face of Twenty-First Century Capitalism*. New York and London: New Press, 2006.

———. "Wal-Mart: A Template for Twenty-First Century Capitalism." Pp. 3–30 in *Wal-Mart: The Face of Twenty-First Century Capitalism*, edited by Nelson Lichtenstein. New York and London: New Press, 2006.

Lo, Clarence. "Countermovements and Conservative Movements in the Contemporary U.S." *Annual Review of Sociology* 8 (1982): 107–34.

———. *Small Property Versus Big Government: Social Origins of the Property Tax Revolt*. Berkeley and Los Angeles: University of California Press, 1990.

Lofland, John. *Social Movement Organizations: Guide to Research on Insurgent Realities*. Hawthorne, N. Y.: Aldine de Gruyter, 1996.

Lofland, Lyn H. *The Public Realm: Exploring the City's Quintessential Social Territory*. New York: Aldine de Gruyter, 1998.

———. *The Commodification of Public Space*. College Park, Md.: Urban Studies and Planning Program, University of Maryland, 2002.

Logan, John R. and Harvey L. Molotch. *Urban Fortunes: The Political Economy of Place*. Berkeley and Los Angeles: University of California, 1987.

Lowe, Michelle and Neil Wrigley. "Towards the New Retail Geography." Pp. 3–30 in *Retailing, Consumption and Capital: Towards the New Retail Geography*, edited by Michelle Lowe and Neil Wrigley. London: Longman, 1996.

Lubell, Sam. "Is There Hope for the Big Box?" *Architectural Record* 193, no. 8 (2005): 68–76.

Mattera, Philip and Anna Purinton. *Shopping for Subsidies: How Wal-Mart Uses Taxpayer Money to Finance Its Never-Ending Growth*. Washington, D.C.: Good Jobs First, 2004.

McGraw, Thomas K. "Competition and 'Fair Trade': History and Theory." *Research in Economic History* 16 (1996): 185–239.

McSpotlight. "The McLibel Trial." Pp. 254–64 in *McDonaldization: The Reader*. 2d ed., edited by George Ritzer. Thousand Oaks, Calif.: Pine Forge Press, 2006.

Merritt, Lani. "Common Cause: A Comparative Case Study of Three Alabama Communities Organizing Against Landfills." *Southern Rural Sociology* 17 (2001): 134–58.

Meyer, David. S. and Suzanne Staggenborg. "Movements, Countermovements, and the Structure of Political Opportunity." *American Journal of Sociology* 101, no. 6 (1996): 1628–60.

Micklethwait, John and Adrian Wooldridge. *The Company*. New York: Modern Library, 2003.

Miles, Steven and Ronan Paddison. "Urban Consumption: An Historiographical Note." *Urban Studies* 35, no. 5/6 (1998): 815–23.

Miller, George. *Everyday Low Wages: The Hidden Price We All Pay for Wal-Mart, A Report by the Democratic Staff of the Committee on Education and the Workforce, U.S. House of Representatives, Representative George Miller*. 16 February 2004.

Mitchell, Lawrence E. *Corporate Irresponsibility: America's Newest Export*. New Haven, Conn.: Yale University Press, 2001.

Mobert, Mark. "Co-Opting Justice: Transformation of a Multiracial Environmental Coalition in Southern Alabama." *Human Organization* 60 (2001): 166–77.

Molotch, Harvey. "The City as a Growth Machine: Toward a Political Economy of Place." *American Journal of Sociology* 82, no. 2 (1976): 309–30.

———. "Media and Movements." Pp. 71–93 in *The Dynamics of Social Movements*, edited by M. Zald and J. McCarthy. Cambridge, Mass.: Winthrop Publishers, 1977.

Mottl, Tahi L. "The Analysis of Countermovements." *Social Problems* 27, no. 5 (1980): 620–35.

Mullins, Patrick, Kristin Natalier, Philip Smith and Belinda Smeaton. "Cities and Consumption Spaces." *Urban Affairs Review* 35, no. 1 (1999): 44–71.

Murphree, David W., Stuart A. Wright, and Helen Rose Ebaugh. "Toxic Waste Siting and Community Resistance: How Cooptation of Local Citizen Opposition Failed." *Sociological Perspectives* 39, no. 4 (1996): 447–63.

Mutz, Diana C. *Hearing the Other Side: Deliberative versus Participatory Democracy*. New York: Cambridge University Press, 2006.

Nace, Ted. *Gangs of America*. San Francisco: Berrett-Koehler, 2003.

National Main Street Center. http://www.mainstreet.org (9 July 2005).

Neumark, David, Junfu Zhang, and Stephen Ciccarella. "The Effects of Wal-Mart on Local Labor Markets." Discussion paper no. 2545. Institute for the Study of Labor (Bonn, Germany), 2007.

Nissen, Bruce. *Fighting for Jobs: Case Studies of Labor-Community Coalitions Confronting Plant Closings*. Albany: State University of New York Press, 1995.

Norman, Al. *Slam-Dunking Wal-Mart*. Atlantic City, N.J: Raphel Marketing, 2003.
———. *The Case Against Wal-Mart*. Atlantic City, N.J.: Raphel Marketing, 2004.
North, Peter. "'Save our Solsbury!': The Anatomy of an Anti-Roads Protest." *Environmental Politics* 7, no. 3 (1998): 1–25.
Oldenburg, Ray. *The Great Good Place*. New York: Paragon House, 1991.
Ortega, Bob. "Wal-Mart to Settle Dispute in Michigan Involving In-Store Price Comparisons." *Wall Street Journal*, 21 March 1994.
———. *In Sam We Trust: The Untold Story of Sam Walton and How Wal-Mart Is Devouring America*. New York: Times Business, 1998.
Overstreet, Thomas R., Jr. *Resale Price Maintenance: Economic Theories and Empirical Evidence*. Bureau of Economics, Federal Trade Commission. Washington, D.C.: U.S. Government Printing Office, 1983.
Peterson, Mark and Jeffrey E. McGee. "Survivors of 'W—day': An assessment of the impact of Wal-Mart's invasion of small town retailing communities." *International Journal of Retail & Distribution Management* 28, no. 4/5 (2000): 170–80.
Piven, Francis and Richard Cloward. *Poor People's Movements*. New York: Vintage, 1979.
Plein, L. Christopher, Kenneth E. Green, and David G. Williams. "Organic Planning: A New Approach to Public Participation in Local Governance." *Social Science Journal* 35, no. 4 (1998): 509–23.
Plotkin, Sidney. "Enclave Consciousness and Neighborhood Activism." Pp. 218–39 in *Dilemmas of Activism: Class, Community, and the Politics of Local Mobilization*, edited by Joseph M. Kling and Prudence S. Posner. Philadelphia: Temple University Press, 1990.
Porter, Douglas R. *Managing Growth in America's Communities*. Washington, D.C.: Island Press, 1997.
Portz, John. *The Politics of Plant Closings*. Lawrence: University Press of Kansas, 1990.
Posner, Prudence S. "Introduction." Pp. 3–20 in *Dilemmas of Activism: Class, Community, and the Politics of Mobilization*, edited by Joseph M. Kling and Prudence S. Posner. Philadelphia: Temple University Press, 1990.
Putnam, Robert D. *Bowling Alone: The Collapse and Revival of American Community*. New York: Simon and Schuster, 2000.
Quinn, Bill. *How Wal-Mart Is Destroying America (and the World) and What You Can Do About It*. 3d ed. Berkeley, Calif.: Ten Speed Press, 2005.
Ragin, Charles. *The Comparative Method: Moving Beyond Qualitative and Quantitative Strategies*. Berkeley and Los Angeles: University of California Press, 1987.
Raine, George. "Southern California Supermarkets, Union Reach Accord." *San Francisco Chronicle*, 27 February 2004.
Raines, John C., Lenora E. Berson, and David McI. Gracie. *Community and Capital in Conflict: Plant Closings and Job Loss*. Philadelphia: Temple University Press, 1982.
Randle, William. "Professors, Reformers, Bureaucrats, and Cronies: The Players in *Euclid v. Ambler*." Pp. 31–69 in *Zoning and the American Dream*, edited by Charles M. Haar and Jerold S. Kayden. Chicago: Planners Press, 1989.
Relph, Edward. "Place." Pp. 906–22 in *Companion Encyclopedia of Geography*, edited by Ian Douglas, Richard Huggett, and Mike Robinson. London and New York: Routledge, 1996.

Ritzer, George. *McDonaldization of Society: An Investigation Into the Changing Character of Contemporary Social Life.* Thousand Oaks, Calif.: Pine Forge Press, 1993.

———. "The McDonaldization Thesis: Is Expansion Inevitable?" *International Sociology* 11, no. 3 (1996): 291–308.

———. *Enchanting a Disenchanted World: Revolutionizing the Means of Consumption.* Thousand Oaks, Calif.: Pine Forge, 1999.

Rohe, John. "USA—What Went Wrong." *Historic Preservation Forum* (Spring 1997): 36–40.

Ruane, Eugene T. and Robert J. Gray. *Community Responses to Population Growth and Environmental Stress: A National Inventory of Local Growth Management Strategies.* Washington, D.C.: Population-Environment Balance, 1987.

Rucht, Dieter. "Mobilization Against Large Techno-Industrial Projects: A Comparative Perspective." *Mobilization: An International Journal* 7, no. 1 (2002): 79–95.

———. "Movement Allies, Adversaries, and Third Parties." Pp. 197–216 in *The Blackwell Companion to Social Movements*, edited by David A. Snow, Sarah A. Soule, and Hanspeter Kriesi. Malden, Mass.: Blackwell, 2004.

Sale, Kirkpatrick. *Human Scale.* New York: Coward, McCann & Geoghegan, 1980.

Schifrin, Matthew. "The Big Squeeze." *Forbes*, 11 March 1996.

Schiller, Zachary, Wendy Zellner, Ron Stodghill II, and Mark Maremont. "Clout! More and More Retail Giants Rule the Marketplace." *Business Week*, 21 December 1992.

Schor, Juliet. *Do Americans Shop Too Much?* Boston, Mass.: Beacon Press, 2000.

Schumaker, Paul D. "Policy Responsiveness to Protest-Group Demands." *Journal of Politics* 37 (1975): 488–521.

Schwarzer, Mitchell. "The Spectacle of Ordinary Building." Pp. 74–90 in *Sprawl and Suburbia: A Harvard Design Magazine Reader*, edited by William S. Saunders. Minneapolis: University of Minnesota Press, 2005.

Sealts, Amy. "Signatures Place Zoning Issue on November Ballot." *Putnam County Sentinel*, August 2, 1995.

Seligman, Brad. "Patriarchy at the Checkout Counter: The *Dukes v. Wal-Mart Stores, Inc.*, Class-Action Suit." Pp. 231–42 in *Wal-Mart: The Face of Twenty-First Century Capitalism*, edited by Nelson Lichtenstein. New York and London: New Press, 2006.

Shaffer, Ron, Steve Deller, and Dave Marcouiller. *Community Economics: Linking Theory and Practice.* 2d ed. Ames, Iowa: Blackwell, 2004.

Shaffer, Sherrill. "Firm Size and Economic Growth." *Economics Letters* 76 (2002): 195–203.

———. "Establishment Size by Sector and County-Level Economic Growth." *Small Business Economics* 26 (2006): 145–54.

Shemtov, Ronit. "Taking Ownership of Environmental Problems: How Local Nimby Groups Expand Their Goals." *Mobilization* 4, no. 1 (1999): 91–106.

Simmons, James and Nancy Stark. "Backyard Protest: Emergence, Expansion, and Persistence of a Local Hazardous Waste Controversy." *Policy Studies Journal* 21, no. 3 (1993): 470–91.

Sklair, Leslie. *The Transnational Corporate Class.* Oxford, England: Blackwell Publishers, 2001.

Smith, Graham. *Deliberative Democracy and the Environment.* London and New York: Routledge, 2003.

Smith, Hedrick and Rick Young. "Is Wal-Mart Good for America?" Alexandria, Va.: PBS Video, 2004.

Sokolow, Alvin D. "The Changing Property Tax in the West: State Centralization of Local Finances." *Public Budgeting & Finance* (Spring 2000): 85–104.

Sprawl-Busters. http://www.sprawl-busters.com.

Starr, Amory. *Naming the Enemy: Anti-corporate Movements Confront Globalization.* London and New York: Zed Books, 2000.

Stone, Kenneth. *Competing with the Retail Giants: How to Survive in the New Retail Landscape.* New York: John Wiley, 1995.

Stone, Kenneth, Georgeanne Artz, and Albert Myles. *The Economic Impact of Wal-Mart Supercenters on Existing Businesses in Mississippi.* Mississippi State University Extension Service 2002.

Stowe, Stacey. "Connecticut Finds More Labor Law Violations at Wal-Mart." *New York Times,* 18 June 2005.

Tolbert, Charles M. "Minding Our Own Business: Local Retail Establishments and the Future of Southern Community." *Social Forces* 83, no. 4 (2005): 1309–28.

Tolbert, Charles, Michael D. Irwin, Thomas A. Lyson, and Alfred R. Nucci. "Civic Community in Small-Town America: How Civic Welfare Is Influenced by Local Capitalism and Civic Engagement." *Rural Sociology* 67, no. 1 (2002): 90–113.

Troy, Mike. "Wal-Mart is Tops in HBA Price Study." *DSN Retailing Today,* 28 October 2002.

Tsoukas, Haridimos. "David and Goliath in the Risk Society: Making Sense of the Conflict Between Shell and Greenpeace in the North Sea." *Organization* 6, no. 3 (1999): 499–528.

Turning Point Project. "Global Monoculture." Advertisement in the *New York Times,* 15 November 1999.

U.S. Census Bureau, *Census of Business (Retail Trade) 1963.* Washington, D.C.

U.S. Census Bureau, *1990 Census of Population and Housing, Summary of Social, Economic and Housing Characteristics.* Washington, D.C.

U.S. Census Bureau, *Census of Retail Trade 1972.* Washington, D.C.

U.S. Census Bureau, *Census of Retail Trade 1982.* Washington, D.C.

U.S. Census Bureau, *Census of Retail Trade 1992.* Washington, D.C.

U.S. Census Bureau. *Statistical Abstract of the United States: 2002.* Washington, D.C.

U.S. Census Bureau. *Statistical Abstract of the United States: 2003.* Washington, D.C.

U.S. Census Bureau. *Statistical Abstract of the United States: 2004–2005.* Washington, D.C.

U.S. Census Bureau. *Statistical Abstract of the United States: 2008.* Washington, D.C.

U.S. Census Bureau. *Statistics of U.S. Businesses: 2002.* http://www.census.gov.

U.S. Census Bureau, "Population Estimates for Places." http://www.census.gov.

U.S. Census Bureau, "Fact Sheet, Census 2000." http://factfinder.census.gov.

U.S. Department of Labor, Bureau of Labor Statistics, "Local Area Unemployment Statistics." http://www.bls.gov/lau.

Urry, John. *Consuming Places.* London: Routledge, 1995.

Useem, Jerry. "One Nation Under Wal-Mart." *Fortune,* 3 March 2003.

Vance, Sandra S. and Roy V. Scott. *Wal-Mart: A History of Sam Walton's Retail Phenomenon.* New York: Twayne, 1994.

Vidich, Arthur J. and Joseph Bensman. *Small Town in Mass Society: Class, Power and Religion in a Rural Community*. Princeton, N.J.: Princeton University Press, 1958.
Wal-Mart Annual Report. Various years.
Wal-Mart Proxy Statement. Various years.
Wal-Mart: The High Cost of Low Price (documentary film). Robert Greenwald et al. New York: Retail Project, 2005.
Walsh, Edward and Sherry Cable. "Litigation and Citizen Protest After the Three Mile Island Accident." *Research in Political Sociology* 2 (1986): 293–316.
Walsh, Edward J., Rex Warland, and C. Clayton Smith. *Don't Burn It Here: Grassroots Challenges to Trash Incinerators*. University Park: Pennsylvania State University Press, 1997.
Walton, Sam with John Huey. *Sam Walton, Made in America: My Story*. New York: Doubleday, 1992.
Weber, Max. *The Protestant Ethic and the Spirit of Capitalism*. New York: Scribner, 1958.
———. *Economy and Society*. Berkeley and Los Angeles, Calif.: University of California Press, 1978.
Weir, Tom. "Wal-Mart's the 1." *Progressive Grocer*, 1 May 2003.
West's Encyclopedia of American Law. St. Paul, Minn.: West Publishing Group, 1998.
Whyte, William H. *The Social Life of Small Urban Spaces*. Washington, D.C.: The Conservation Foundation, 1980.
———. *City: Rediscovering the Center*. New York: Doubleday, 1988.
Worpole, Ken. *Towns for People: Transforming Urban Life*. Buckingham, England: Open University Press, 1992.
Wrigley, Neil and Michelle Lowe. "New Landscapes of Consumption." Pp. 311–14 in *The Economic Geography Reader*, edited by John Bryson, Nick Henry, David Keeble, and Ron Martin. Chichester, England: John Wiley and Sons, 1999.
Wylie, Jeanie and David C. Turnley. *Poletown: Community Betrayed*. Urbana: University of Illinois Press, 1990.
Wynne, Derek and Justin O'Connor. "Consumption and the Postmodern City." *Urban Studies* 35, no. 5/6 (1998): 841–64.
Zald, Mayer N. and Bert Useem. "Movement and Countermovement Interaction: Mobilization, Tactics, and State Involvement." Pp. 247–72 in *Social Movements in an Organizational Society*, edited by Mayer N. Zald and John D. McCarthy. New Brunswick, N.J.: Transaction Books, 1987.
Zellner, Wendy. "How Wal-Mart Keeps Unions at Bay." *Business Week*, 28 October 2002.
Zimmerman, Ann and Kris Maher. "Wal-Mart Warns of Democratic Win." *Wall Street Journal*, 1 August 2008.
Zovanyi, Gabor. *Growth Management for a Sustainable Future*. Westport, Conn.: Praeger, 1998.
Zukin, Sharon. *The Cultures of Cities*. Cambridge, Mass.: Blackwell, 1995.
———. "Urban Lifestyles: Diversity and Standardization in Spaces of Consumption." *Urban Studies* 35, no. 5/6 (1998): 825–39.

Index

anticorporate activism, local, 201–7; and enclave politics, 204; limitations of, 205–6
anti–Wal-Mart movement, 203–4
A&P (Great Atlantic and Pacific Tea Company), 49n29
Ashland, Wisconsin, 129–43; Alfsen, Vic, 130, 139; Ante, Fran, 130, 137; Ashland Area Chamber of Commerce, 138; Ashland County, 129–30, 158–59; Benchmark Group, 131–32, 133; Birtch, Jeff, 131; Centres Inc., 130–32, 143; Citizens for the Right to Vote (CRV), 140; city administrator issue, 138, 139–40, 141; *Daily Press*, 138, 139; Downtown Development Corporation (DDC), 136; downtown and downtown merchants, 130–31, 135–37; east side/west side antagonism, 139; election of 1990, 134, 141–42; framing by opponents, 159; Highway 2 site, 130, 131–32, 135, 139, 142; Highway 2 site homeowners and landowners, 133, 135, 141–42, 161n42; Highway 13 site, 131, 139; King, John "Berry," 130, 131, 133, 142; Main Street committee, 135; Melin, Ed, 142; nearby residents, 132, 137; Northwest Regional Planning Commission (NWRPC), 130; opponents, 135–38; Pointer Development Corporation, 130, 131, 133, 142–43; quality of life, 138; retailers, independent, 130–31; supporters, 132–35; tactics of opponents, 136–37; zoning, 131–32, 142

Basker, Emek, 53, 56
Bensman, Joseph, 4
Bernstein et al., 54
Blanchard, Troy, 57
big box stores. *See* superstores
big retailers. *See* corporate retailers
Boggs, Carl, 202, 205

Cable, Sherry, 14
category killers, 31
chains: growth of, 29; and McDonaldization, 197
Chandler, Jr., Alfred D., 193

*Page numbers for figures and tables are *italicized*.

civil rights movement, 10
class, 168–69
community, 3–4
community-corporate conflicts, 6–10; conditions for success, model of, 177–81; environmental degradation, 7, 205; interlocal competition, 6, 204–5; and local state, 187–90; plant closings, 6, 204; urban development, 7, 205
community welfare, Wal-Mart's effect on, 55–58
comparative historical method, 19–20
consumption, 36; hypertrophy of, 195–97; spaces of, 65
corporate blunders, 172, 174. *See also* corporate weaknesses
corporate model, 8–9
corporate retailers, 33, 190–97; and competition, 37; and control, 193; and efficiency, 37; and fakery, 194–95; and homogenization, 194; and hypertrophy of consumption, 195–97; and organizational size, 191–92
corporate weaknesses, 174–77
corporations, 4–6; characteristics of, 5–6; public opinion of, 209n54
counter social movement organizations, 15, 171–72. *See also* shoppers

Davidson, Sharon M., 56
debate, 180; and deliberative democracy, 182
decision making, 183
deliberative democracy, 22, 181–85; examples of, 182
department stores, 61–62
discount merchandisers, 33; and pricing, 39–40; Wal-Mart, 40–41
disruption, effectiveness of, 13
downtown: effect of superstores on, 62–67; importance of, 62–63; as public space, 65

Drucker, Peter, 32
Dunham-Jones, Ellen, 61

economic conditions, local, 168
edge city, 70n43
enclave politics, 202, 204–5
establishment, definition of, 28
Eureka, California, 1, 129, 143–59; balloon track, 144–45, 149, 157–58; Berg, Patty, 150, 151–52; California Coastal Commission (CCC), 145, 147; Davis, Daphne, 146–47, 158; downtown, 144; economic conditions, 143; economic development, 151–54, 157–58, 159; Eureka Citizens, Businesses and Wal-Mart Stores for Responsible Economic Planning, 148; Eureka City Council, 153, 158; Flemming, Nancy, 154–55, 158; framing by opponents, 151, 153, 159; Friends of Humboldt County, 146, 150, 155–56; Greater Eureka Chamber of Commerce, 153; Hamblin, Ken, 145, 154; harbor, 143, 152, 156–58; *How Wal-Mart is Destroying America*, 146; Humboldt County, 143; Humboldt County Board of Supervisors, 153–54; Lin, Cynthia, 146, 148; Measure J, 147, 155–58; Mintier & Associates, J. Laurence, 157; Neely, Bonnie, 150; Norman, Al, 147, 150, 158; opponents, 149–54; organizations opposed, list of, 151; Quinn, Bill, 146; Redwood Region Economic Development Commission, 154; reports and studies, 157–58; Rose, Harvey, 154–55; sales tax revenue, 154; supporters, 148–49; tactics of opponents, 151, 155; tactics of supporters, 155; Think Twice/No on Measure J, 150–53; *Times-Standard*, 147, 154, 156; Union Pacific Railroad, 144; Wal-Mart, blunders by, 146, 156; zoning, 145, 147–48, 152

evidence of widespread opposition, 169–70

firm, definition of, 28
framing, 13–14, 170

Galanter, Marc, 14
Gamson, William, 12–13
Gehl, Jan, 64
general merchandise stores, 29, *30, 31,* 31–32
Gifford, Kathie Lee, 204
Gig Harbor, Washington, 71, 72–81, 93–94; approval process, 73–74; Barr, Rick, 73; CB (Coldwell Banker) Commercial, 73; Copeland, Les, 77, 78; Eyrse, Lois, 75; framing by opponents, 93; Gig Harbor-Peninsula Area Chamber of Commerce, 74, 78; Huckell/Weinman, 73; Morfee, Tom, 76, 78, 79; Morford, Brian, 74–75; opponents, 75–77; Pacific Public Affairs, 78; *Peninsula Gateway,* 76–77, 78, 79; Peninsula Neighborhood Association (PNA), 74, 75–76, 77, 78, 80; Pierce County, Washington, 73; quality of life, 93; supporters, 74–75, 94; tactics of opponents, 93–94; Washington Land Design, 73; Webber, Billie, 72; Wilbert, Gretchen, 72, 76; zoning, 73
Gillham, Oliver, 60
Glass, David, 41
Goetz, S., 57
grocery market, 50n52
growth machine, 16–18, 102, 115, 167
growth management, 45–46
Gruidle, John, 56

Huxtable, Ada Louise, 65–66

independent retailers: goals of, 193; Wal-Mart's effect on, 55–58

Jacobs, Allan B., 64
Jacobs, Jane, 63
jobs, 53–54; quality of, 54; wages, 54

Kline, Steven, 56

land use, 207n5; regulation of, 188–89. *See also* zoning
law suits. *See* legal challenges
legal challenges, 14, 167
Lichtenstein, Nelson, 9
local decision making, 180. *See also* decision making
local social movement organizations, 10
local social movements, 10–11, 206
local state. *See* state, local
Lofland, Lyn, 66
Lubell, Sam, 60

Main Street. *See* downtown
malls, 62, 65, 66, 194
Matthews, Todd L., 57
McDonaldization: and chains, 197; and corporations, 198; defined, 9; examples of, 197; resistance to, 197–201; and retailing, 198–201; spread of, 198; Wal-Mart as example of, 9, 198. *See also* rationalization
McLibel trial, 200
media, 15, 170–71
mobilization of opponents, 166–67
model of conditions for success. *See under* community-corporate conflicts

newspapers. *See* media
NIMBY (Not In My Back Yard), 8, 108, 202
Norman, Al, 46, 51, 69n32; and Eureka, 147, 150, 158, 159

Oldenburg, Ray, 66–67
Ottawa, Ohio, 99, 111–25; Albright, Robert, 113, 121; Anandale Development Corporation, 122–23; Concerned Citizens Coalition (CCC),

115–17; framing by opponents, 116, 124; Gilb, Michael, 121, 122; growth machine, 115; Heitmeyer, Marie, 112–13; Kuhlman, Martin, 113, 121; Laudick, David, 117; local merchants, 117–18; Maag, Kenneth, 120; Macke, Timothy, 118; McDowell, S. Scott, 118; Meyer, J. Dean, 120; nearby residents (*see* Concerned Citizens Coalition); New Creation Lutheran Church, 122–24; Niese, Richard, 113; Oakes, David, 113, 121; opponents, 115–19; Ottawa Area Chamber of Commerce, 119; Perry Street site, 112; Philips Display Components Company, 111, 114; Putnam County, Ohio, 111; Putnam County Community Improvement Corporation (CIC), 113, 122; Putnam County Sentinel, 119; Schmiedebusch, Thomas, 116–17; shoppers, 125; Stone, Kenneth, 123; supporters, 113–15; tactics of opponents, 124; voters, issue submitted to, 122; Williams, Jack, 118; zoning, 112, 116–17, 121, 122–23

partial successes, 172–73
Peterson and McGee, 56
Petoskey, Michigan, 71, 81–93, 93–94; approval process, 82–84; Bear Creek, township of, 82, 83, 90, 94; Bear Creek Mall, 82, 83; downtown, 85, 87, 88; Elder-Beerman, 82, 84, 90, 92–93; Emmet County (Michigan), 82, 83; Foster, Al, 89; framing by opponents, 93; Germond, William, 86, 91; Gunlock, Bo, 82, 92; Gunlock, Randy, 82, 84; Gunlocks (Bo and Randy), 86, 88–89; legal challenge, 91, 92–93; Litzenburger, Diane, 87; Meyer, Dale, 90–91; nearby residents, 90–91; Northern Michigan Hospital, 84; opponents, 85–87; Petoskey Gaslight-Downtown Association, 87; *Petoskey News-Review*, 88; Petoskey Regional Chamber of Commerce, 87; planned unit development (PUD), 83–84, 92; Putters, Max, 90; quality of life, 86; RG Enterprises, 82, 84, 86, 87, 92; shoppers, 88–89, 91; sprawl, 85, 93; supporters, 88–90, 94; tactics of opponents, 93–94; Urban Sprawl Alliance (USA), 85–86, 92; Wyckoff, Mark, 90; zoning, 83–84, 87, 89, 90, 92

planners, survey of, 3
Plotkin, Sydney, 202
police power, doctrine of, 188
population, 25n37
power center, 34, 62
pricing, politics of, 36–40; predatory pricing, 37–38, 48n28; price discrimination, 38–39; resale price maintenance, 39, 49n30, 49n32
public realm, 66
public space, effect of superstores on, 62–67
publicity, 180; and deliberative democracy, 184
Putnam, Robert, 57

railroad yard. *See* Eureka: balloon track
rationalization: of the built environment, 62, 65–66; and corporations, 5; and McDonaldization, 9, 197; of retailing, 28–32; of spaces of consumption, 65; spread of, 198; and superstores, 33–34, 61. *See also* corporate retailers; McDonaldization
real estate interests. *See* growth machine
regulatory checkpoint, 179–80; and deliberative democracy, 184
research methods, 18–20
retail development, 35–36; and hypertrophy of consumption, 196

retail industry: concentration in, 33; and manufacturers, 32; rationalization of, 28–32; restructuring of, 28–32; sales, 27–28; size of, 28; and technology, 28; as zero-sum game, 58–59. *See also* chains
retail trade, *29, 30*
Ritzer, George, 197, 198–99
Rohe, John, 60
Rummel, Amy, 56
Rupasingha, Anil, 57

scenic appeal, threat to, 168
Service Employees International Union (SEIU), 203
Shaffer, Sherrill, 57
shoppers, 88–89, 168, 199. *See also* counter social movement organizations
siting controversies, 15–16; and outcomes, 16. *See also* growth machine
Sklair, Leslie, 196
Smith, Graham, 181
small business, criticism of, 5
small merchants. *See* independent retailers
snobbery, accusations of, 75, 108
social movements: common features of, 10; outcomes of, 12–15
social movements, local. *See* local social movements
sprawl, 45, 59–61, 85; defined, 59
Sprawl-Busters Alert, 19, 46
state, local, 187–90; and community-corporate conflicts, 188; as mediator, 189–90
stationery stores, 31, *32*
Stone, Kenneth, 56, 123
supercenters, 44–45
superstore controversies, 7–10, 43–47; and enclave politics, 202; explanation for success of opponents, 165–77; and local state, 188–90; outcomes of, 11–18, 21–22; and zoning, 189

superstores, 33–34; and the built environment, 59–67; definition of, 2; design of, 60–61, 69n36, 79; objections to, 2, 8; size of, 60, 80; and sprawl, 59–61
survey of local officials, 23n4
Swaminathan, H., 57
symbolic power, 176–77

tax laws, 34–35, 162n75
third places, 66–67
Tolbert, Charles, 57
Tsoukas, Haridimos, 176

unions, 45, 54
United Food and Commercial Workers (UFCW), 45, 50n52, 76, 203

variables: combined, 173–74; environmental, 165–66; explanatory, 166; key, 169–72; with uncertain effects, 166–69; under control of the social movement organization, 165
Vidich, Arthur J., 4

wages. *See* jobs
Wal-Mart, 40–43; arguments in favor of, 52–55; blunders by, 172, 174; and control, 193; economic impact of, 68–69n16; effect on merchants and community welfare, 55–58; as example of McDonaldization, 9; and fakery, 194–94; fiscal impact of, 55; growth of, 31, 41–42, *42*, 44; jobs, 53–54; low costs, 49–50n48; and manufacturers, 32; merchandise, selection of, 52–53; movement against, 203; prices, 52–53, 67n2, 67n3, 68n4, 68n5; resistance to, 3; sales, 40; shopping options, 52–53; subsidies for, 55; tactics of, 167–68, 174; tax revenue, 54–55; and technology, 43, 208n29; as template business, 9, 204; treatment of workers, 207n12

Walsh, Edward, 14
Walton family, 42, 195
Walton, Sam, 40–44, 61, 106, 195
Weber, Max, 197
West Bend, Wisconsin, 99–111, 124–25; Bohn, David, 101, 102; Capelle, John, 109; Citizens Advocating Appropriate Planning (CAAP), 104–6; Copeland, Les, 103, 107; crime, 105; Department of Community Development (DCD), 101, 102, 109; downtown, 107; employers, local, 104; Fox Ridge subdivision, 100, 101, 104, 108; framing by opponents, 124; growth machine, 102, 124–25; 2010 Land Use Plan, 101, 105–106, 108; Miller, Michael, 100, 102, 107, 109, 110; Murphy, Todd, 101, 103, 106, 108, 110; nearby residents (*see* CAAP); opponents, 104–6; Pearson, Betty, 102–3, 110; supporters, 102–4, 107–8; tactics of opponents, 124; traffic, 104–5; Valley Avenue site, 100; Washington County, Wisconsin, 100; West Bend Area Chamber of Commerce, 102; West Bend Corporate Center, 110–11; *West Bend Daily News*, 102, 109; zoning, 100, 104, 107–8
Whyte, William H., 63

zero-sum game. *See under* retail industry
zoning, 11, 178–79; and local state, 188–89

About the Author

Stephen Halebsky is an assistant professor of sociology at the State University of New York (SUNY) College at Cortland. His research has focused on the politics of retail development, efforts to enhance community quality of life, and the relationship between big business and society. He worked in the corporate world for many years before joining academia. He has published several journal articles and is coauthor, with Gary Green and Anna Haines, of *Building Our Future: A Guide to Community Visioning*.